## Commendations: Key issues in Women & Work

'According to the feminist lobby, women in general are an exploited group and the difference in their employment experience compared to men represents the outcome of male oppressive power rather than free choice. Using an unusually extensive range of data drawn from a number of disciplines and countries Dr Hakim explodes a number of myths. For example, women are not becoming so similar to men that gender differentiation loses its rationale. Apart from the dramatic increase in part time work, female employment has not increased dramatically over the last 150 years. There is little evidence that housewives are exploited in the sense of working longer hours in total than men. Unpaid or voluntary work is undertaken as much by men as by women. Women's rates of labour turnover exceed those of men by 50%. There are important differences in work commitment and orientation with women less concerned than men to maximise earnings at the expense of working conditions. In short, this book *should be essential reading for those interested in the operation of the labour market, including economists, psychologists and lawyers as well as sociologists.*'

*Professor P J Sloane, Jaffrey Professor of Political Economy, University of Aberdeen.*

'This impressive review is essential background reading for all employment and discrimination lawyers.'

*Professor B A Hepple, Master of Clare College, University of Cambridge*

# Key Issues in Women's Work

# CONFLICT AND CHANGE IN BRITAIN SERIES
# – A NEW AUDIT

**Series Editors Paul Rock and David Downes (London School of Economics)**

The series provides reports on areas of British life conventionally conceived to be conflict-laden. It assesses the scale and character of the conflict in those areas, considering new or little heeded evidence, balancing the claims of different commentators and placing such conflict in its historical and social context, allowing intelligent judgements to be made. It provides prognoses about the likely development of that conflict; and ascertains what measures have been taken to manage it and what success they have met with; drawing on international experience where helpful.

*Already published volumes include*
Vol. 1    John David **Youth and the Condition of Britain: Images of Adolescent Conflict** (1990)
Vol. 2    Nigel Fielding **The Police and Social Conflict: Rhetoric and Reality** (1991)
Vol. 3    Brendan O'Leary and John McGarry **The Politics of Antagonism: Understanding Northern Ireland** (1993)

*Later volumes will include*
John Carrier & Ian Kendall **Health and the National Health Service**
Rod Morgan **Rethinking Prisons**
Christopher Husbands **Race in Britain**

CONFLICT AND CHANGE IN BRITAIN SERIES
– A NEW AUDIT

4

# Key Issues in Women's Work

Female heterogeneity and the polarisation of women's employment

CATHERINE HAKIM

ATHLONE
London & Atlantic Highlands, NJ

First published 1996 by The Athlone Press Ltd
1 Park Drive, London NW11 7SG and
165 First Avenue, Atlantic Highlands, NJ 07716

*British Library Cataloguing in Publication Data*
A catalogue record for this book is available
from the British Library

ISBN 0-485-80009-8 hb
ISBN 0-485-80109-4 pb

*Library of Congress Cataloging in Publication Data*
Hakim, Catherine.
    Key issues in women's work : female heterogeneity and the
polarisation of women's employment / Catherine Hakim.
        p.   cm. -- (Conflict and change in Britain series)
    Includes bibliographical references and index.
    ISBN 0-485-80009-8 (hardcover). -- ISBN 0-485-80109-4 (pbk.)
    1. Women--Employment--Great Britain.   2. Sex discrimina-
tion in employment--Great Britain.   3. Sex role in the work
environment--Great Britain.   4. Labor policy--Great Britain.
I. Title.   II. Series.
HD6135.H35   1996
331.4′0941--dc20                                        96-3351
                                                           CIP

Typeset by Bibloset

Printed and bound in Great Britain by the University
Press, Cambridge

For WRH

# Contents

# Series Editors' Preface

Few subjects have proved more contentious than women's employment. The grounds for the debate for the past century and a half were eloquently expressed by Charlotte Bronte's Jane Eyre: "Women are supposed to be very calm generally; but women feel just as men feel; they need exercise for their faculties, and a field for their efforts as much as their brothers do; they suffer from too rigid a restraint, too absolute a stagnation, precisely as men would suffer; and it is narrow-minded in their more privileged fellow-creatures to say that they ought to confine themselves to making puddings and knitting stockings, to playing on the piano and embroidering bags." If we substitute housework and child-care, scrubbing floors and taking in laundry, this passage would have embraced the lot of most working-class women as well.

From this position in the mid-19th Century, women have faced an appallingly uphill struggle to gain formal equality with men in entry to the labour market and in opportunities for self-advancement within it. The current conventional wisdom is that reality falls far short of genuine equality. Women remain discriminated against in the market-place; tied to inferior positions; and are saddled with two roles – primary responsibility for domestic affairs as well as for their work outside the home – which conflict to the detriment of each other. The only answers lie in far better provision of child care support in the community, in schools and in the workplace; and for far more democratic sharing of responsibilities inside the home.

Is it possible to quarrel with so widely accepted a view of the history and current state of female employment? Catherine Hakim finds this picture badly flawed, and she does so on the basis of evidence about trends in and attitudes towards employment which is publicly available and yet remains widely ignored. The tendency for feminist myths to replace the patriarchal has, in her view, seriously

distorted our understanding of the issues at stake in female employment. She brings a wealth of evidence and analysis to bear on these
questions which cannot be ignored in future debate. Her approach
is not that of the professional controversialist, seeking acclaim by
simply inverting conventional wisdom. She is a dispassionate and
rigorous scholar who writes with great clarity about matters all too
easily obscured by preconceptions. Yet she does not duck difficult
issues or mince words about those who do. Her career has included
work in the Department of Employment as a Principal Research
Officer and the Directorship of the National Social Science Archive
at the University of Essex; and over two decades she has produced
a distinguished sequence of academic studies and official reports
on occupational segregation and other employment issues. If her
conclusions are to be challenged, the evidential basis on which they
rest must be taken fully into account rather than side-stepped.

*David Downes*
*Paul Rock*
London School of Economics

# List of figures

# List of tables

# List of cases

*Barber v. Guardian Royal Exchange Assurance Group*, 262/88 [1990] ICR 616 ECJ; [1990] IRLR 240; [1990] 2 All ER 600
*Bilka-Kaufhaus v. Weber von Hartz*, 170/84 [1987] ICR 110 ECJ; [1986] 2 CMLR 701; [1986] 5 ECR 1607; [1986] IRLR 317
*Commission v France* 312/86 [1988] ECR 6315
*Francovich v Italian Republic* [1992] IRLR 84
*Meade-Hill and another v. The British Council*, [1995] IRLR 478
*R v Secretary of State for Employment, ex parte Equal Opportunities Commission*, [1994] IRLR 176
*R v Secretary of State for Employment, ex parte Seymour-Smith*, [1994] IRLR 448 DC
*R v Secretary of State for Employment, ex parte Seymour-Smith*, [1995] IRLR 464
*Rinner-Kühn v. FWW Spezial-Gebaudereinigung GmbH & Co. KG*, 171/88 [1989] IRLR 493 ECJ
*Stadt Lengerich v. Helmig* (15 December 1994) ECJ

# Acknowledgements

I wish to thank Duncan Gallie for providing special tables from the 1992 PSI survey of employment in Britain which were used in Tables 4.7 and 4.8. I wish to thank Sheila Jacobs for providing special analyses of the 1980 Women and Employment Survey from her unpublished D.Phil. thesis, including the analyses that provide the basis for Tables 5.2 and 5.3. I wish to thank Simon Burgess for providing special analyses of the General Household Survey data used in Table 5.6. I would like to thank the Office of Population Censuses and Surveys (OPCS) for allowing me use of the OPCS Longitudinal Study and members of the LS Support Programme at the Social Statistics Research Unit, City University, for assistance with accessing the data which is used in Table 6.4. I thank OPCS and the ESRC/JISC/DENI programme for creating and providing access to the 1% and 2% Samples of Anonymised Records from the 1991 Census of Population, the ESRC Census Microdata Unit at Manchester University and the Computing Service staff at Manchester and ULCC and the London School of Economics for help with processing these huge datasets which provided the basis for Table 6.3. I thank Bob Hepple for comments on an early draft of Chapter 7. I am indebted to Norman Stockman, Norman Bonney, Xuewen Sheng and Masami Shinozaki for bringing the Chinese and Japanese surveys used in Tables 4.5 and 4.6 to my attention.

The following appear in this book by permission:

Tables 2.1, 2.2 and 2.3 reprinted from Hakim, 'Workforce restructuring, social insurance coverage and the black economy', *Journal of Social Policy*, June 1989, by permission of Cambridge University Press.
Tables 6.1. 6.2 and 6.6 reprinted with minor changes from Hakim,

'Explaining trends in occupational segregation', *European Sociological Review*, September 1992, by permission of Oxford University Press.

Table 6.5 reprinted from Hakim, 'A century of change in occupational segregation 1891-1991', *Journal of Historical Sociology*, December 1994, by permission of Blackwells.

Figures 1 and 2 reprinted from Main 'The lifetime attachment of women to the labour market' in *Women and Paid Work*, 1988, by permission of Brian Main and the Institute for Employment Research, University of Warwick.

# Abbreviations

| | |
|---|---|
| BSAS | British Social Attitudes Survey |
| DI | Dissimilarity Index |
| EC | European Commission |
| ECJ | European Court of Justice |
| ESRC | Economic and Social Research Council |
| EU | European Union |
| FES | Family Expenditure Survey |
| GHS | General Household Survey |
| ILO | International Labour Office of the United Nations |
| LFS | Labour Force Survey |
| NES | New Earnings Survey |
| NLS | National Longitudinal Surveys (of Labour Market Behaviour) |
| OECD | Organisation for Economic Cooperation and Development |
| OPCS | Office of Population Censuses and Surveys |
| PSID | Panel Study of Income Dynamics |
| SAR | Sample of Anonymised Records |
| SCELI | Social Change and Economic Life Initiative (ESRC research programme) |
| SNA | System of National Accounts of the United Nations |
| TUC | Trades Union Congress |
| USA | United States of America |
| WES | Women and Employment Survey |

*Abbreviations used in tables*

| | |
|---|---|
| .. | Data not available |
| * | Less than 0.5% |
| FT | full-time |
| PT | part-time |
| M | men |
| W | women |

# 1
# Explaining women's subordination

Are women today oppressed? Or do they now have the best of both worlds - taking jobs when they like, on an equal basis with men, but retreating to the sanctuary of the home to revert to their other role as homemaker and mother whenever they please? This book is about the choices women make, the diversity of these choices, and their consequences.

There are good reasons for optimism. History looks quite different when viewed from women's perspective. The Second World War may have been a disaster for men, but it was beneficial for women, breaking down job barriers and creating new openings. The 1960s brought the contraceptive revolution, giving women control over their fertility and opening up the option of voluntary childlessness. The 1970s brought equal opportunities legislation, in particular the Equal Pay Act 1970 that produced a 10 per cent increase in women's earnings as compared with men's. The 1980s brought the impact of European Union policies and European Court of Justice decisions insisting that the principle of non-discrimination between men and women, in particular in all aspects of pay, had to be fully implemented in Britain as in the rest of Europe. With the post-War decline of manufacturing industry, the economy shifted towards greater emphasis on service sector industries, all offering more congenial work environments to women. Post-War developments have created a new and beneficial social and economic situation for women.

On the other hand the *potential* for change does not seem to have born fruit. Men and women are still segregated in different occupations, with women concentrated in what is often described as a 'job ghetto' of low grade, low-paid work. A substantial sex differential in earnings still remains, even if smaller than before. Men seem always to have the upper hand, so that it is more of a struggle for women to get what they want. In practice, it is argued, women remain disadvantaged and dissatisfied with their lot.

This book offers a more empirically grounded review of developments in the post-War period than is offered by most recent texts on women's employment, and thus a more informed assessment of the main theories accounting for women's social and economic position today. It presents a new analysis of women's position in the labour market and of the social changes currently under way in all industrial societies, not just in Britain. The focus is on women's choice between paid employment and full-time homemaking, and on women's position within the workforce. The choices women make seem to be changing, prompting vigorous debate over the nature of the changes and their consequences.

The focus is paid employment in the market economy and the terms 'work' and 'employment' are used interchangeably throughout the book for stylistic variation and simplicity. As the next chapter demonstrates, strictly speaking work covers a broader range of activities than employment.

## Key issues in women's employment

Is it really necessary for women to go out to work to gain equality with men? Are they not doing enough work in the home and raising children? It is often argued that women's work has been systematically undercounted and undervalued, giving a false impression of women's contribution to the economy: first, that national statistics fail to fully reflect the hidden wage work of women – as family workers, in home-based employment and in the informal economy; second, that national statistics do not even attempt to record women's domestic work, caring work and voluntary work. Chapter 2 reviews the evidence for these two arguments and finds them not proven. It shows statistics on unpaid work are readily available and rarely show women to do more of it than men.

The alternative view is that women have been gaining economic equality with men as levels of female employment rose steadily from the 1950s onwards. Women's gains have been men's losses, as women steal men's jobs and feminise them. Men are displaced, socially as well as economically. Chapter 3 examines the feminisation of the workforce and finds that jobs have been defeminised as well as being demasculinised. Apart from the post-war creation of a segregated part-time workforce, there have been no substantial changes in the level of female employment for over 150 years.

Do women really want paid employment? It has become received wisdom in recent years that they do, that any differences that might have existed in men's and women's work orientations, work commitment and ambitions have now faded away. Women want interesting jobs and well paid work just as much as men, but are prevented from getting them by discrimination, overt and covert. Chapter 4 reviews the evidence on work orientations and how they are changing. Attitudes to the sexual division of labour in the home are examined in cross-national perspective to show how differential sex roles are being remodelled rather than abandoned. One sex role stereotype that seems most resistant to change is the idea that power and authority are in some way a male prerogative.

If women's labour force attachment had really been increasing in recent years, as is so often stated, we would expect to see increasing employment stability and continuity of employment among women. A review of the evidence in Chapter 5 shows on the contrary that the sex differential in labour turnover rates has not changed in twenty years and that women's employment profiles display rising *discontinuity*.

The key explanation offered by patriarchy theory for women's disadvantaged position within the workforce is that occupational segregation is used to restrict women to a female job ghetto of low-paid work, so that women invariably earn less than men. Chapter 6 reviews the evidence to find that in this area there has been far more change, all of it to women's advantage, than feminist theory admits. A review of the impact of legislation in Chapter 7 confirms the importance of equal opportunities policies, but shows the law to be a two-edged weapon. Overall, women made real gains in the 1980s and 1990s which cannot be explained solely by equal pay and opportunities legislation. We must thus consider the competing theories explaining women's social and economic position and assess how effective they are in accounting for current developments.

## Theoretical perspectives

Much recent theorising on women's position has been misinformed, has rested on reviews of the evidence that are incomplete, mistaken or one-sided. Perhaps this is not surprising. A full assessment of the empirical evidence has to be grounded in economics as well as sociology, anthropology, demography and psychology. Few of those who contribute to the expanding field of women's studies have a sufficiently broad disciplinary base, for example to appreciate the contribution from economics and rational choice theory as well as psychology. This has resulted in misunderstandings about theory and evidence, down to the level of confusion about the basic concepts of work and employment, as shown in Chapter 2. In some cases the errors are less excusable, as illustrated in Chapter 5 by the problem of sample selection bias which is rather more common, and hidden, in sociology than in economics.

There is no shortage of theories claiming to explain women's subordinate position in the labour market and at home. All of them are plausible, have some element of truth in them. Very few of them have been subjected to rigorous testing in a wide range of cultures. In *Theorising Patriarchy* Sylvia Walby reviews the enormous number of theories that have been offered in the last twenty years to explain women's subordinate position in society and the workforce or, as she puts it, women's exploitation and oppression. However her review, like so many, discusses theories in terms of their intellectual merits and explanatory adequacy. At the end of the day the key test of theory is against reality. Theory that rests on inadequate or selective evidence is weak, no matter how coherent a world view it offers. Following Einstein, theory is not right or wrong. Theory is either useful, or not useful, in making sense of the world, helping one to understand change processes and formulate further questions to address. On this basis, there are three main theories that are currently useful for understanding women's social and economic position. The most important competing theories today are Steven Goldberg's theory of the inevitability of male dominance and patriarchy based on psycho-physiological processes; Heidi Hartmann's theory of men's collective organisation to further their own interests against those of women through trade unions, the legal system and political organisations, as illustrated by a pattern of occupational segregation that is to men's advantage; and Gary Becker's rational choice theory of the allocation of time and labour to domestic work and employment based on the role specialisation of husband and wife. Between them these theories cover the full range of explanations so far offered: physiological, psychological, sociological and economic.

The pattern of women's employment, and non-work, remains central to any theory. Women's position in society as a whole is jointly determined by their access to, role and status in paid employment and the status accorded to their reproductive and domestic role. In industrial societies women's economic position in the workforce is gaining importance relative to non-market domestic and child-care functions. Various theories link the segregation of men and women in paid employment to the domestic division of labour between husband and wife. An adequate theory must be able to explain patterns of sex-based occupational segregation, in particular the *vertical* job segregation that finds men concentrated in the higher-status and higher-paid positions. It must also be able to account for the domestic division of labour, and women's choices between the full-time domestic role and some combination of paid employment and non-market work.

### Patriarchy and male dominance: Goldberg

Goldberg's theory of the *Inevitability of Patriarchy* and male dominance based on psycho-physiological processes was originally published in 1973 and has been the subject of intensely critical debate since then. A much more precise, developed and persuasive (though repetitive) version of his theory was published in 1993 under the new title *Why Men Rule*. Goldberg focuses on the impact of physiology on social attitudes and behaviour, in particular the effect of male hormones such as testosterone as a source of sex differences in motivation, ambition and behaviour. He argues that testosterone and other differences in male physiological development make men generally more self-assertive, aggressive, dominant and competitive. In consequence they invariably seek to obtain the top positions in any hierarchy, such as the top positions in political or other public leadership hierarchies, the highest status jobs or roles in the workforce, sport, the arts, crime or any other area of social activity with a hierarchy of status and power that prompts competitive behaviour.

A second element of his theory points to the effect of hormonal and other physiological differences in shaping the character of private heterosexual relationships, and the mutually-reinforcing and supporting *congruence* between personal styles in the public and private arenas. Sex differences that have their roots in physiology and are developed by the socialisation process create an emotional expectation or preference for *male dominance* in personal and sexual relationships. Private heterosexual relationships set a pattern for relationships between men and women in the workplace. At the minimum, this creates an invisible barrier to establishing egalitarian and relaxed work roles and relationships that are not 'coloured' by patterns in the sexual arena. At the worst, sex roles and styles of behaviour established in heterosexual relationships carry over into role expectations and behaviour patterns in the workplace, consciously or subconsciously.

Goldberg is sometimes wrongly classified as an evolutionist sociobiologist and castigated for evolutionary theories he does not address and for exaggerations of his own theory that he does not offer. His approach is similar to that of Rossi (1977) who sought to incorporate the influence of physiological factors in interaction with social and cultural factors to explain why women actively seek greater involvement in childcare than do men, especially in the first six years of a child's life, although she refers to evolutionary theory that Goldberg eschews completely. Goldberg set out to explain why men invariably get almost all the top jobs and top positions in *all* societies, past and present. In his first book the emphasis was on anthropological research evidence showing that no society had ever existed in which women ruled. In his more recent book the emphasis shifts to contemporary societies and the evidence that within the workforce vertical job segregation is pronounced. All other hierarchies are also dominated by men. Goldberg points out that exceptional women sometimes reach the top, Golda Meir and Margaret Thatcher being two examples. However the exceptions will remain exceptions unless social and cultural factors start to overcome the influence of hormonal differences in the development of children and adolescents. He accepts that determined social engineering might achieve this; but it remains to be seen. The Israeli *kibbutzim* failed in their efforts to alter sex-role differentiation; socialist Russia and China failed to eliminate vertical job segregation; egalitarian and family-friendly policies in Sweden artificially reduced earnings differentials but again did not reduce vertical job segregation. Physiological differences between males and females do not fully determine behaviour, they only create dispositions which may be valued or belittled, encouraged or discouraged by a society. Similarly Goldberg is not saying that men are necessarily more able, competent or effective in using positions of power and authority, only that they are *motivated to seek* such positions with greater determination and persistence than women, and are more prepared to make sacrifices to get there, in terms of effort and foregoing other activities or benefits.

As a result, patriarchy is universal in that authority and leadership are, and always have been, associated with the male in every society. He defines *patriarchy* as any system of organisation (political, economic, industrial, financial, religious or social) in which the overwhelming number of upper positions in hierarchies are occupied by males. Patriarchy refers only to suprafamilial levels of organisation. Authority in familial and dyadic relationships is a manifestation of the psychophysiological reality he labels *male dominance*.

The attraction of Goldberg's theory is that it is simple, specific and provides a *sufficient* explanation of vertical job segregation in the workforce and of male domination in politics and other public hierarchies. It is the only theory that can explain some of the more inconvenient facts about women as well as men, such as the apparently universal preference for a *male* superior or boss, as noted in Chapter 4. His theory is also consistent with Chodorow's (1978) and Gilligan's (1982, 1993) theory of qualitative personality differences between men and women. Gilligan describes men as being more individualistic, achievement-oriented, detached from others, oriented more towards power, distinctive activity and success. She argues that women define themselves in terms of personal relationships, are unselfish, concerned about fulfilling the needs of others and feel powerless. Along with Miller (1976) she describes women as accepting subordinate relationships with men (1993: 168). Gilligan insists that women's greater interest in social relationships is invariably benign, consisting of a concern to *care* for others rather than a detached curiosity or a desire to manipulate and control others emotionally. The empirical validity of her work has been questioned (Treadwell, 1987: 280-1; Beutel and Marini, 1995: 438). Despite all this, Gilligan's thesis has been accepted with positive acclaim rather than being rejected as 'sexist' in the same way as Goldberg's thesis and other theories that acknowledge important gender differences in personality and behaviour.

Goldberg also offers a novel explanation for the fact that male occupations tend to be the most highly paid. The explanation usually offered is that male-dominated occupations are rewarded disproportionately well and female occupations are undervalued and less well paid. This theory led to demands for equal pay for work of equal value policies (Treiman and Hartmann, 1981). Another explanation is that workers queue for jobs and as (male) employers invariably prefer men over women if men are available, men get the cream of the jobs and women end up in the worst paid jobs (Reskin and Roos, 1990). Goldberg points out that if these theories were true, there would be no male-dominated occupations that paid substantially less than women's occupations. In fact, there are many male jobs that are low status and low paid. Male roles are not high status because they are male, Goldberg argues. It is simply that *any* role that acquires high status (as indicated by high earnings) will attract more men than women, so will *become* male-dominated as a result of its' position in the hierarchy (Goldberg, 1993: 108). Men never need to be encouraged to apply for promotion, whereas women do. The example is often quoted of the job advert that failed to attract any women applicants at all until the salary was reduced by half in a readvertisment (Hakim, 1979: 50).

Goldberg points out (1993: 106) that sexual differentiation in motivation to attain high status positions is statistical and probabilistic, like other attitudes and behaviour differences, rather than an absolute difference. Socialisation in childhood and adolescence magnifies and enhances psychological and personality differences to create the discrete qualitative differences observed between adult men and women. Physiology does not determine but predisposes towards ambitious competitiveness in males far more than in females but there is variation around the two averages. Other writers have also criticised the misleading use of averages to describe and differentiate male and female behaviour and attitudes, as averages hide the large overlap between the two groups in terms of behavioral styles; however they have also emphasised the striking differences between men and women's testosterone levels and the much larger variation in male levels (Treadwell, 1987: 269, 278). Within-group variation for men is almost as large as the sex differential, a finding which may help to explain male homosexuality. More important, the sex differential in testosterone levels is substantial enough to contribute some part of the explanation for sex differences in everyday behaviour.

Goldberg's theory of patriarchy and male dominance is universalistic and proven, in that there has never been a society in which women normally held all the most senior posts or filled most high status non-maternal roles. It is a theory that offers only one avenue of change, through intensive socialisation to eliminate sex differentiation. It is a more useful theory than Firestone's (1974) theory that women's reproductive functions make them physically and socially vulnerable while they are bearing or rearing children, at the minimum restricting their activities and potentially allowing men to take advantage to dominate and subordinate them. In this case childlessness offers one obvious avenue of escape. Another is for women to organise collectively to ensure that childbearing is rewarded at an appropriately high level, in social and/or economic terms. The fact that they have not done so, and produce babies without adequate compensation is itself informative. Women who provide a commercial baby production service, selling the produce for substantial sums of money are criticised, never praised, by women as well as men; women who fail to honour these deals and decide they cannot bear to give the child away are even admired. Women actively collude with men in treating as deviant venal sexual activity and reproduction. Even feminists accept the labelling of prostitutes as deviant and exploited rather than liberated from the yoke of marriage, being far more concerned with the sexual double standard that fails to treat male customers as equally deviant (Smart, 1976; Downes and Rock, 1988: 273-292). Indeed rape, which is rare, and largely confined to Western industrial society, attracts far more attention than prostitution (Smart and Smart, 1978; Walby, 1990), a universal occupation providing regular employment for thousands of women. It appears that *women*'s sex role attitudes and behaviour are resistant to change.

The reasons for women's failure to organise as effectively as men to promote their interests has been developed further by Hartmann.

## Patriarchy, male organisation and job segregation: Hartmann

A classic short paper by Hartmann first published in 1976 provides the essential framework for theories that place patriarchy centre stage as the key explanatory factor. Hartmann defined *patriarchy* as men's domination of women, specifically men's control over women's labour as illustrated by historical developments in trade union policies in Britain and the USA. Subsequently she extended her concept of patriarchy to include heterosexual marriage, women's economic dependence on men, male-dominated social institutions, the domestic division of labour, women's disproportionate share of housework and childcare, all creating the potential for conflicting rather than harmonious interests between spouses or between men and women (Hartmann, 1979, 1981). Hartmann's theory was developed by Walby, first in a historical analysis of the role of British trade union policy to exclude women from paid employment and restrict them to the less well paid areas of work through occupational segregation (Walby, 1986) and then in a broader theoretical statement (Walby, 1990). Walby defines patriarchy as a system of inter-related social structures and practices through which men dominate, oppress and exploit women (1990: 20). She sets out how patriarchy operates through the private household, the labour market, heterosexuality, culture, male violence towards women as illustrated by rape, and through state support for the ideology of patriarchy, as illustrated by laws that restrict women's employment and control divorce, through welfare state regulations that impose traditional sex roles.

Social class and social stratification have been the main concepts used in sociological theory on social inequality, whereas economists focus on earnings or income inequality. A voluminous literature struggled to incorporate explanations of gender inequality with Marxist theories of social stratification, exploitation and the value of labour power (Walby, 1990; Fine, 1992). Fine (1992) insists that the oppression of women can be adequately incorporated into class analysis, but the general consensus is that it is more useful to treat capitalism and patriarchy as theoretically separate but interacting. Hartmann views capitalism and patriarchy as broadly in harmony much of the time, while Walby sees them as being in conflict more often.

Hartmann's theory of patriarchy places explicit emphasis on occupational segregation as the key mechanism used by men to restrict and constrain women's access to income and earnings, thus rendering them financially dependent on men, forcing them to become domestic servants for their husbands. Hartmann recognises that this is not the only mechanism, just the main one. The separation of the workplace from the home brought about by the development of modern industry also meant that many women ceased to be gainfully employed. However the ideology of the sexual division of labour became a force in its own right, leading women and men to prefer feminine and masculine jobs and to men refusing to be formally subordinate to a woman in the workplace (Hartmann, 1976: 151, 154, 164, 168-9), as demonstrated by studies of women's employment in male jobs during World War II (Milkman, 1987: 9, 157-9) and other historical studies of the USA and Britain (Matthaei, 1982: 187-232; Bradley, 1989: 225-230; Strom, 1989). Walby differentiates the two mechanisms used by men to limit women's access to earnings: total exclusion from the market economy and wage labour; and the segregation of male and female workers within the workforce, restricting women to the lower-paid jobs. Both policies are seen as ensuring that men have more financial power in the home and in the labour market.

Walby claims that the exclusion strategy was dominant in nineteenth century Britain while the segregation strategy is most influential in twentieth century Britain, as illustrated by the segregation of full-time and part-time work today. This is the basis of her thesis that patriarchy has changed and developed from the *private patriarchy* which characterised the nineteenth century, with women excluded from paid work, devoting their time instead to domestic work and rearing children for the benefit of an individual patriarch (that is, their husband), to the *public patriarchy* of twentieth century Britain in which large numbers of women are now in employment but collectively exploited by employers who pay women workers wages below the level that would be expected in terms of women's human capital (in essence, their qualifications and work experience). Our analysis of the evidence on the feminisation of the workforce in Chapter 3 shows that Walby's theory of the historical development of patriarchy is simply not supported by the facts on trends in female employment. A fuller critique by Fine (1992: 52-66) questions the power of trade unions to impose their will on employers who wanted to hire cheaper female labour. Fine also argues that protective labour legislation that excluded women from working in the mines and at night was motivated by a wider range of social concerns than a patriarchal desire to restrict women to the homemaking role alone. Trade union policies were also irrelevant to women employed in domestic service and exclusively female occupations such as dressmaking and sewing, which remained the most important occupations for women well into the twentieth century. Finally, the exclusionary strategy of the marriage bar lasted until well into the twentieth century: in Britain, Holland and other European countries the exclusion of married women from employment was only made unlawful by the sex discrimination and equal opportunities legislation of the 1960s and beyond. More puzzling, trade union policy on unequal pay is downplayed by Walby (1986: 214-7, 1990: 51, 162). Milkman (1987: 77-83, 158) shows that pay equity is the more important issue in industries where the work cannot easily be stereotyped as male or female. Grint (1988) shows that job segregation strategies were not necessary as long as trade unions maintained unequal pay for women doing the same jobs as men. Lower wage rates for women had been traditional in agriculture and were carried over into manufacturing industry and white-collar work, with female wages being 50-60% of male rates. Even when formally in favour, trade unions generally remained opposed to equal pay for women, overtly or covertly, right up to the Equal Pay Act 1970 pushed through by a woman minister, Barbara Castle, in a Labour government (Grint, 1988: 101-105; Castle, 1993: 409-412, 427). In sum, the key changes in policy all occurred in the post-war period, with simultaneous legislation on unequal pay, exclusion and segregation, in Britain and other industrial societies. Walby's attempt to develop a dynamic theory of patriarchy fails on the evidence.

We thus return to Hartmann's original simple and elegant account of patriarchy as male organisation to further their interests against those of women, especially to control women's wage work, which remains the basis for most formulations today. Exclusion, segregation and unequal pay all achieve the same purpose of limiting women's access to earnings and the independence of spirit that comes with an independent income. The key element of Hartmann's theory which no-one challenges is the idea that men organise collectively to further their own interests against those of women through the labour market, laws, political organisations, culture and ideology. Male solidarity and male organisation are the key factors, which Walby (1986) and Milkman (1987) illuminated further in their research on trade union strategies in Britain and the USA. It is less important whether trade unions used exclusion, segregation or unequal pay strategies, and less important that their strategies sometimes failed, than to underline that male solidarity is high, that men organise collectively to advance their own interests, and that men perceive a conflict of interests between men and women much of the time. Walby added to this the point that women also organise collectively to advance their own interests against those of men, at least occasionally, that women are not purely passive actors in their own lives (Walby, 1990: 58, 87-88, 93, 125-6). However Grint (1988) concludes that this was never the most important factor in achieving change, which was largely forced by the changing industrial composition of the economy.

The idea that women make real choices is developed further by Becker and other human capital theorists.

## Rational choices within families: Becker

Rational choice theory (sometimes termed rational action theory or exchange theory) is simply economics applied to social institutions which are more commonly studied by sociologists or political scientists, such as the family or voting behaviour. The most well known area of rational choice theory is the 'new home economics' and human capital theory which studies non-economic aspects of the family, including the sexual division of labour in households, the supply of wives' labour to the market economy, decisions about investments in children, decisions about marriage and divorce. Most of the time economics treats the family, or household, as a single undivided unit, a black box, that makes choices about work or leisure, production or consumption in order to maximise its utility (satisfaction or valued benefits, not only money). The novelty was to open up the black box of the family, to study and model how decisions are made within it to maximise collective and individual utility. It has to be remembered that economics relies on scarce resources as its starting point. It is not possible for everybody to have exactly what they want all of the time. If it were, we would be in paradise, the word choice would have no meaning and we would have no need for social science. Therefore we study how people make decisions that get the best 'deal' possible out of the options and constraints that confront them. Rational choice theory focuses on the personal or mutual advantage individuals gain through cooperative exchange. It assumes people know what they value (have stable preferences) and act rationally to achieve their aims, to maximise or optimise their desires. The main problem is that the theory can veer towards tautology: whatever happens must have been desired and preferred, otherwise people would have done something else. But this is a general problem of economics rather than of rational choice theory.

The key text is Becker's *Treatise on the Family*, originally published in 1981 and reprinted in 1991 with additions, in particular a paper on the sexual division of labour first published in 1985. The book had not been welcomed enthusiastically by sociologists, who felt uncomfortable with the application of clear-headed logic to social institutions that are idealised in Western culture as structured around loving relationships, which are assumed to be incompatible with reason. The 1985 paper argued that if they work at all, most married women economise on the effort expended on paid employment by seeking less demanding jobs. It prompted an immediate rejection by some sociologists as having no empirical basis (England and McCreary, 1987; Bielby and Bielby, 1988) although others showed the thesis to be vindicated by research on the characteristics of part-time workers in Britain (Hakim, 1991, 1993b; see also Bradley, 1989: 226). Becker argues that even if a husband and wife are intrinsically identical they gain from a division of labour between employment and household work, with one specialising more in employment and the other specialising more in domestic work. The sexual division of labour is mutually advantageous because it is efficient, and raises the productivity of the person who specialises in domestic work as well as the productivity of the person who specialises in employment. Even small initial differences between people, such as the fact that only women bear children and this gives them a small edge on subsequent childcare, would cause a sexual division of labour which, extended over the years, would produce an enormous gender gap in earnings, even in the absence of discrimination. Becker does not deny that discrimination exists in the labour market and that husbands may exploit their wives. Indeed he argues that logically the entire difference in average earnings between men and women could be classified as due to discrimination and other sex differences which cause the sexual division of labour, even though differences in human capital may be the immediate, visible explanation.

Becker argues that the sexual division of labour in the home leads women to invest less and men to invest more in their human capital: education, training, career development and work experience. It leads wives to choose jobs that are less effort intensive and are generally compatible with domestic responsibilities. It causes occupational segregation since wives will seek jobs that are less demanding even if they work full-time. These processes affect single men and women as well as married couples if they anticipate marriage and parenthood, as most do.

There are two obvious sources of change in this theory. First, Becker assumes that childcare is a major element of household work, any decline in fertility rates being offset by parents investing extra time and effort to produce higher quality children. On the other hand, raising a single child does not generally require the same investment of time and effort as raising four children, and single children are now quite common, even outside China. Further, intentionally childless couples have a qualitatively different bargain, with far less incentive to adopt differentiated sex roles if both have decided to invest in careers. If their careers are sufficiently rewarding, this may compensate for a loss of efficiency in their domestic work due to both partners being amateur cooks and so forth. Second, Becker is obliged to assume that individuals have stable preferences. In fact, preferences sometimes change markedly over the life cycle. Women who have children early in life can become bored with motherhood at a young enough age to initiate a late-start career. Women who invest in a career may become disenchanted with the 'rat race' and retire to the haven of domestic life and motherhood and learn to cook. Generational changes in the attractiveness of the homemaker role and in the relative returns to paid employment and homemaking can alter the precise balance in the sexual division of labour. Chapter 4 explores the evidence on changing attitudes to the sexual division of labour in Britain and other countries.

Finally, Becker himself notes that the family is becoming a less and less important institution as functions are transferred out of it. Education and training, social insurance against unemployment or sickness, health care, entertainment and social activities in clubs and other organisations – all are provided by public sector or commercial organisations, reducing reliance on families for these services. Commercial goods and services are usually available, at least in large cities, to replace many domestic goods and services. The volume of work done in the home is increasingly a matter of choice, and the outcome of negotiations over who does it becomes less predictable.

Becker's thesis is the fullest development to date of human capital theory and models formulated originally by Mincer (1962) and extended by others seeking to explain the characteristics of female labour force participation with reference to the family division of labour (Mincer and Polacheck, 1974; Mincer, 1985; Blau and Ferber, 1992: 34-71, 141-187). All treat women as a single homogenous group with interrupted work histories due to their family role. Human capital theory is useful for analyses of female employment, especially for explaining earnings and differences in earnings between men and women (Blau and Ferber, 1992: 34-71, 141-187). The earnings gap between men and women is due in large part to differences in work experience and employment-related investments, as noted in Chapters 5, 6 and 7. Unfortunately human capital theory became somewhat discredited, especially among sociologists, by one particular application. Polachek (1979) tried to explain the segregation of men and women in the workforce as being due to women choosing occupations with lower penalties for discontinuous employment histories, arguing in effect that job choices were rational and efficient, a thesis that has repeatedly been refuted, in somewhat different formulations, for the USA (England, 1982, 1984; Corcoran, Duncan and Ponza, 1984) and for Britain (Hakim, 1996) for reasons set out in Chapter 6. In addition, sociologists reject it because the emphasis on explaining women's behaviour with reference to family roles is sometimes seen as sexist and linked to discredited Parsonian functionalism (Walby, 1990: 30-32). However the approach is in fact very similar to the sociological idea of household work strategies with husband and wife making joint decisions about the allocation of time to employment, informal work, household production and domestic work (Pahl, 1984), the key difference being that Pahl shows how household work strategies vary across the lifecycle and in response to events such as unemployment of the breadwinner. This seems to be another instance where the concepts and language used by economists and sociologists differ more than the substance of their ideas, so that a fruitful theoretical synthesis is feasible (England and McCreary, 1987).

**Britain as a case study**
In the following chapters we assess the usefulness of these theories in accounting for the empirical evidence on developments in female employment in Britain and other industrial societies in recent decades. Just as methodological triangulation produces more reliable research results than studies based on a single method, theoretical triangulation gives us a firmer grasp of the influences on women's

choices and changes in behaviour (Sayer, 1984: 219-228; Hakim, 1987: 144-5). The three theories are complementary rather than mutually exclusive choices in a zero sum game. They identify areas where change is unlikely, such as vertical job segregation, and areas where change is most possible, such as the precise shape of the sexual division of labour. They point to women's failure to organise collectively as problematic. Taken together, they warn us against automatically equating differences between men and women with inequality or subordination. In a civilised society differences are valued rather than just tolerated. Social equality does not require clone-like similarities across all actors and social groups.

In any event this is unlikely in Britain which is a multi-cultural and multi-ethnic society. Although formally Christian, Britain is one of the most secular societies in Europe and has substantial communities of Jews, Moslems, Buddhists, Hindus, Jains, Sikhs, Ismailis, Rastafarians and Shintoists. The full diversity of cultures and communities is illustrated by the fact that in London one can sample the cuisines of almost every country in the world in some 1400 restaurants with a distinctively non-English character. Britain retains richly diverse regional and social class cultures that confuse and mystify newcomers (Mikes, 1966) as well as a large Asian community and a black community with distinctive roots in the Indian subcontinent and the West Indies. It is indicative that for the 1991 UK Population Census the self-completion forms for private households were printed and issued in no less than twelve languages in addition to English and Welsh: Arabic, Bengali, Chinese, Greek, Gujerati, Hindi, Italian, Punjabi, Somali, Turkish, Urdu, and Vietnamese. Few countries can match this public demonstration of recognition and acceptance of ethnic minority groups. This cultural diversity makes Britain interesting to study, but it also leads us to expect diversity and difference in choices rather than homogeneity in preferences and responses to social and economic change. There is no such thing as a representative Englishman or woman, and no single set of norms to which everyone conforms.

A focus on the relatively unregulated British labour market offers another advantage. To the astonishment of most Europeans there are no laws specifying annual holiday entitlement, maximum daily hours of work or part-time work hours. Neither a carpenter nor a hairdresser requires qualifications or a license before starting work. European labour markets can seem over-regulated to British eyes due to heavy reliance on statute law. Britain appears to be a case of unregulated chaos and anarchy in the eyes of the European Commission. In reality common law, collective bargaining, custom and practice combine to produce much the same regulation of the labour market (Hepple and Hakim, 1996), but on a much more flexible basis than with statute law – as illustrated by the decades required to delete sexist laws in countries which introduced them during the Great Depression. Change and development can happen more easily in Britain, unconstrained by regulations that impede innovation, whether good or bad. Britain can almost be regarded as a kind of ongoing natural experiment. The obvious example is the early development of part-time jobs, which could not be created in the Netherlands, for example, until the law was changed to allow this innovation. The advantage to the Netherlands was that they then designed and shaped the direction of policy on part-time work very carefully indeed (European Commission, 1994: 117), whereas policy in Britain has been piecemeal, often reacting to developments rather than shaping them. Theory attempts to formulate what happens *all other things being equal*, that is, in the absence of major constraints limiting choice or forcing choice in particular directions. So the British case is a theoretically important case study of labour market processes.

# 2
# Marginal work and domestic work

In all industrialised societies, except for the Scandinavian countries, far fewer women than men participate in the labour market. It is widely believed that women's work rates have been increasing throughout the twentieth century, especially in the post-War decades, so that this difference in participation rates is falling across Europe, and may eventually be eliminated. Chapter 3 examines this idea in some detail. An alternative thesis, addressed in this chapter, is that national statistics are faulty and ideologically biased: women's work has been systematically undervalued and undercounted, giving the false impression that work rates are now higher than in the recent past. Women have always worked, it is argued, often longer hours than men. Due to the undervaluation of women's work, national statistics provide an incomplete picture of women's full contribution to the economy and of their role in society.

The idea occurs occasionally in historical research, with historians and sociologists claiming that the true volume of female employment was higher, in their case-study areas and industries, than was shown in contemporary (national) population census statistics (Roberts, 1984: 230; Bose, 1987: 96-7, 103-7, 115; Nyberg, 1994). The thesis became a central feature of discussions of women's role in the development process, on the need for more comprehensive statistical information on household production as well as work in the market economy in order to fully monitor the changing location of productive work and its impact on women as well as men (Boserup, 1970: 160-7; Beneria, 1981; Beneria and Sen, 1981; Redclift, 1985). The thesis was also a feature of the domestic labour debate in the 1970s, a lengthy exploration of the social and economic significance and value of women's domestic labour in capitalist society (Fine, 1992: 169-191), a debate that was restricted to theoretical analysis and speculation by the limited empirical data on domestic work, apart from case-studies (Oakley, 1974). Restricted may be the wrong word here; theoretical speculation is often wilder when it is not informed by reality.

A seminal article by Beneria (1981, 1988) provides the most detailed and persuasive presentation of the thesis. Unlike many others, Beneria is fully cognizant of the economic conceptual framework underlying labour market statistics, the practical difficulties involved in operationalising new conceptual frameworks, and the continuous efforts of bodies like the International Labour Office to improve labour force statistics. Her informed discussion concludes that censuses and surveys should be redesigned to collect information on all productive labour, for two reasons. First, to counteract the ideological undervaluation of women's work and to give recognition to the long hours of labour in which women are engaged. Second, to inform development strategies and programmes in the Third World (Beneria, 1988: 384-5, 388-9). Waring (1988) offers a more passionate and extensive presentation of the thesis, incorporating a critique of economic concepts and theory, of statisticians' practices, and of the United Nations System of National Accounts which institutionalises all these errors and imposes them, imperialistically, on developing countries.

In this chapter we assess this thesis in the light of the available empirical evidence. The focus is limited to Britain and other industrialised countries, so we do not address the issues relating to the development process. There are two logically separate elements in the thesis, which are often conflated in debates. First we address the thesis that women's *market* work is undercounted, due to under-reporting and relative invisibility. Second, we address the thesis that women's *non-market* work is undervalued and hence not counted. For completeness, we also look at voluntary work, a type of work that falls between domestic and market work and is institutionalised in industrial society.

There is no suggestion that national censuses and surveys undercount women's full-time year-round employment. All the debates focus on what we can broadly describe as women's marginal work, work that is relatively less visible, or more difficult to count because it is part-time, seasonal, irregular or combined with domestic work - types of work that differ from the standard male profile of full-time year-round gainful work. Because of this, we first need a clear understanding of definitions of work, and the practical rules applied at the boundary line to separate work and non-work. The next section reviews the basic conceptual framework on which national labour statistics rest, and which are so often the source of misunderstandings and confusion. Following this, we examine the available evidence on *marginal work*: general studies of marginal work, then data on types of marginal work that are most likely to be hidden, invisible and undercounted, such as family helpers, home-based work and the informal economy. Voluntary work is treated as a separate category, as it is highly public and visible, yet always excluded from labour force statistics. We then examine the available evidence on *household work*: domestic work, reproductive and other caring work. Finally, research on the social status of the housewife, treated as an occupation like any other, sheds new light on the whole debate. We show that overall, any undercount in British data is very small. More important, marginal work and domestic work are not exclusive to women.

## Work and employment: the conceptual framework

Labour market statistics are collected within the theoretical framework of economics. Sociologists have never even tried to produce an alternative framework, the closest being the idea of national social and economic indicator systems that were developed in the 1960s and 1970s. More specifically, the concept of economic activity is based on the United Nations System of National Accounts (SNA) to ensure that employment statistics and production statistics are consistent and can be analysed jointly (Dupre, Hussmanns and Mehran, 1987; Hussmanns, 1989). Sociologists, historians, social geographers and others regularly overlook this fact; assume that 'official' statistics are shaped solely by political ideology and public administration needs; offer critiques that are wide of the mark and draw inappropriate conclusions because they have not bothered to acquaint themselves with the basic economic concepts that are operationalised in employment statistics. For example Oakley (1974) thought it necessary to show that housework is work. Nyberg (1994: 153) suggests that statisticians collect data on any 'interesting' topic, in line with personal prejudices. In Britain, there is a long tradition of challenging the perceived political bias of national statistics produced by the state apparatus and exposing their role in maintaining cultural hegemony (Irvine, Miles and Evans, 1979).

*Work* is any productive activity, any activity that produces goods or services. *Employment* is any work done for pay or profit, any work producing goods or services that are traded in the market economy. The key distinction is between *market* work and *non-market* work. Economists are fully aware that domestic work and work in the subsistence economy are productive work, and ideally would like to measure the value of all types of work. Market work can be assigned a monetary value with reference to earnings or profits from traded goods or services. It is a great deal easier to collect data on market work than on the work that produces goods and services consumed immediately within the household or bartered with neighbours, for example. No theoretical distinction is made between formal and informal economic activity: casual childminding for a neighbour is market work if it is paid for, just like any commercial supply of childcare services. Informal economic activity is still market work, even if its casual nature makes it difficult or impossible to measure reliably, even if its value in GNP is too trivial for the effort and cost of data collection to be justified, so that it is allowed to slip through the net. The economic character of the conceptual framework is reflected in the modern terms 'economically active' and 'economically inactive', usually shortened to 'active' and 'inactive', in the same way as 'gainful work' and 'employment' are regularly replaced by the simpler term 'work'. The term 'inactive' is misunderstood by non-economists to mean 'idle' when it is applied to full-time housewives. But students in full-time education are also classified as 'inactive' and no-one suggests that they are idle. It is immediately obvious that some of the misunderstandings and arguments are due to sensitivity and doubts about exactly how much necessary work housewives do in industrial societies. No-one doubts the massive workloads of women in Third World countries, especially in the agricultural sector and in rural areas (Boserup, 1970; United Nations, 1995). Like all work, housework expands to fill the time available (Friedan, 1963: 233-257) and full-time housewives devote more time to housework irrespective, even at weekends, to prove how useful they are (Vanek, 1974).

Most household activities are not work but personal activities, such as eating, sleeping, personal grooming, studying, taking part in sport or maintaining social relations within the family and with neighbours. The substitution rule or third-person criterion is used to distinguish between activities in the fuzzy borderline area between work and non-work. If an activity would lose its value (utility) if a substitute did the task, it is not work. An activity is deemed productive if it can be performed by a third person, someone other than the one benefiting from it (Hawrylyshyn, 1977; Goldschmidt-Clermont, 1990: 280; Mogensen, 1990: 14-19; Thomas, 1992: 17). Studying is not work, because the value of it would be lost if the task was performed by a substitute. Playing with one's child, gardening or cooking a special dish would all be personal activities rather than work if their performance by a third person would spoil the pleasure of them. Routine cleaning is more likely to be work, if the same purpose would be achieved by having a substitute do it. The dividing line between productive non-market activity and personal activities can be a very fine one within the household, and can depend on personal taste. One person buys a power tool to use in household tasks to enjoy the exercise of skill it demands, particularly if the activity differs from their normal day job. Another person does the same thing purely to save on the labour costs of getting these tasks performed commercially. For many people, both objectives are combined, in varying degrees. This means there is no simple rule of thumb to divide productive work from 'leisure' activities, thus providing fertile ground for sociologists to explore the theoretical problems of defining the meaning of work, employment and leisure (Pahl, 1984, 1988; Harding and Jenkins, 1989; Erikson and Vallas, 1990; Mogensen, 1990: 371-418). In the past household work included a lot of market-oriented production work, on the family farm or in the family business, shop or other enterprise. In industrial society most domestic work is consumption work, with goods and services produced for immediate consumption within the household, so that productive work in the household context is less easily identified.

The two key features of any operational definition of employment are the time reference period and the hours threshold applied. At present, the most common reference period is one week, but in some surveys one year is used. Obviously, the number of people identified as being in employment is higher the longer the reference period. Questions that ask about 'usual' occupation or activity are in practice using a reference period of a year or longer. Similarly, the lower the threshold of hours worked, the higher the number of people identified as having paid work. At present, the ILO recommendation, followed in almost all European labour force surveys, is to use a minimal threshold of just one hour's work in the last week, which means that large numbers of marginal workers are counted into the workforce – if they remember to mention the one hour's gainful work in response to an interviewer's enquiry. In recent decades, and in other countries, much higher thresholds have been used – such as a minimum of 13 hours' work a week, a minimum of 15 hours in the last two weeks or, for unpaid family workers, at least a third of usual weekly hours in the job (Beneria, 1988: 375; Hussmanns, 1989: xiv; ILO, 1990a,b). Surveys that collect information about 'usual' or 'main' occupation or activity are generally referring to the activity which takes up most hours in the week and ignoring any secondary jobs or activities. This approach generally increases the numbers of women classified as housewives, whereas the one hour a week threshold for paid work classifies everyone with marginal jobs as being in the workforce rather than inactive, following the rule that economic activity always takes precedence over inactivity.

The utility of the one hour a week minimalist definition of employment is now being questioned by statisticians, sociologists, economists and international bodies. In a chaotically unfruitful discussion of labour statistics with the House of Commons Select Committee on Employment in May 1995, two representatives of the British Royal Statistical Society (RSS), Professors Bartholomew and Moore, explained that they would press for changes to the ILO recommendations for national Labour Force Surveys. In particular, the RSS felt that one hour a week was too low a threshold to meaningfully classify someone as being in employment (Employment Committee, 1995: para 124). Hakim has argued that for sociological analysis, the appropriate focus is on someone's *main* activity, which locates them within the social structure, reflects and shapes their ideas and values, provides the basis for personal identity and for other people's perceptions of them and their social status. Thus marginal workers, who work very few annual hours, due to working part-time and/or part-year, might be counted in national surveys, for monitoring purposes, but would be excluded from analyses of the employed workforce. Marginal workers would be classified by their principal activity as students or housewives (Hakim, 1993a: 112-3). Attempts to create a consistent time series on female employment 1951-1981, especially for part-time work, led Joshi and Owen (1987) to question the value of a headcount measure given variable coverage of women's part-time and marginal work.

Following a detailed analysis of working hours across Europe, the European Commission concluded that people working less than 10 hours a week should be treated as a somewhat different, marginal category; that the label of part-time work should be reserved for people working 10 to 29 hours a week; the label full-time work being reserved for people working average weekly hours of 30 and over (European Commission, 1994: 116). This classification ensured that people working slightly reduced hours, such as the so-called 'part-time' workers in Sweden who work a six-hour day and 30 hour week, would be correctly grouped with full-time workers, thus ending a long-standing misunderstanding in cross-national economic comparisons. Variation in the incidence (or reporting) of marginal work had distorted international comparisons, it was found (European Commission, 1994: 116-118). In sum, the one hour a week minimum limit is questioned on economic, sociological and statistical grounds.

As most censuses and labour force surveys are carried out in the spring, harvest work and other seasonal work are not covered at all. Since the primary aim of these data collections is to monitor *trends* over time, this does not matter: by comparing the size of the workforce in spring each year you are comparing like with like and any upward or downward trend is reliable. Obviously a spring census tells you nothing about the numbers of people doing harvest work; a separate survey would be needed for that. For this reason *continuous surveys*, with interviews carried out throughout the year, are becoming popular, as they can yield averages across the year or data for particular quarters of the year (Hakim, 1987a: 77-81). In the long term, there is increasing interest in the year instead of the week as the reference point for data on employment and working time, as well as in data on lifelong working hours (Bosch, Dawkins and Michon, 1994: 5-15), and alternative measures to the conventional economic activity rate are often proposed (Hakim, 1993a: 108-114). But even in the USA, where annual work profiles have been collected for many decades, the data are rarely used except to show the discrepancy between single-time and year-round employment profiles (Mellor and Parks, 1988; Clogg et al, 1990; see also Table 3.4).

These definitions, and the economic framework, have been developed over more than a century. Early population censuses applied a quite different *social* classification of main activity which included full-time domestic work and full-time studying alongside gainful work. In Britain, for example, full-time unpaid domestic work was listed as an occupation in the census classification up to 1871; however 42% of women were counted as having another occupation in the relevant professional, commercial, agricultural or industrial class up to 1871 (Hakim, 1980: 556-7; Hakim, 1993a: 98-101). The classification of family workers varied between censuses, but they were generally included as gainfully occupied. By 1911, wives engaged full-time and exclusively in domestic work were classified as outside the workforce. These and other changes reflected the move away from the nineteenth century concern with documenting and understanding the changing social structure towards the twentieth century focus on the cash economy and market work (Hakim, 1980: 571). The focus on the market economy emerged earlier in the USA census (Davies, 1980: 594).

The relatively unregulated British labour market allows many forms of marginal work to emerge and flourish, then disappear, in line with the economic cycle, to a far greater extent than is possible in heavily regulated labour markets in other European countries, such as Germany. Studies of the informal economy, the black economy and clandestine employment regularly find that there is less of it in Britain than, say Italy, because the relative absence of regulation allows marginal employment to come and go in the formal economy, instead of pushing it into the shadows (De Grazia, 1980, 1984). In some EU countries part-time work and temporary jobs were not legal options until the law was changed, prompting a massive increase (Hakim, 1990a,b).

**Marginal market work in Britain**
There is no doubt that women's market work is undercounted, to some extent. However the size of the undercount is small; the volume of excluded work, measured in hours or earnings, is tiny; and the main reason for the undercount is the unwillingness of women themselves, or their husbands, to report small amounts of gainful work, since it does not constitute their *main* activity and social identity. The problem has been exaggerated by social scientists who did not have the skills to measure its impact, which is small.

It is well known that particular national surveys exclude people with very low earnings due to the way the data are collected. For

**Table 2.1** People with earnings below the National Insurance (and tax) thresholds, Great Britain, 1985–86

|  | The proportion (%) of workers in each category with earnings below the thresholds | | |
|---|---|---|---|
|  | Employees | Self-employed | Total |
| Full-time workers | 0.3 | 6.8 | 1.0 |
| Part-time workers | 24.1 | 52.3 | 26.3 |
| All in employment | 6.4 | 16.1 | 7.3 |
| Men | 1.7 | 6.5 | 2.3 |
| Women | 12.1 | 48.8 | 14.0 |
| All in employment | 6.4 | 16.1 | 7.3 |

Source: Family Expenditure Survey merged data for 1985 and 1986. See notes at Table 2.

example the New Earnings Survey (NES) only collects earnings data for people who pay income tax, thus excluding people with earnings below the tax threshold. As part-time work has expanded, the number of people thus excluded has increased since the NES was initiated in 1968. By April 1992, there were 2.75 million women employees in Britain with earnings below the level where income tax becomes payable; of these, 2.25 million earned less than the lower threshold at which social insurance taxes (termed National Insurance contributions in Britain) became payable. Independent estimates from the Family Expenditure Survey (FES) showed about 75% of these women were married women; 20% were single women and 5% were lone parents. In spring 1994, it was estimated that one-fifth of part-timers were excluded from the NES due to the tax threshold. Various other estimates have been produced from these two sources at different times, most of them too broad-brush to give a picture of numbers, trends and whether more women than men are excluded from the surveys. The most detailed and reliable estimates so far available are provided by Hakim (1989b) based on special analyses of FES merged data for 1985 and 1986 (Tables 2.1 and 2.2); earnings and tax allowances were also uprated to provide estimates for the 1987/88 tax year (Table 2.3).

Women constitute the great majority of people with very low earnings, and this is due almost invariably to working part-time hours rather than to very low hourly earnings in full-time jobs. Unexpectedly, the results also show that about one-quarter of people

**Table 2.2**  Characteristics of people with earnings below the National Insurance (and tax) thresholds, Great Britain, 1985–86

|  | Employees | Self-employed | Total |
|---|---|---|---|
| Men | 11 | 7 | 18 |
| Women | 67 | 15 | 82 |
| All in employment | 79 | 21 | 100 |
| Full-time workers | 3 | 7 | 10 |
| Part-time workers | 76 | 14 | 90 |
| All in employment | 79 | 21 | 100 |
| Aged under 19 years | 9 | 1 | 9 |
| 19-24 years | 4 | 1 | 5 |
| 25-59 years | 66 | 20 | 86 |
| 60 and over | * | * | * |
| All in employment | 79 | 21 | 100 |

\* Less than 0.5 per cent.

**Source:** Family Expenditure Survey merged data for 1985 and 1986. Data for persons aged 16 or more with gross earnings below the lower personal tax threshold (£42.50 per week for 1985 and £45 per week for 1986) and with zero National Insurance contributions (*N* = 1146). Information on usual earnings was used for employees, and information on earnings as reported for people who are self-employed in their main job. But note that part-time self-employed people with tiny earnings (less than £5.00 per week in 1985 and 1986) and with no other employment are classified as unoccupied rather than as self-employed from 1982 onwards in the FES, and are hence excluded from this table. Part-time work is defined as normally occupying 30 hours a week or less including overtime regularly worked.

with very low earnings are self-employed rather than employees, many of them full-time workers (Table 2.3). The self-employed are a small minority of the workforce but, contrary to stereotype, they have a disproportionate share of low earners (Tables 2.1 and 2.3).

Some people have other tax deductions in addition to the basic 'personal allowance' tax deduction which is treated as the income tax threshold. So the total numbers not paying any income tax at all are slightly larger than those below the basic tax threshold: 3 million rather than 2.9 million (Table 2.3). It is notable that about half of all part-time workers, both employees and self-employed, pay no income tax at all and would pay only a tiny amount of social insurance taxes. This is consistent with the repeated research finding that many wives, whose earnings are supplementary to their husband's earnings, intentionally keep their earnings below the taxable level. The easiest way of doing this is to work less than

**Table 2.3** National estimates for workers who earn less than the National Insurance and/or income tax thresholds

| | People with earnings below the 1987/88 National Insurance threshold | | | People earning less than 1987/88 basic tax thresholds | | | People who are working but are non-taxpayers | | | Base No. |
|---|---|---|---|---|---|---|---|---|---|---|
| | No. (thousands) | % | % of total | No. (thousands) | % | % of total | No. (thousands) | % | % of total | (thousands) |
| **All working** | **2,154** | **100** | **8.9** | **2,913** | **100** | **12.1** | **3,095** | **100** | **12.9** | **24,062** |
| Full-time employees | 71 | 3 | 0.4 | 199 | 7 | 1.2 | 276 | 19 | 1.6 | 16,984 |
| Part-time employees | 1,598 | 74 | 34.6 | 2,067 | 71 | 44.7 | 2,084 | 67 | 45.1 | 4,633 |
| Full-time self-employed | 223 | 1 | 11.8 | 348 | 12 | 18.4 | 436 | 14 | 23.2 | 1,882 |
| Part-time self-employed | 262 | 12 | 45.6 | 299 | 10 | 52.1 | 299 | 10 | 52.1 | 573 |
| All employees | 1,669 | 77 | 7.7 | 2,266 | 78 | 10.5 | 2,360 | 76 | 10.9 | 21,617 |
| All self-employed | 485 | 23 | 19.7 | 647 | 22 | 26.3 | 735 | 24 | 29.9 | 2,455 |
| All full-time | 294 | 14 | 1.6 | 547 | 19 | 2.9 | 712 | 23 | 3.8 | 18,866 |
| All part-time | 1,860 | 86 | 35.8 | 2,348 | 81 | 45.4 | 2,383 | 77 | 45.9 | 5,206 |
| All men | 329 | 15 | 2.4 | 540 | 19 | 3.9 | 697 | 23 | 5.0 | 13,846 |
| All women | 1,825 | 85 | 17.9 | 2,373 | 81 | 23.2 | 2,398 | 77 | 23.5 | 10,219 |

**Source:** National estimates based on 1985 Family Expenditure Survey data for workers aged 16 to 54 years, but with earnings uprated to 1987 levels (using the average rise in earnings in the intervening period) and applying 1987/88 tax and National Insurance thresholds and tax allowances. The 1987/88 National Insurance threshold was £2,030 p.a. for employees and the same figure was used for the self-employed for convenience. The 1987/88 basic tax threshold was £2,425 for all persons except the minority of married men (who constituted only 38.5% of the labour force in 1987) for whom it was £3,795. Other tax allowances may be claimed in addition to the basic tax allowance (for example for mortgages), so that the number of working non-taxpayers will always be higher than the number of people with earnings below the basic tax thresholds. In this analysis, mortgage tax allowances have been attributed to husbands rather than to wives in the case of married persons. As the analysis is based on FES data, large numbers of part-time self-employed people with tiny earnings (less than £5.00 a week in 1985 and 1986) and working less than 30 hours a week are automatically excluded from the results.

full-time hours, or to vary the hours worked so that annual earnings remain tax-free. Comparing these results for 1987/88 with the more recent data quoted earlier for 1992 shows that there was an increase of about 0.4 million women with earnings below the tax threshold over this four year period.

The FES is a continuous survey that goes to some trouble to obtain comprehensive income and expenditure data for households, which is why the FES data on workers with low earnings is more complete than in most other surveys (Hakim, 1982: 108-114). Consistent results were also obtained from a special survey – the 1980 Women and Employment Survey (WES) – which went to great lengths to identify all types of paid work done by women, including the relatively invisible jobs done at home such as childminder, mail order agent, outwork and seasonal work. The 1980 WES survey found that 14% of *non-working* women between the ages of 16 to 59 years said they did such work – that is, about one in eight women who had already said they did not have a job and would be classified as 'inactive' on the conventional definition admitted later, in response to specific prompts, that they were doing occasional paid work of this nature (Martin and Roberts, 1984: 8-10, 31-2; see also Kay, 1984). Applying the figure of 14% to the total of 11.3 million economically inactive women aged 16 and over shows that 1.6 million women who would not report themselves as working were in practice earning small sums of money from marginal jobs. On average, these jobs involved only five hours work a week, and earnings of £4.10 a week or on average just over £200 a year in 1980, placing them far below the thresholds at which income tax and social insurance tax would be applied. Most important of all, these women were classified as non-working throughout the 1980 WES survey, rather than being reclassified as part-time workers. Pilot work confirmed that they could not meaningfully be asked the questions put to women with paid jobs. More significantly, the vast majority (90%) of these women did not think of themselves as 'working' – their work was too irregular or insignificant in its effects on their lives. The authors concluded that marginal work was of too limited importance, both in terms of the numbers of women who do such work and the hours of work and earnings involved, to merit further research attention or to suggest changes to the conventional classification of economic activity. If all the women doing marginal work were to be included in the workforce, this would have raised the female economic activity rate by 4 percentage points. The average of 5 hours work a week meant that these 1.6 million women contributed the equivalent of 200,000 extra full-time workers to a workforce of 24 million, an almost negligible addition.

Similar results are obtained from other surveys. The British General Household Survey (GHS) and the British Social Attitudes Survey (BSAS) have both found it necessary to adopt a lower limit of at least 10 hours' work a week for some or all of their questions on labour market experiences, as the questions make little sense to marginal workers. Since its initiation in 1983, the BSAS has classified everyone working less than 10 hours a week as economically inactive rather than in employment. Some 15% of women classified as 'looking after the home' are marginal workers; their exclusion depresses economic activity rates for women aged 18-59 years by 4% overall (Witherspoon, 1988: 180-1). One advantage of this approach is that it automatically excludes schoolchildren and students with part-time jobs from analyses of the workforce. Some students have Saturday-only jobs, which can consist of an eight-hour day, while others have jobs delivering newspapers to private households, and a variety of other jobs involving a few hours a week. The proportion of students with such jobs rose sharply from one-fifth to over one-third in the 1980s (Hutson and Cheung, 1991). By 1991 students and schoolchildren aged over 16 years accounted for some 600,000 part-time jobs, ten per cent of the total (Naylor and Purdie, 1992: 158). Confusingly, the LFS count of people in employment is in fact a count of *jobs*, including jobs held by students in full-time education, who are not strictly part of the workforce.

In sum, people doing very small amounts of market work are knowingly excluded from some surveys, such as the NES, with regular estimates produced of the numbers excluded by the design of the survey. Other surveys include them, and fill the information gap. Regular surveys, like the FES and BSAS, and special surveys, like the 1980 WES, have all measured the size of the undercount and found it to be tiny in terms of the hours and earnings involved. Large numbers of people do tiny amounts of work for pay or profit, thus allowing commentators the option of claiming a large undercount on a headcount basis. Finally, the LFS routinely identifies large numbers of people working less than 10 hours a week, in Britain and other EU countries (Watson, 1992). It appears that these are mainly employee jobs done on a *regular* basis, in contrast with the more *intermittent* nature of the jobs that do not get included in the labour force count.

International comparisons show that marginal work, defined as working for no more than ten hours a week, is concentrated in countries with large and increasing numbers of part-time workers: the Netherlands, Denmark and the UK, with 15%, 6% and 8% of female employees respectively being marginal workers. In Germany, only 4% of female employees are marginal workers, and in all other European Union member states the percentage is under 3%. Marginal workers account for a large part of cross-national differences in rates of part-time working; when they are excluded, part-time work varies much less across Europe (European Commission, 1994: 115-118). In most industrial countries, the majority of part-time employees work half-time hours: 20-29 hours a week. However the second most important type is the marginal job of under ten hours a week, which is clearly a qualitatively different category (OECD, 1994: 77-86). Within Europe, Denmark has the second highest rate of part-time work among men, consisting typically of marginal jobs (OECD, 1994: 80), which explains why they have exceptionally high turnover rates (Hakim, 1996: Table 8). The exclusion of marginal workers from labour market analyses would thus greatly improve cross-national comparisons.

The diversity of part-time work is concealed by the practice of reporting average weekly hours for each type of worker (Table 2.4). The long-term decline in *usual* work hours is not necessarily reflected in *actual* weekly hours worked, as overtime working rises and falls in line with the economic cycle. The averages give the impression that part-timers work a fairly constant 15-17 hours a week in employee jobs, 13-14 hours a week in self-employment jobs, and 8-10 hours a week in second jobs (Table 2.4). In reality one-quarter of part-timers are marginal workers working 1-10 hours a week, while one-third work half-time hours that can approach those of full-time workers (Naylor, 1994: Table 5).

**Family workers**

The thesis that women's market work is undercounted is sometimes argued on the basis of female family workers not being counted in national censuses and surveys. The most well documented example is Nyberg's (1994) study of female family helpers on Swedish farms

**Table 2.4** Average actual weekly hours worked 1979-1994

|                          | 1979 | 1983 | 1988 | 1992 | 1994 |
|--------------------------|------|------|------|------|------|
| Full-time employees      | 39   | 38   | 39   | 37   | 38   |
| Part-time employees      | 17   | 16   | 15   | 15   | 16   |
| Full-time self-employed  | ..   | 50   | 43   | 40   | 39   |
| Part-time self-employed  | ..   | 14   | 14   | 13   | 13   |
| Unpaid family workers    | ..   | ..   | ..   | 18   | 15   |
| Employees: second jobs   | 10   | 9    | 9    | 9    | 9    |
| Self-employed: second jobs | 12 | 10   | 9    | 10   | 9    |

**Source:** Derived from Table 2 in Butcher and Hart (1995: 216) reporting Great Britain Labour Force Survey data for Spring 1979 to 1994.

in the twentieth century, for which there is only a brief summary in English of the full research report in Swedish. Bose (1987) also rests her case for an undercount in USA censuses primarily on female part-time family labour on farms not being counted in the 1900 Census whereas it was counted from 1940 onwards. However Nyberg's study is unique in providing concrete data on the hours worked by Swedish farmers' wives taken from surveys carried out at regular intervals by the Swedish farmers' association. The surveys sought to document the total volume of hours worked on Swedish farms for input-output accounts which were used to lobby the government for subsidies and other assistance to farmers. Thus Nyberg is able to present trend data on the proportion of farmers' wives who participated in agricultural work (which varied from 50 to 95 per cent) and on the average annual work hours they contributed, by size of farm. The work was almost invariably part-time work, typically milking, and it declined rapidly over time with mechanisation. In general, wives contributed a larger volume of work on small farms and a smaller volume of hours on large farms where mechanisation was more common and hired labour more often employed. Nyberg shows that trends in female family labour cannot be studied through census data in Sweden, due to the census practice of recording only full-time regular work in main occupations, a practice that was retained up to 1950. From 1960 onwards, part-time work in family farms and family businesses was counted, so that the labour supplied by wives and other family helpers began to be documented.

Nyberg recalculates labour force participation rates for married women including family workers and shows that the rates were as high in 1880 and 1900 as in 1980 at about 50%, but they declined to a low point of around 25% in the 1950s. The sexual division of labour which created the full-time housewife is shown to be a transitory phenomenon in Sweden. Like Bose (1987: 108), Nyberg goes on to note that survey definitions have now swung too far towards inclusiveness in Sweden, as large numbers of women are counted among the employed, even though they are at home full-time, on extended parental leave, thus giving a misleading impression of equality between men and women in economic activity rates. Nyberg goes on to claim that censuses measure above all changing values and ideologies about women's market work rather than real changes in women's participation in the labour force (Nyberg, 1994: 153-4).

Family workers were identified as a separate employment status in British censuses up to 1971 (Hakim, 1982: 35) although they were not always separately identified in the published statistics (Hakim, 1980: 562). As the status became increasingly rare, the information ceased to be collected in the census from 1981 onwards. Family workers are also declining in the rest of the European Union but remain important in Greece (13% of all employment in 1990), Spain, Italy and Portugal (3-5%), Belgium, France and Ireland (2-3%). Thus information is collected in the LFS in almost all EU member states, and comparative analyses are published periodically (Meulders, Plasman and Plasman, 1994: 130-146). From spring 1992 the British LFS also began identifying family workers as a separate category and found some 180,000 in Britain, 50,000 men and 130,000 women; 30,000 were in agriculture; 63,000 in retail distribution, hotels and catering; 24,000 were in the construction industry, where wives often take responsibility for business accounts and correspondence; and 62,000 in other industries (Chamberlain and Purdie, 1992: 487; see also Watson, 1994: 241). Average hours are very similar to those of other part-time workers and are declining (Table 2.4). In Britain, about 70 per cent of family workers are female. The proportion varies from half in Ireland, where many are unmarried sons or daughters working in a family farm or business to 100% in Denmark where virtually all are wives (Meulders *et al*, 1994). Family workers constitute a small share of women's employment: less than 10 per cent in all EU countries in 1990 except for Greece where they reached 28%. In the USA, time use surveys from the 1920s onwards show that women in rural areas spent an average of only 10 hours a week on farm work (gardening, dairy activity and the care of poultry), making it an almost marginal activity (Vanek, 1974). By 1981, family workers accounted for less than 1% of total employment, down from almost 3% in 1950, and fewer than half were in agriculture. Over 70% were female, many of them doing white-collar work for a family business (Daly, 1981).

When Britain returned to collecting data on family workers in 1992, the Employment Department was forced to assess how they had been classified previously in the LFS, and what difference the new classification made. Just under a quarter would have been defined as employees or self-employed before 1992 and 11% would have been classified as unemployed; a two-thirds majority would previously have been counted among the economically inactive (Butcher and Hart, 1995: 213). This proves that identifying a separate category of family worker in surveys increases the number of people (most of them women) who are counted as employed rather than out of the labour force. However it also proves that the omission was unimportant: the addition of 120,000 previously uncounted people to a workforce of 25 million is negligibly small, a bare half of one per cent (1% for women and only 0.3% for men). Family workers do not account for any significant element of female employment in modern industrial society, and this seems unlikely to be reversed, given women's preference for jobs which give them some degree of financial independence from their spouse.

Family labour is productive market work in that the goods and services produced by the family business are traded in the cash economy. The constant emphasis on it being *unpaid* in the sense of not wage-earning is irrelevant. Family labour is work for profit rather than for pay, as few are paid a regular wage. However family labour has none of the other characteristics of market work. Workers cannot be dismissed if the quality of work is poor; they cannot be made redundant; their hours are not fixed. There is none of the competitiveness or discipline of wage labour; family workers are not selling their labour in the wider labour market. Because they are not wage-earners and pay no taxes, they are excluded from virtually all social welfare benefits, such as unemployment compensation or disability benefit (Meulders et al, 1994: 146). In many respects they resemble voluntary workers or housewives working for their own family rather than wage-earners.

**Home-based work**

Family work may be in terminal decline but home-based work more generally is undergoing a regeneration and renewal. The separation of home and work imposed by the industrial revolution and the creation of large manufacturing establishments is slowly being reversed as the service sector replaces manufacturing as the main source of employment. Information technology allows white-collar jobs to be done at home, or almost anywhere and the telephone network begins to replace public transport systems as a means of getting the work and the worker together.

There is an extensive literature on the manufacturing homework that was the focus of public concern and legislative controls in late nineteenth century Britain and survived in small numbers throughout the twentieth century (see for example Allen and Wolkowitz, 1987; Boris and Daniels, 1989). From the 1970s onwards, but particularly after the 1980s when personal computers and laptops revolutionised home-based work, traditional manufacturing homework was supplemented, and overtaken by white-collar homework: professional, artistic and clerical work carried out as a personal or family business or undertaken for employers on variable contractual terms. A major research programme on home-based work in Britain carried out by the Employment Department documented these developments and their social, economic and policy implications (Cragg and Dawson, 1981; Hakim and Dennis, 1982; Leighton, 1983; Huws, 1984; Kay, 1984; Hakim, 1985, 1987b, 1988b). There is also much speculation about future trends, some predicting a revival of cottage industry (Applebaum, 1987; Meulders *et al*, 1994: 147-159).

The invisibility of homework is said to contribute to an undercount of women's market work. Unlike family labour, this is work done directly for pay or profit, so there is no doubt it should be reported as employment in national censuses and surveys. The main reason for under-reporting is simply that the work is irregular and regarded as too casual to constitute 'a proper job' (Hakim, 1988b: 619). There is no suggestion that home-based work that is regular and full-time is under-reported.

Surveys of home-based work invariably reveal large overlaps between home-based work, self-employment, work in a family business, second jobs, part-time and intermittent work, leading to some confusion in the literature over numbers in each category. Only a detailed personal interview survey can attempt to separate out all

**Table 2.5** People working at home in their main job by occupation and industry, 1994

Thousands

|  | All | Men | Women |
|---|---|---|---|
| Managers and administrators | 152 | 68 | 84 |
| Professionals | 76 | 44 | 32 |
| Associate professional/technical | 110 | 51 | 58 |
| Clerical & secretarial | 135 | * | 130 |
| Craft and related | 49 | 19 | 30 |
| Plant & machine operatives | 21 | * | 18 |
| Other | 118 | 20 | 98 |
| Manufacturing industries | 85 | 20 | 65 |
| Non-manufacturing industries | 577 | 191 | 368 |
| Who they work for: |  |  |  |
| an outside organisation | 124 | 39 | 85 |
| on their own account | 330 | 127 | 203 |
| a family business | 185 | 38 | 148 |
| Employees and self-employed working in own home - subtotal | 664 | 212 | 452 |
| Unpaid family workers working in their own home | 53 | * | 44 |
| People doing paid work in different places with home as a base | 1678 | 1359 | 320 |
| All others working in own home or using home as a base - subtotal | 1731 | 1368 | 364 |
| Total - All home-based work | 2395 | 1580 | 816 |

**Source:** Labour Force Survey, Great Britain, Autumn 1994 not seasonally adjusted, as reported in *Employment Gazette*. Figures below 10,000 shown as *.

these overlapping aspects, and this has so far been too small a labour force minority to justify more than occasional studies. Population censuses (Felstead and Jewson, 1995) and the Labour Force Survey (Meulders et al, 1994: 147-159) simply identify everyone who does gainful work in domestic premises or uses their home as a base for work carried out elsewhere. Self-employed plumbers, consultants or salesmen, for example, may do their accounts at home, but do most of their work elsewhere. In Britain there were 2.4 million people working at home or from home as a base in 1994 (Table 2.5) about 10 per cent of the workforce, a substantial increase on the figure of 1.7 million or 7 per cent of the 1981 England and Wales workforce (Hakim, 1988b: 613). Of these, 1.7 million were working from home as a base, most of them men; 53,000 were family workers, all of them women; and 664,000 were homeworkers, most of them women, with clerical work the largest single occupation (Table 2.5). Virtually identical figures have been obtained each year since the questions were introduced into the LFS in 1992. The stability of the figures seems to invalidate the notion of substantial under-reporting, which should cause more random variation. Despite the large numbers, homework remains marginal work for women: two-thirds work less than 16 hours a week and have short job tenures. In contrast, most men work full-time and have long job tenures (Hakim, 1988b: 615-7). The sex differentials that characterise the main workforce are simply duplicated among homeworkers.

The expansion of second jobs in the 1980s in Britain and the USA is linked to the growth of home-based work, stimulated by recession and the growth of sub-contracting as well as new technology (Stinson, 1990). Between 1984 and 1995, the number of second jobs grew from 0.7 million to 1.2 million in Britain, although average hours remained constant at 9 hours a week (Table 2.4), making them marginal jobs. Men and women are equally likely to have second jobs, although women began to outnumber men in the 1980s (Naylor and Purdie, 1992: Table 11).

**The informal economy**
Definitions of the informal economy vary from country to country, but the term usually refers to small-scale enterprises producing goods and services that may be under-represented in national statistics on the economy and the workforce, because of the small scale and informal character of the activities involved (Thomas, 1992). In developing countries, the term refers to small street traders, for example. In industrial society the concept embraces all types of marginal work, small family enterprise and home-based work that might be under-recorded in national statistics. Yet as we have already demonstrated, data can be produced on all these groups, if necessary, at least in Britain. Thomas (1992) draws a distinction between the *informal economy*, the *irregular sector*, which involves some illegality, such as tax evasion or the avoidance of minimum wage laws, and the *criminal sector*, where the output itself is illegal, such as the manufacture and sale of drugs. Others group all three types of activity together under the label of 'clandestine', 'secondary',

'hidden', 'black', 'informal', 'underground', 'parallel' or 'twilight' economy, meaning all economic activity that goes unrecorded in national accounts statistics (De Grazia, 1980, 1984).

There has been increased interest in the informal economy in recent years. In developing countries the informal sector is argued to be the engine of economic growth, which should be assisted, even if regulations are sometimes ignored. In industrial society, there is concern that if the picture presented by national economic statistics is seriously incomplete, attempts to manage the economy may have unintended consequences. Italy is invariably taken as the prime example in Europe of an economy with a large and growing informal sector with substantial evasion of tax and labour laws (De Grazia, 1984). In the relatively unregulated British labour market there are few laws for small enterprises to avoid – for example there is no national minimum wage, no laws laying down holiday entitlements or maximum daily or weekly working hours (Hepple and Hakim, 1996). Employment contracts that would be classified as illegal in other EU countries are perfectly legal in Britain so, in a sense, Britain lacks any substantial irregular sector because it lacks the body of restrictive legislation that stimulates and defines it. For example a homeworker whose earnings over the year remain below the basic personal tax-free allowance has no need to 'declare' or 'register' her activities and no need to pay any taxes. Too often it is assumed that any 'unreported' work is necessarily unlawful, or that any marginal work or second job automatically involves substantial tax evasion, as did Pahl (1984: 247) in his survey of informal household work (Hakim, 1989b: 484-5) and as do many other sociologists (Harding and Jenkins, 1989). There seem to be more incorrect assumptions masquerading as knowledge and more unscientific research reports on the informal or 'black' economy than on any other subject (Hakim, 1989b: 483-494).

As demonstrated earlier (Tables 2.1-2.3), there are large numbers of marginal workers in Britain, most of them women, whose short work hours and low total earnings leave them outside the income tax and social insurance systems. All of these people can be labelled as working in the informal economy. All could be suspected of tax evasion and hence incorrectly labelled as being in the black economy (Hakim, 1989b). Adding together the 2 million workers with earnings low enough to leave them outside the tax and social security net (Table 2.3) who are excluded from some surveys but included in others and the 1.6 million non-working women with small earnings from occasional jobs gives a total of some 3.6 million people whose earnings are low enough to classify them as marginal workers, invisible to the income tax and social welfare systems. Making some allowance for non-working men with similarly small earnings (for example students with part-time jobs) brings the total to about 4 million marginal workers who could be classified in the informal economy. Clearly there are huge numbers of *people* doing small amounts of paid work who may not appear in the Labour Force Survey and similar large scale surveys which do not have any special questions probing about marginal activities. However the number of *hours worked* are too trivial to make a great difference to conventional measures of the size of the labour force and the *earnings* involved are too small to dramatically alter their financial dependence on others.

A 1981 study that set out to display the size and importance of the informal economy in Britain in fact proved its insignificance. Even though informal work was defined very loosely as any work that had ever been done for the household by friends, relatives or neighbours, whether on the basis of reciprocal exchange or payment, half of all households had *never* used this source of labour for any household task (including periodic tasks like car maintenance, house maintenance and repairs, decorating, gardening and window-cleaning) and another third had only used it once. Only 16 per cent of all households had ever used informal labour sources (paid or unpaid) on two or more occasions, compared to one-third using commercial firms for the same household tasks. Virtually all household tasks are done by members of the household themselves normally, which is hardly surprising (Pahl, 1984: 237-241).

### Seasonal and temporary work

The final category of marginal work is seasonal, casual and other temporary jobs. These jobs may well involve full-time work, in contrast with the short part-time hours involved in homework, family work and most other forms of marginal work. The argument is that they are undercounted because they are not year-round jobs, because they are short-term and intermittent, as illustrated by seasonal work in harvesting or in summer holiday resorts. The argument seemed plausible before the advent of continuous year-round surveys such as the General Household Survey and, following its adoption of a rotating sample design in 1984, the Labour Force Survey (Hakim, 1987a: 80-81). However the continuous surveys do not yield significantly higher measures of female employment than the time-specific measures from the spring census and LFS.

The LFS shows that in general women are more likely than men to take seasonal, temporary and casual jobs: from 1984 to 1994 about 4-6% of all female employees had short-term jobs compared to 2-3% of male employees (Beatson, 1995: 10). Men and women had almost identical rates for fixed-term contract jobs, which rose from 1.5% of employees in 1984 to 3.5% by 1994. So there is a small undercount of women's seasonal and casual jobs in the spring LFS data, but the summer and autumn LFS results show the effect to be very small indeed. Even in the summer months the percentage of temporary jobs rises to only 7-8% of all employee jobs. The absolute increase is about 200,000 jobs divided fairly equally between men and women, a relatively small addition to the 1.4 million year-round total for all temporary workers, which is again split fairly evenly between men (600 thousand) and women (800 thousand). The key differences between men and women doing temporary jobs are that men are more likely to be working full-time whereas many women take part-time temporary jobs; men are more likely to say they are really seeking a permanent job while women are more likely to actively choose a non-permanent job.

In sum, temporary contracts of all types are a small and fairly stable element of the British workforce, increasing minimally from 5.3% to 6.5% between 1984 and 1994, and these jobs are done almost equally by men and women. The failure to include part-year work in time-specific economic activity rates does not seriously under-represent women's employment. More importantly, the sex differential is small, so men and women are affected almost equally.

**Non-standard employment**
There is no suggestion that censuses and surveys undercount regular full-time jobs. In previous decades, this was the only type of job counted, due to the emphasis on people's main activity or usual occupation. Now, however, definitions have been broadened so that even a single hour's work for pay or profit in a week allows

someone to be classified as economically active rather than inactive. A great deal of part-time, intermittent work is now pulled into the definition of employment. Given the overlaps between home-based work, family labour and other types of marginal work, the total potential undercount is probably little over the 4 per cent estimate for all forms of women's marginal work obtained from national surveys, as noted above, with a similar figure for men. The two key points are, first, that the undercount is far more trivial than this headcount suggests if we take account of the low hours and earnings involved and, second, that men's marginal work is also undercounted. Men's marginal work consists of students' part-time jobs and the second jobs of those in employment. The problem is not exclusive to women and does not reflect an ideological bias against the types of marginal work done by women. It arises from the practical difficulties and costs of measuring very marginal work, set against the low benefits of its inclusion. Surveys repeatedly show that the main impediment is people's natural unwillingness to treat a couple of hours' work a week done on an informal 'own account' basis as equivalent to the full-time permanent employee job which still provides the common notion of 'a proper job' in Britain, what the OECD refers to as 'standard' employment and what the European Commission calls 'typical' employment. As standard employment declines, statistical surveys have become more adept at identifying and measuring all types of non-standard employment which replace it, which is why there is now good data on the diverse forms of marginal work identified above.

To overcome the substantial overlaps between all types of non-standard and marginal employment, the analysis in Table 2.6 provides an overview, dividing the whole workforce into just two categories: full-time permanent employee jobs (standard employment) and all other types of work (non-standard employment). All the self-employed are allocated to the non-standard category. Most self-employed men are working very long full-time hours in permanent jobs; however most self-employed women are working relatively short part-time hours (Table 2.4) – so the self-employment category is very mixed, especially as it includes people who are labour-only subcontractors as well as people in business on their own account (Hakim, 1988a). However most non-standard jobs in Britain are part-time employee jobs; self-employment, non-permanent jobs and family workers all contribute small numbers.

**Table 2.6** Trends in non-standard employment in Britain 1981-1993

| | Thousands and percent | | |
|---|---|---|---|
| | All | Men | Women |
| 1981 Employed workforce | 23,606 | 14,093 | 9,512 |
| Full-time permanent employees | 16,639 | 11,581 | 5,058 |
| as % of employed workforce | 70% | 82% | 53% |
| All other workers | 6,967 | 2,512 | 4,454 |
| as % of employed workforce | 30% | 18% | 47% |
| 1983 Employed workforce | 22,943 | 13,565 | 9,379 |
| Full-time permanent employees | 15,655 | 10,896 | 4,759 |
| as % of employed workforce | 68% | 80% | 51% |
| All other workers | 7,288 | 2,668 | 4,620 |
| as % of employed workforce | 32% | 20% | 49% |
| 1987 Employed workforce | 24,257 | 13,958 | 10,299 |
| Full-time permanent employees | 15,560 | 10,616 | 4,944 |
| as % of employed workforce | 64% | 76% | 48% |
| All other workers | 8,697 | 3,342 | 5,355 |
| as % of employed workforce | 36% | 24% | 52% |
| 1993 Employed workforce | 25,381 | 13,934 | 11,446 |
| Full-time permanent employees | 15,685 | 10,204 | 5,480 |
| as % of employed workforce | 62% | 73% | 48% |
| All other workers | 9,693 | 3,729 | 5,964 |
| as % of employed workforce | 38% | 27% | 52% |

**Source:** Labour Force Survey data for Great Britain, Spring 1981, 1983 and 1987 reported in Hakim (1990: 165) Table 1 and Spring 1993 Labour Force Survey for the United Kingdom, reported in Watson (1994: 240) Table 1.

Throughout the 1980s the female workforce was divided almost equally between standard and non-standard jobs. In 1981 standard jobs predominated (53%); by 1993 non-standard jobs dominated female employment (52%). Among men, the loss of full-time permanent jobs was more dramatic, as they declined from 82 per cent to 73 per cent of all jobs, with non-standard jobs rising from less than one-fifth (18%) to one-quarter (27%) by 1993. In the workforce as a whole standard jobs outnumber non-standard jobs by two to one in Britain. In the European Union as a whole the ratio is the same, varying from four to one in Luxembourg to one to two in Greece due to high levels of self-employment in family farms and businesses (Hakim, 1987c: 554, 1990a: 173-9, 1990b: 179).

The substitution of part-time for full-time jobs is examined more closely in Chapter 3. Here we simply note that with all its limitations as a time-specific count, the spring LFS seems to be working well in identifying non-standard or atypical forms of employment and in measuring trends over time in comparison with conventional jobs. Women's employment in Britain already consists *mainly* of non-standard jobs. Increasing this count to make allowance for the more marginal types of non-standard employment would enhance this trend slightly.

**Voluntary work**

Voluntary work is a separate category of activity falling between market work and domestic work. As the label implies, voluntary work is definitely productive activity which easily passes the third person test. Yet it has never been counted in national labour force surveys. On the face of it, voluntary work provides the strongest example of women's contribution to society at large (not just their own families and friends) being under-reported and under-valued. It also provides the strongest refutation of the argument, because there are no differences between the voluntary work contributions of men and women, either in Britain or in the USA. The undercount affects men just as much as women, arguably more.

Voluntary work is important in developing as well as industrial societies, but the ILO had no hesitation in continuing to exclude it from labour force statistics in its latest review, along with domestic work (Dupre, Hussmanns and Mehran, 1987: xiv). They noted that in most countries volunteer workers contribute to private non-profit organisations which supply various social services to their community such as child and elderly welfare, education and medical related services. Sometimes emergency services such as sea rescue and fire services are also organised on a volunteer basis. Furthermore, in many developing countries, particularly in rural areas, household members often provide work on a volunteer basis for community development, such as filling ditches, cleaning tanks and flood prevention. The purpose of voluntary work is to provide a service to others and is typically defined as any work undertaken without coercion for an organisation either in an unpaid capacity or for a token payment.

Information on voluntary work in Britain was first collected in 1981, then again in 1987 and 1992 in the GHS (OPCS, 1983: 160-180; Matheson, 1990; Goddard, 1994). The 1992 GHS defined voluntary work as unpaid work, except for the refund of expenses, which is done through a group or on behalf of an organisation of some kind. It should be of service or benefit to other people or the community and not only to one's family or personal friends. The definition was explicitly intended to exclude informal caring of family or friends and help to neighbours which is potentially reciprocal. The definition also excluded fostering children, contributing to collections for charity, attending fund-raising events, doing jury service, acting as blood-donors, voluntary work organised by a school for a student to gain work experience, work done for a trade union or political party. The three British surveys yield almost identical results. There is almost no change over time in voluntary work. The extent and the pattern of voluntary work in the USA are almost identical to the results for Britain (Blau and Ferber, 1992: 56-59).

Once neighbourly activities and services to friends and family are excluded, voluntary work is relatively rare. In 1992, one-quarter (24%) of people aged 16 or over said they had done some kind of voluntary work through or on behalf of a group in the 12 months before interview. One in six (16%) had done so in the four weeks before interview. Men and women were equally likely to do voluntary work: 21% and 27% respectively had done so in the year before interview; men contributed an average of 17 hours' voluntary work within the preceding four weeks compared to women's average of 15 hours. It was not necessarily those who had most time to spare who were most likely to volunteer, as volunteering was strongly associated with higher educational qualifications and higher grade occupations. People who were in employment were more likely to do voluntary work than the economically inactive (27% versus 20%). Women working part-time were most likely to do voluntary work and full-time housewives were one of the groups least likely to volunteer (37% and 22% respectively). This means that voluntary work does not even out the differences between the working and non-working populations (Matheson, 1990: 9-11; Goddard, 1994: 4-6). On the contrary, it enhances the polarisation already manifested in paid work. If voluntary work for political parties, trade unions, employers' associations and professional associations are added into the picture, it is clear that men do more voluntary work than women, as men tend to dominate active membership of these organisations.

A 1980 survey of one community in Britain provides information on voluntary work for relatives, friends and neighbours of the sort which is potentially reciprocal and excluded from the GHS surveys, such as house repairs, babysitting, shopping and gardening. Men and women were equally likely to do such work (25% in each case); employed men and full-time housewives were most likely to do jobs for relatives, friends and neighbours; men most often helped with house repairs and women most often provided domestic services or did sewing, but both did a wide range of voluntary work tasks (Pahl, 1984: 248-251).

The absence of any substantial sex differential in voluntary work is worth underlining because the failure to measure women's voluntary work has been given special emphasis in critiques of labour force statistics and the SNA (Waring, 1988: 113-5) and is popularly believed to be important. What this tells us is that women are highly conscious of all their own activities but largely oblivious of the equivalent activities of men. No doubt the reverse is also true. This means that virtually everyone feels their contributions are not fully highlighted and appreciated. It seems we are dealing here with a problem of human nature, not a problem specific to women. The idea that women are unique in doing a substantial volume of voluntary work has no basis in reality. Men do just as much voluntary work as women, whether formally organised or informal neighbourly work, and on some definitions men do more. In contrast, there is no doubt that women do the majority of domestic work, which is also not represented in national labour force statistics.

**Domestic work**

Economists have always thought it desirable to include household production work in national accounts. The sole reason for not doing so has simply been the methodological difficulty of measuring the value of household work, or indeed any non-market non-traded work for which there are no prices (Goldschmidt-Clermont, 1982, 1987, 1990). Transfers of production occur between the household sector and the market economy, causing GNP to rise and fall while the actual amount of goods and services available to the population does not change. For example a sizeable share of laundering moved from the household to commercial enterprises in the late 1920s and early 1930s; it then moved back to households as appropriate equipment became available. In the past, clothing for women and children was usually made at home; today they are purchased ready-made from commercial establishments despite the electric sewing machine. In contrast, power tools for home use have created a new Do-It-Yourself industry of house repairs and decorating dominated by men. These changes cannot be identified when GNP measures exclude household production. However difficulties in measuring the value of household work are real. The number of hours of work can be misleading, given flexibility in the housewife's use of time. Domestic work can be carried out with different degrees of intensity, efficiency and productivity, interspersing it with leisure time and other breaks. Domestic work carried out by hired labour invariably requires far fewer hours than are typically reported by housewives, and wives in employment spend half as much time on housework as do full-time housewives (Vanek, 1974). The measurement of domestic work must rely on the number of hours expended, and hence time use data, but there is no direct or constant relationship to output (Myrdal and Klein, 1968: 34-7; Vanek, 1974; Goldschmidt-Clermont, 1989).

As Hawrylyshyn (1977: 84-5) pointed out it is only the *minimum required time* for an activity that constitutes the work element; additional time is only devoted to an activity if it provides satisfaction and pleasure (utility, in economic terms). In practice, an hour of household time may combine production and consumption, indirect and direct utility. In the same way that a car provides both transport and status, cooking may provide a meal to eat but also a relaxation. She concludes that the minimum necessary time for domestic work is most closely approximated by the hours allocated to it by women in full-time employment, who are obliged to be more efficient than full-time housewives (1977: 91). Unfortunately none of the time use surveys tells us what the minimum time required for domestic work is. They do not even address the question. The answer can only be estimated from indirect evidence.

Studies of the activities of full-time housewives reveal a remarkable lack of concern with efficiency; on the contrary tasks are constantly expanded into huge amounts of unnecessary make-work (Friedan, 1963; Oakley, 1974: 85, 110, 121; Pahl, 1984: 112, 228-9, 256). One notable finding from Oakley's landmark study is that the extra work did not arise from housewives seeking to upgrade the skill content of their work, for example by cooking more complex or unusual dishes, but from endlessly repeating the same unskilled tasks. For example full-time housewives cleaned and shopped daily instead of weekly, washed and ironed sheets twice a week, insisted on giving all their children a fresh set of clothes every day, vastly increasing the volume of laundry and ironing (Oakley, 1974: 92-112). Variations in hours spent on domestic work are *not* explained by the number of children being cared for, access to labour-saving equipment and other amenities, or the purchase of more services in the market (Oakley, 1974: 94, 110-112; Blau and Ferber, 1992: 55). One explanation for the reluctance of husbands to help with domestic work is the knowledge that there should be no need for it if efficient work methods were used. Full-time housewives often create a self-imposed domestic slavery which cannot be blamed on men (or patriarchy), especially as the majority of wives say they are satisfied with their husband's contribution to housework and childcare (Martin and Roberts, 1984: 101-2; Pahl, 1984: 112, 257, 269).

A recent British study showed that full-time housewives spend over three times as many hours on cleaning as do women with full-time jobs; they also spend almost twice as many hours on preparing meals. Overall, women with full-time jobs spend about half as much time on domestic work: 18 hours a week on average compared to 30 hours a week reported by full-time housewives. Domestic work is defined here as house cleaning and tidying, meal preparation, washing up after meals, repairs, gardening, shopping and laundry, but not time spent on childcare which is discussed separately below. Husbands contribute a relatively unvarying 10 hours a week of domestic work, an increase on earlier decades. Overall couples who both work full-time spend 28 hours a week on domestic work compared to 40 hours a week in homes with a full-time housewife (Horrell, 1994: 207-212). Averages reported for the USA are very similar: wives do 25 hours of housework per week and husbands do 7 hours a week (Brines, 1994: 670). In broad terms about half the full-time housewife's hours are attributable to inefficiency, huge amounts of unnecessary make-work or to activities done for pleasure rather than necessity. Further evidence comes from comparisons of time spent on housework by single people. Unmarried women were found in one study to do twice as many hours of housework as unmarried men in 1975, a large reduction on 1965, when they did three times as many hours (Stafford, 1980: 58). Single women spend 50 per cent more time on domestic work than single men, an average of three hours a day instead of just two (Mogensen, 1990: 110). This suggests that one-third or more of the time spent on housework by women consists of optional extras, that is consumption work.

All these results rely on time use surveys which require respondents to complete diaries reporting their activities for each 15 minute section of the day, typically for a period of one week. Anyone who has been obliged to complete such time use diaries for an employer knows that the description or classification of activities in time use accounts is open to just as much, perhaps more, manipulation and bias as responses to interview surveys; if the purpose of an enquiry is not clear, people apply their own assumptions. The validity of subsequent researcher coding of reported tasks and activities as 'work' or 'leisure' can also be doubtful, given that the classification of an activity depends very much on why it is done and for whom. Finally, people do not naturally perceive activities in terms of blocks of time, as required by time use surveys, but in terms of tasks to be performed and responsibilities to be remembered (Pahl, 1984: 128, 256, 1988: 744-7). The 'objectivity' of time budget data is not all it is claimed to be (Anderson, Bechhofer and Gershuny 1994: 157-8, 205-7, 271-2; Robinson and Gershuny, 1994). This invisible problem of data validity is just as important as the more frequently discussed problem of obtaining data for fully representative national samples (Mogensen, 1990: 31, 371-418). Most dubious of all is the practice of *imputing* data on unpaid household work hours from a single time use survey to earlier and later years, as Fuchs (1986) and Leete and Schor (1994) have done. Data from conventional interview surveys can in practice be as good as or better than time use survey data.

Thomas (1992: 13-47) provides an invaluable review of the economic theory, data collection problems and research results on household work and subsistence production. He sets out the current UN System of National Accounts (SNA) rules which list many primary production activities that should be included in national income accounts, distinguishing these from what might be called consumption work in the household. He explains why this work is conventionally excluded from GDP; reviews the arguments now offered for estimating its value within national accounts; sets out the methods used to do so; and the results obtained. For developed countries, the total value of household work ranges widely from 9% to 48% of GDP, although most estimates cluster in the 20-30% range. For developing countries, estimates are somewhat higher, in the range 23% to 49% of GDP. It is often noted that there is no tax on the imputed income from household work and that, if domestic work can be valued, it should be taxed in order to remove the fiscal bias in favour of couples with a full-time housewife (Gronau, 1980: 411; Stafford, 1980: 59).

The higher value of domestic work in industrial societies is explained by the greater importance of consumption work. As Galbraith (1975: 45-53) pointed out, the conversion of women into a crypto-servant class was an economic accomplishment of the first importance. Menially employed servants were available only to a minority of the preindustrial population. The servant-wife is available, democratically, to almost the entire male population. Women's labour to facilitate consumption facilitates indefinitely increasing consumption levels in capitalist society, legitimated by the notion that lifestyle expresses individual personality and cultural capital. The great achievement of Western capitalism has been to persuade women that housework and homemaking are an expression of their femininity (Friedan, 1963; Oakley, 1974, 1976: 128; Matthaei, 1982), in sharp contrast with values and ideas in other cultures. This may explain why hours spent on housework peaked in the 1960s, before the second wave of feminism questioned the need for it and prompted a decline (Hartmann, 1981). However domestic consumption is labour intensive and time-consuming in Western industrial society, fuelled especially by the purchase of housing, automobiles and consumer durables, all requiring care and maintenance (Mogensen, 1990: 100, 111).

Trends in domestic work are strongly influenced by social class. Gershuny (1983a: 149-151, 1983b: 38, 1988: 587) has shown that time spent in domestic work (including childcare) shows opposing trends when analysed by social class. Over the last 50 years, working class women have come to do less domestic work, due to time-saving devices like the washer-dryer and drip-dry shirts. In contrast, middle and upper class women now do far more domestic work, since they no longer have servants to do it for them. Working class women also spend less time in employment too, due to part-time work options, and more educated women enter employment more often. As the leisured class has become the overworked class and the working class now does far less work of any kind, the working class has more leisure than the middle class (Gershuny, 1993: 581). Up to 1980, men did roughly one-third as much domestic work (including childcare) as did women (Gershuny, 1983a: 145) and women did one-third to one-half as much paid work as did men (Joshi et al, 1985: S171), producing a certain balance. From the 1970s onwards, longitudinal data for a dozen industrial societies including Britain show that economic growth (as measured by GDP) produces contrasting trends among men and women: total hours of employment decline among men and rise among women while total hours of domestic work (broadly defined) rise for men and decline for women – leading to a long-term convergence in total work hours of men and women (Gershuny, 1992: 15-20, 1993: 583) as predicted twenty years ago by Young and Willmott (1973).

Adding together market work, domestic and childcare work, the evidence for the 1970s onwards is that wives and women generally do *fewer* total work hours than husbands and men generally (Stafford, 1980: 58; Blau and Ferber, 1992: 53; Coleman and Pencavel, 1993). From the 1970s onwards, wives without paid employment had the shortest total work hours, shorter than wives with market work, even though they spent more hours on domestic work than employed wives (Blau and Ferber, 1992: 53). There is little evidence that wives generally, or full-time housewives, are exploited in the sense of working longer hours in total than men.

**Reproductive and caring work**
A century ago, child-bearing and childcare dominated married women's adult lives, except for the very rich (Lewis, 1984), in part because few people lived beyond the age of 50. Today, families of 16, 12, 8 and even 4 children are almost unheard of. Very few women will have more than two or three children; many will have only one child; and voluntarily childless couples are becoming a feature of Western industrial society (see Chapter 5). Childbearing and childcare are no longer the dominant activities of adult women. They occupy a small proportion of the lifecycle, even if they become overwhelmingly full-time activities for a few years. The expansion of compulsory education up to age 16 in Britain, 18 in some European countries, means that childcare is a full-time activity for only the first 4-6 years of a child's life, about ten years with two children. Discussions of domestic labour often emphasise women's reproductive work, overlooking the fact that this now forms a tiny element of household work over the whole lifecycle, which is dominated by year-round domestic work and

periodic house and car maintenance (Pahl, 1984: 223, 273-5; Fine, 1992: 186-7).

A 1986 study found that childcare occupied on average 19 hours a week for full-time housewives, 7 hours a week for women working part-time and 1 hour a week for women working full-time, compared to 6 hours a week for non-working men, 4 hours a week for men working part-time and 1 hour a week for men working full-time (Horrell, 1994: 209). On average, childcare accounted for 10% of weekly time for housewives, 4% and 1% of weekly time for women working part-time and full-time respectively, and for 3%, 2% and 1% respectively of men's weekly time. Given differentiated sex roles, as shown in Chapter 4, women do the bulk of childcare, but even so, averaged across all women aged 20-60, childcare represents a tiny fraction of adult life. Producing children may still be a major feature of women's lives in terms of personal identity and attitudes.

The decline in childcare work is being replaced to some extent by the care of elderly relatives, which is potentially more time consuming and burdensome. A mother's care of her children is based on unreasoning love and affection, at least some of the time, in most cases. Care of the elderly is based on love and obligation. The dependency of children does not last long, but people caring for the elderly cannot look forward to a bright future. The elderly can only be expected to get more frail, more unreasonable and more dependent, and one never knows when the caring activity will end. Compared with childcare, care of the elderly is a heavier and less rewarding burden.

Nationally representative data on informal caring was collected in the 1985 and 1990/91 GHS and in the 1991 British Household Panel Survey. All three surveys yield almost identical results (Green, 1988; OPCS, 1992; Arber and Ginn, 1995; Corti and Dex, 1995). Men and women are equally likely to be caring for a sick, disabled or elderly person living with them (4%) or living in another household (10%-15%) and they are equally likely to devote over 20 hours a week to caring (4%). Most commonly, the person cared for is a spouse living with the carer, or else parents or parents-in-law. Differences in caring between men and women are generally small and caring responsibilities are only weakly associated with employment patterns among men and women. However caring responsibilities can have more dramatic consequences for men's employment than for women, who are more often full-time housewives anyway and can more readily get part-time jobs. The popular stereotype of caring work being an almost exclusively female activity is unfounded. Men are as likely to be carers as women. The reason why women dominate in terms of absolute numbers of carers is simply that women live longer than men.

## Status of the housewife and househusband

The entire debate on the undercounting of women's productive work is in one sense irrelevant. The main reason for the issue being treated as important is that women feel the status of the housewife has diminished; they therefore seek a revaluation of their role and status by underlining the marginal market work done by women and the productive element in their domestic work. A more direct approach to the issue would simply be to assess the social status of the housewife and whether the role has in reality fallen in status in the post-War decades.

The conventional social stratification theory response to this question says that the wife, along with any children in the home, takes her social status from the male income-earner's occupation. The housewife's Social Class (in Britain) or Socio-Economic Status (in the USA) is taken from the husband, and is thus independent of the quantity and value of any domestic work done in the household. Indeed a housewife traditionally has higher status the less domestic work she does herself and the more such work is given to servants, as this implies greater wealth from the husband's activity, whatever his occupation. As the workforce becomes more highly qualified, there is a long term drift upwards in the entire Social Class structure, with an increasing proportion of professional, technical and managerial occupations and fewer unskilled occupations. Collectively, housewives must have risen in status too, in parallel with the upward drift in the class structure in the post-War period. In this perspective, housewives cannot have *fallen* in status.

The alternative view is that most people are aware that the housewife's job as housekeeper and mother has shrunk in size in Western industrial society, leaving time free for other activities. Wives are expected to do other things as well, instead of being 'just a housewife' in the sense of an exclusive life-long role. Wives who are full-time homemakers have thus lost status in some subtle way. True or false?

To answer this question we must resort to a study carried out in 1972 in the USA, the only large-scale study that included the housewife among the list of occupations to be ranked in prestige and status by respondents (Bose, 1985; Bose and Rossi, 1983). Studies of occupational status in Britain have been limited to male workers and occupations (Goldthorpe and Hope, 1972, 1974). The extrapolation of occupational status scores from data for male occupations to typically-female occupations has been accepted, *faute de mieux*, but creating a status score for the housewife has not been attempted. A study carried out in the USA offers somewhat indirect evidence on the status of the housewife in Europe, as there may be subtle differences between Europe and North America, but it is the best data available.

The main focus of Bose's study was the relationship between occupational segregation and occupational prestige, that is, whether female occupations tend to be ranked as lower in status than male occupations. The study combined experimental design with survey research, with randomly varying descriptions of 110 occupations presented to a sample of householders living in Baltimore who were asked to rate each occupation's prestige on a scale from 1 to 9. (The study included a survey of college students' occupational prestige ratings, but these results are ignored here as unrepresentative of anyone except this minority group.) The innovation was that the list of occupations included 'housewife', 'househusband' and 'person living on state welfare', and a separate chapter of the report was devoted to the social status of these non-working positions (Bose, 1985: 44-57).

The somewhat surprising result was that the housewife was accorded higher social status than any of the labour market occupations that corresponded roughly to domestic work (Table 2.7). Within a scale that ranged from a high of 90 for college professor to a low of 8 for parking lot attendant, the housewife had an average occupational prestige score of 51, well above the score of 25 for a paid housekeeper, 39 for a hairdresser, 15 for a laundry worker and 12 for a maid, but below the score of 63 for a social worker and 65 for a primary school teacher. This high status score applied only to the traditional female homemaker; the househusband was accorded very low status indeed: a score of 15 compared to 51

**Table 2.7** Average status of housewife, househusband and related occupations

| Occupation | Prestige score | Occupation | Prestige score |
|---|---|---|---|
| Secondary school teacher | 70 | Hairdresser | 39 |
| Administrative assistant | 68 | Housekeeper | 25 |
| Primary school teacher | 65 | Boardinghouse keeper | 24 |
| Hotel manager | 64 | Short order cook | 22 |
| Social worker | 63 | Waitress | 22 |
| Private secretary | 61 | Babysitter | 18 |
| Dental assistant | 55 | Laundry worker | 15 |
| Office secretary | 51 | Maid | 12 |
| **Housewife** | **51** | **Househusband** | **15** |

**Source:** Derived from Tables 4.1 and 4.2 in Bose (1985: 48, 50) reporting average prestige scores awarded by householder sample for occupations without descriptions of the incumbents.

for the housewife, reflecting the fact that the non-working male is not yet a legitimate role in society. However there was no consensus on the housewife occupation, which had the largest variance in scores in the study (1,018), followed by the artist role (a variance of 876), followed by a dozen occupations with variances in the 600 range: coalminer, farmer, househusband, landscape gardener, social worker and sociologist. These occupations cover diverse grades of work, so it is clearly something about the occupations themselves that creates confusion or disagreement on where they should be placed on a prestige scale.

Lack of consensus on the housewife's status was also reflected in the marked divergence of opinion between men, who gave it a score of only 41, and women, who gave it an above average score of 61. No other occupation attracted such a marked sex difference in prestige rating. The male rating placed the housewife role much closer to equivalent jobs in the labour market, such as hairdresser or housekeeper. The female rating placed it closer to white-collar typically-female jobs in the labour market, such as secretary (Table 2.7). It seems that men evaluated the housewife in terms of her domestic functions and activities. Women gave her a 50 per cent average mark-up in prestige, which was stronger than their general tendency to give higher gradings to female occupations (Bose and Rossi, 1983: 329).

These results demonstrate the ambivalence that surrounds the housewife role in Western industrial society, and confirm that women rate the role much higher than men do. They also explain why the full-time housewife role is attractive to working class women, for whom it represents a higher status position than the manual jobs they have access to in the labour market, and is unattractive to middle class or professional women, for whom it represents a drop in status compared with their occupational prestige scores (Bose, 1985: 50-1).

One of the best-known studies of the housewife is Oakley's (1974, 1985, 1976) case study of 40 young mothers of young children in a London suburb in 1971, almost all of them full-time housewives. Oakley concluded that three-quarters of these mothers were dissatisfied with domestic work, due to the long hours of work and perceived low status of the housewife role. Mothers who had previously been employed in high status jobs were most dissatisfied with domestic work. Middle class women perceived themselves as mothers and wives with interests beyond the home, rather than housewives, and enjoyed looking after their children; in contrast, working class women displayed positive attachment to and identification with the housewife role but were at best ambivalent about looking after their children. Attachment to the housewife role was associated with far longer hours devoted to domestic work and, paradoxically, with greater job satisfaction. Domesticity was seen as feminine and the sexual division of labour in the home was seen as natural by these mothers. They valued the autonomy of the housewife role, and being 'your own boss'. There was little evidence that these mothers longed to return to employment, and they had no sympathy with the women's liberation movement (Oakley, 1974: 42-3, 72, 106-112, 120-133, 166, 176, 182-92). This richly detailed study has been taken as representative of housewives generally, and dissatisfaction with domestic work has been interpreted as dissatisfaction with the housewife *role*. Both conclusions are incorrect.

Oakley's study of non-working mothers of young children is not representative of housewives generally, either for 1971 or the 1990s. The GHS and LFS both show that across the two decades 1973-1993, among women aged 16 to 59 years who were economically inactive, only one-third had a child aged under 5 years; only half had a child aged under 10 years. Among non-working wives living with their spouse, less than half had a child under 5 years at home. If we add the 6 million wives aged 60 and over, virtually all of whom are non-working housewives, to the 3 million inactive women of working age, the mothers of young children shrink to a small minority of the total. Over half of all wives have no dependent children at home; four-fifths of wives have no child aged under 5 years at home. Oakley's sample of housewives was biased towards domestically-oriented mothers, a subgroup of all housewives. It appears that the dissatisfaction they expressed was due primarily to the long hours of childcare work at this stage of the lifecycle (Pahl, 1984: 273-5).

Bonney and Reinach (1993) also point out that Oakley's study was not representative of British housewives generally, most of whom do not have young children to care for, so that Oakley's portrayal of housewives as rebelliously dissatisfied was misleading. Using a large representative 1986 survey dataset, Bonney and Reinach showed that among 500 full-time homemakers aged 20-59 years only 16 per cent said they planned to return to full-time employment at some point in the future. The vast majority (84%) of housewives saw homemaking as their principal activity in the long term: 37 per cent intended never to return to employment and 47 per cent were only interested in part-time jobs eventually. Only half the sample had any young children to care for; the rest simply regarded themselves as permanent homemakers. Attitudes towards the housewife role, and the disadvantages of being without a paid job revealed that the majority did not regret the lack of a job and found being at home satisfying. There was no sign that the role was perceived to be of low prestige and social recognition as Oakley had concluded. The main disadvantages of the homemaker role were reported by everyone to be the social isolation and, for those who had children, the heavy workload entailed in caring for young children. The young mothers in the sample spent a median of 73 hours a week on childcare compared to only 28 hours a week on domestic work (a distinction that Oakley fails to make in her study). Even so, no more than one-quarter of any group of housewives expressed general dissatisfaction with their situation (Bonney and Reinach, 1993: 616, 619, 621-2, 626). The 1990 BSAS also found no evidence that women looking after their children at home full-time were dissatisfied, or that a majority wished to join the labour market instead (Witherspoon and Prior, 1991: 151). Oakley's study is revealed as seriously misleading in its conclusions due to sample selection bias (see Chapter 5) – in this case a focus on only one stage of the lifecycle. The same problem arises with Hochschild's (1990) study of 50 North American couples both working full-time and with a child aged under 6 years, who experienced even greater workloads than did Oakley's full-time housewives.

## Conclusions

Marginal work for pay or profit, some of it carried out in the informal economy, is fully measured in some national surveys but is undercounted in others, despite the one hour a week minimalist definition of employment. Almost all marginal work involves so few hours and such low earnings that it remains below the tax threshold, exempt from deductions. Its inclusion would add only 4 percentage points to current female work rates in Britain. However the utility of the one hour a week definition of employment is now widely questioned, as it reclassifies into the workforce students in full-time education, people retired on employer pensions as well as women whose main activity is full-time homemaking.

Domestic work produces a large volume of goods and services consumed immediately within the household which would represent a substantial addition to GDP as measured by market work. However there is still no agreed method for valuing non-market work and valuations of domestic work vary hugely. A substantial and growing proportion of domestic activity also consists of consumption which is not work as identified by the third person test. Women in Britain do more than half of all domestic work; men contribute between one-quarter and one-third on average. Both in domestic work and in marginal work the sex differential is smaller than popularly believed. However domestic work and family labour, while productive, differ fundamentally from wage work in the competitive market economy. Whereas wage work is social and abstract, domestic labour is private and individual-specific. The absence of competition in the domestic labour market means there are no norms to set minimum labour time for tasks. There is no rigid distinction between work and leisure, between production and consumption. There is no pressure to increase productivity or to reduce costs and no external control over the production process (Fine, 1992: 169-191). Only market employment allows work to be separated from family relationships and ascribed roles, with increases in individual productivity (Goldin,

1990: 11, 119). The sex differential in domestic work mirrors the sex differential in market work, and the long-term trend is towards convergence in the hours of paid and unpaid work done by men and women.

Throughout this review of all forms of marginal and non-market work, differences between men and women have been small or non-existent. In some areas, such as home-based work, men dominate. Among family workers, women dominate. Voluntary work of all types is done equally by men and women. Caring work is done equally by men and women, although women do more childcare. Marginal and non-market work are visible, counted, done by men as well as women, and do not markedly alter the overall picture on workloads. Criticisms of the ideological bias of the economic conceptual framework for labour statistics have been ill-informed and have often rested on a lack of familiarity with the basic concepts of labour economics and economic sociology.

The argument that women's work is undercounted can most fruitfully be reformulated as an argument in favour of a more informative classification of the main activities of people classified as economically inactive. At present people in full-time education are usually separately identified, but the retired are often not. And the majority of prime-age non-working people are not differentiated at all at present, not even to distinguish those with young children at home from the rest. More information would obviously be useful on what housewives do with their time. This is now a genuine question. If feminists want to see proper valuations of women's domestic work, this will mean a lot more prying into private lives, to assess efficiency, quantity and quality of outputs instead of guesstimates of time allocation at the end of each day. This seems an unlikely development in the near future.

In sum, labour statistics in Britain stand up to close scrutiny, even for research on female employment, which is always more difficult and demanding. In terms of their accessibility, quality and variety, Britain is the envy of some European countries. We have a solid information base for the remainder of our analysis.

# 3
# Feminisation of the workforce

The idea that women's employment has been steadily rising for many decades in Britain, certainly throughout this century and possibly longer, and particularly since the watershed of the Second World War, has become a commonplace, part of received wisdom, endlessly repeated and never questioned. This chapter examines the feminisation of the workforce and its consequences. Has women's entry to the workforce driven men out, by taking their jobs? Has the feminisation of the workforce laid the foundation stone for greater equality between men and women in the workplace? And has the nature of work itself been changed by women's increasing presence in an environment that was for some decades heavily masculine? The answers to these questions are inter-related, and sometimes surprising. Undoubtedly there have been massive changes in the economy and the labour force since the 1950s. But behind the easily remembered rising economic activity rates for women, especially married women, there have been more complex changes in the composition and characteristics of the workforce that undermine expectations for social and economic changes resulting from women's increased presence in the workforce.

**The rise of part-time jobs**
In 1985 the *Journal of Labor Economics* published a valuable comparative analysis of trends in female employment in seven European countries (Britain, France, Germany, Holland, Sweden, Italy and Spain) plus the USSR, the USA, Japan, Australia and Israel. Summarising the results, Mincer (1985: S5) noted that historically, the shrinkage of farm, family business and other household-based employment and its eventual replacement by employment outside the home and independent of the spouse creates a U-shaped trend in aggregate female workforce participation that can take a long time to materialise. In Sweden, the changeover from a heavily agrarian

economy to an industrial economy continued until well into this century, so that the low point of the U-shaped trend was in the 1950s when economic activity rates fell to about 25%, as shown in Nyberg's study discussed earlier (see Chapter 2). In Britain, the low point was not very low, and it lasted a long time, from about 1881 to 1921, when work rates fell to one-third of adult women compared with virtually all of adult men (Hakim, 1993a: 93-102). In the mid-nineteenth century female work rates were a constant 42-43% falling to 32% by 1881 and remaining at this level until the Second World War (Table 3.1). The ten percentage point reduction resulted from a combination of a genuine fall in women's work rates and some element of new under-reporting, as working class and middle class families all sought to conform to the ideal of the full-time housewife supported by a husband earning a 'family wage'.

From the 1950s onwards, economic activity rates rose rapidly, from 43% of women aged 15-59 in 1951 to a projected 75% of women aged 16-59 by the year 2006 (Table 3.1). Among ever-married women, the rise seems sharper: from 26% in 1951 to 49% in 1971 and to 71% in 1990 to 1994, whereas male economic activity rates fell from 91% in 1979 to 85% by 1994 (Hakim, 1979: 3, 1993a: 100; Sly, 1994: 405). What this meant in reality was that the abolition of the marriage bar for women allowed them to remain in their jobs after marriage, typically until the first birth, although some returned to work later on. As marriage rates rose over the century, married female workers substituted for unmarried female workers, a process found also in the USA in this period (Oppenheimer, 1970). The female workforce became representative of all women of working age. Female employment has been redistributed across the life-cycle whereas before the 1950s it was concentrated among unmarried younger women (Hakim, 1979).

Full-time work rates changed very little in the post-War decades, while part-time employment grew rapidly (Tables 3.2 and 3.3). Full-time work rates fluctuated around one-third of the age group from 1951 (30%) to 1994 (36%). In the 1980s it looked as if a sustained increase in full-time work rates was taking off, as rates climbed steadily from 33% in 1984 to a high of 38% in 1990. Since then, however, rates have fallen off, leaving an overall picture of stability in women's full-time employment rates (Table 3.2). What this means is that women's full-time employment rates have been

**Table 3.1** Economic activity rates 1851-2006

|      | Men aged 20+ | Women aged 20+ | | |
| --- | --- | --- | --- | --- |
| 1851 | 98 | 42 | | |
| 1861 | 99 | 43 | | |
| 1871 | 100 | 42 | | |
| 1881 | 95 | 32 | | |
| 1891 | 94 | 32 | | |
|      | Adult men* | Adult women* | Men 16-64 | Women 16-59 |
| 1901 | 84 | 32 | 96 | 38 |
| 1911 | 84 | 32 | 96 | 38 |
| 1921 | 87 | 32 | 94 | 38 |
| 1931 | 91 | 34 | 96 | 38 |
| 1941 | - | - | - | - |
| 1951 | 88 | 35 | 96 | 43 |
| 1961 | 86 | 38 | 95 | 47 |
| 1971 | 81 | 44 | 91 | 57 |
| 1981 | 77 | 48 | 89 | 64 |
| 1991 | 74 | 52 | 87 | 71 |
| 1996 | 71 | 54 | 84 | 72 |
| 2001 | 70 | 55 | 83 | 74 |
| 2006 | 69 | 56 | 82 | 75 |

* 1901-11 people aged 10 and over, 1921 people aged 12 and over, 1931 people aged 14 and over, 1951-71 people aged 15 and over, 1981-2006 people aged 16 and over.
**Sources:** Derived from Hakim (1979) Table 1 and Hakim (1980) Tables 1 and 2 based on analyses of Population Census reports for England and Wales or Great Britain 1801–1971, and Ellison (1994) Table 3 presenting mid-year estimates based on 1971 and 1981 Census results and LFS results up to 1993, and labour force projections to 2006 based on these sources. Figures for 1851-1961 relate to England and Wales; figures for 1971-2006 are for Great Britain. Figures are for the 'occupied' population 1801-1951 and for the 'economically active' population 1961-2006. Figures for 1851-1871 exclude people whose sole occupation was unpaid household work (listed as an occupation in these censuses) in order to achieve comparability with other censuses. Figures for the population of working age 1901-1971 are for people aged 15 to 59/64; figures for 1981-2006 are for people aged 16 to 59/64.

virtually stable since 1881, at around one-third of the age group. From 1851 to the mid-1990s, women's full-time employment rate fluctuated only within a 30%-40% range, very similar to the 34-43% work rates in France over the past century (Riboud, 1985). Pott-Buter (1993) shows a remarkable stability in female work rates since 1850 across Europe. There is no evidence here that women have been taking full-time jobs from men, or that changes in female work rates could account for the loss of men's jobs.

**Table 3.2** Full-time work rates among women 1951-1994

Proportion (%) of women of working age who work full-time

| *women aged 20-64 years* | | *women aged 16-59 years* | |
|---|---|---|---|
| 1951 | 30.3 | 1984 | 33.1 |
| 1961 | 29.8 | 1985 | 33.6 |
| 1971 | 29.0 | 1986 | 33.9 |
| 1981 | 31.6 | 1987 | 34.5 |
| | | 1988 | 35.9 |
| | | 1989 | 37.4 |
| | | 1990 | 38.2 |
| | | 1991 | 37.4 |
| | | 1992 | 36.5 |
| | | 1993 | 36.1 |
| | | 1994 | 35.8 |

**Sources:** Population Census data for Great Britain 1951-1981 reported in Joshi, Layard and Owen (1985: S154), and Labour Force Survey data for Great Britain 1984-1991 reported in Department of Employment (1992b: 444), updated with annual LFS reports.

*All* the increase in employment in Britain in the post-War period, from 22 million jobs in 1951 to 25 million in 1995, consisted of growth in female part-time jobs (Table 3.3). By the early 1980s, two million full-time jobs were lost in the male workforce, most of them in manufacturing. Another one million jobs were lost in the female workforce, but then regained by the early 1990s. Overall, the only increase in female employment since the 1950s, and indeed since 1851 or before, is the massive expansion of part-time jobs, from 0.8 million in 1951 to 5.1 million by 1995, echoed by a much smaller growth of part-time jobs among men, reaching one million in the 1990s. The headcount increase in female employment conceals an almost unchanging contribution of total hours worked by women, which remained below 33 per cent until 1980 (Joshi et al, 1985: S171).

The relatively unregulated British labour market allowed part-time work to develop earlier and grow faster than elsewhere in Europe (Joshi et al, 1985), but similar trends are observed in most other European countries (Hakim, 1993a: 431; Meulders et al, 1993, 1994; EC, 1995a: 9-18). The dramatic increase in female employment in Sweden has also been exposed as largely illusory, due to including in the employment count women who are at home full-time with their children on parental leave as well as part-time women (Jonung and

**Table 3.3** Trends in full-time and part-time work, Great Britain 1951-1995

| | Total in employment 000s | Full-time employment 000s | Part-time employment 000s | % part-time |
|---|---|---|---|---|
| **All workers** | | | | |
| 1951 | 22,135 | 21,304 | 831 | 4 |
| 1961 | 23,339 | 21,272 | 2,066 | 9 |
| 1971 | 23,733 | 19,828 | 3,904 | 16 |
| 1981 | 22,881 | 18,977 | 3,905 | 17 |
| 1984 | 23,246 | 18,395 | 4,851 | 21 |
| 1988 | 24,664 | 19,264 | 5,400 | 22 |
| 1991 | 25,294 | 19,667 | 5,627 | 22 |
| 1993 | 24,944 | 18,973 | 5,971 | 24 |
| 1995 | 25,402 | 19,256 | 6,146 | 24 |
| **Women** | | | | |
| 1951 | 6,826 | 6,041 | 784 | 11 |
| 1961 | 7,590 | 5,698 | 1,892 | 25 |
| 1971 | 8,701 | 5,413 | 3,288 | 38 |
| 1981 | 9,146 | 5,602 | 3,543 | 39 |
| 1984 | 9,638 | 5,346 | 4,292 | 45 |
| 1988 | 10,527 | 5,837 | 4,690 | 45 |
| 1991 | 11,072 | 6,230 | 4,842 | 44 |
| 1993 | 11,203 | 6,236 | 4,967 | 44 |
| 1995 | 11,322 | 6,302 | 5,020 | 44 |
| **Men** | | | | |
| 1951 | 15,309 | 15,262 | 47 | * |
| 1961 | 15,748 | 15,574 | 174 | 1 |
| 1971 | 15,032 | 14,430 | 602 | 4 |
| 1981 | 13,736 | 13,374 | 362 | 3 |
| 1984 | 13,608 | 13,050 | 558 | 4 |
| 1988 | 14,139 | 13,429 | 710 | 5 |
| 1991 | 14,222 | 13,438 | 784 | 6 |
| 1993 | 13,741 | 12,737 | 1,004 | 7 |
| 1995 | 14,080 | 12,954 | 1,126 | 8 |

* less than 0.5%

**Sources:** Population census data for 1951-1981 taken from Table 3 in Hakim (1993a: 103). Figures for 1951-1971 refer to people aged 15 and over; figures for 1981 refer to people aged 16 and over. Estimates of part-time workers for 1951, 1961 and 1981 refer to people who described themselves as such. The 1971 figures refer to people who stated they usually worked 30 hours or less per week, excluding overtime and meal breaks; people who did not state hours worked in 1971 are redistributed pro rata between full-time and part-time workers. Labour Force Survey data for 1984-1995 taken from Department of Employment published statistics: spring seasonally adjusted estimates of the employed workforce aged 16 and over. The definition of full-time and part-time work is almost always based on the respondent's own assessment, not on the hours actually worked. The LFS figures include (from 1984) people on employer-based government training programmes for the unemployed and (from 1992) unpaid family workers; the inclusion of these groups slightly increases figures for 1984 onwards, but it does not alter any of the trends, nor does it alter the proportion part-time in any year.

**Table 3.4** Annual work experience profiles in the USA, 1966-1986

| | *Proportion of population of working age in each group* | | | | | | | | |
| | Full-time year-round employment | | | Part-time and/or part-year employment | | | No employment over the year | | |
| | All | M | W | All | M | W | All | M | W |
|---|---|---|---|---|---|---|---|---|---|
| 1966 | 39 | 60 | 20 | 28 | 25 | 30 | 33 | 15 | 50 |
| 1971 | 37 | 55 | 22 | 30 | 29 | 30 | 33 | 16 | 48 |
| 1976 | 36 | 52 | 22 | 31 | 29 | 32 | 33 | 19 | 46 |
| 1982 | 37 | 49 | 26 | 30 | 29 | 31 | 33 | 22 | 43 |
| 1986 | 41 | 53 | 30 | 28 | 26 | 30 | 31 | 21 | 40 |

**Source:** Derived from Table 1 in Mellor and Parks (1988). Full-time year-round workers are those who worked 50 weeks or more during the year and usually worked 35 hours a week or more. That is, they must work full-time hours for at least 25 weeks in the year. About 8% of this group have some weeks of part time work (under 35 hours a week).

Persson, 1993). Only the USA has had a steady and accelerating growth in women's employment (OECD, 1988: 129), although there was little or no growth in married women's average work experience, measured in years (Goldin, 1989, 1990) and there was a 9% decline in women's annual market hours from 1940 to 1988 (Coleman and Pencavel, 1993). In sharp contrast to Britain, all the growth has been in women's full-time year-round employment in the USA and not in part-time part-year employment rates, which have remained stable for men and women for decades (Table 3.4).

**Part-time workers and secondary earners**
The idea that female employment has been rising, to levels close to male work rates, has been read as laying the foundation for greater equality between men and women. In reality the female full-time work rate remained constant for over a century and is still only half the male rate: 36% compared to 70% in 1994 for people of working age. The only innovation is that another 29% of women aged 16-59 years are working part-time compared to 5% of men aged 16-64 years (Sly, 1994: 405). Almost all part-time workers are secondary earners rather than primary earners. There is thus no reason to expect any significant social and economic change from the post-War changes in female employment patterns, in effect, from a rise in secondary earners.

Secondary earners are not earning a living; they are financially dependent on another person, or on state income support, for the basic necessities of life such as housing, food and fuel. Earnings from employment are thus *supplementary* or *secondary* to this other, larger source of income. Primary earners must necessarily obtain a *regular* income to cover basic necessities; they will therefore normally work full-time and continuously. Secondary earners may work on an intermittent basis as well as part-time, and they often work closer to home (Madden, 1981). Secondary earners may take full-time jobs which are relatively low-paid but provide compensating advantages such as convenient hours, an agreeable work environment and pleasant social relations. Secondary earners may even forego earnings completely in favour of voluntary work, educational courses or other activities. Their earnings may be an important contribution to the family budget, providing some flexibility, birthday gifts or the holiday that gives a lift to life. The annual FES reports show that a working wife's earnings typically contribute one-third of household income among couples without dependent children and one-quarter of household income among couples with dependent children in periods when she is working. However the defining factor is not the level of earnings, nor their use. Primary earners are people who may decide to work more or fewer hours, or to vary their work effort in other ways, but for whom the question of whether or not they enter the labour force is not in doubt. Secondary earners are people who may choose to work or not according to a range of considerations, financial and non-financial, and thus have intermittent work histories. Primary earners respond to marginal tax rates, whereas secondary earners are affected by the average rate of tax on the whole of their earnings (Kay and King, 1978: 37). The work decision differs qualitatively between primary and secondary earners, and married women are the most important group of secondary earners.

Barron and Norris (1976) classified all women as secondary earners in the secondary labour force in the 1960s, noting their above-average turnover rates. The secondary earner label is also used more narrowly to refer to marginal workers and discouraged workers who move in and out of the labour market in response to the economic cycle, almost a 'reserve army of labour' classification (Joshi, 1981). The very size, stability and separateness of the part-time workforce in Britain ensures it cannot all be a reserve army of labour (Bruegel, 1979; Beechey and Perkins, 1987). However particular groups of women and men have markedly higher cyclical movements, notably men and women over pensionable age and young mothers, and these are also the groups most likely to work part-time (Joshi, 1981; Owen and Joshi, 1987).

Although numerically important, part-time workers are not a salient sector of the workforce; they are the most unstable members of the workforce; their primary identity is as homemaker or student rather than worker; they are highly satisfied with their jobs; and their contribution to household finances is generally too small to have a major impact on their role and power within the family. All of these consequences are attributable to part-timers being secondary earners. Strictly speaking, we should demonstrate these effects with reference to the distinction between primary earners and secondary earners, as some North American researchers have done (Martin and Hanson, 1985), as this is the variable that differentiates attitudes and behaviour. Unfortunately we have to rely on part-time work as a proxy indicator of secondary earner status, as that is the way data are most readily available.

On average, it takes 2.4 part-time employees to provide the same number of work hours as one full-time employee. Among the self-employed, the ratio is 3 to 1. People in second jobs work the equivalent of a bare one day a week (see Table 2.4). As a result, the real contribution of part-timers to the workforce is much smaller than the headcount suggests. By the mid-1990s, part-time employment accounted for 22% of all jobs, or closer to one-quarter if the part-time self-employed are included. But 5.4 million part-timers still only accounted for 10% of all hours worked (Table 3.5). The self-employed were more important, contributing 15% of hours worked despite a dramatic decline in their average work hours in the 1980s (see Table 2.4). Even though full-time employee jobs have been declining, they still account for three-quarters of total work hours, completely dwarfing part-timers' contribution (Table 3.5).

The low profile of part-timers within the workforce is reinforced by the vast majority of part-time jobs being concentrated within a narrow range of female-dominated occupations (Hakim, 1993b) which function as labour market entry and exit jobs for small numbers of male students and pre-retirement older workers as well as women (Hakim, 1995b: Table 5). Women's part-time jobs

**Table 3.5** The relative significance of part-time employees: jobs and hours

|  |  | 1979 | 1983 | 1993 | 1994 |
|---|---|---|---|---|---|
| Total employment in thousands = 100% | | 24,210 | 22,589 | 24,288 | 24,481 |
| Ttoal hours worked in millions = 100% | | 863.0 | 782.1 | 806.3 | 816.3 |
| Full-time employees | - Employment | 18,411 | 16,298 | 15,945 | 15,872 |
| | as % of total | 76% | 72% | 66% | 65% |
| | Hours worked | 708.1 | 616.3 | 604.8 | 606.4 |
| | as % of total | 82% | 79% | 75% | 74% |
| Part-time employees | - Employment | 4,020 | 3,990 | 5,240 | 5,401 |
| | as % of total | 17% | 18% | 21% | 22% |
| | Hours worked | 70.0 | 63.9 | 79.8 | 83.7 |
| | as % of total | 8% | 8% | 10% | 10% |
| Self-employed | - Employment | 1,779 | 2,301 | 3,103 | 3,208 |
| | as % of total | 7% | 10% | 13% | 13% |
| | Hours worked | 85.0 | 101.9 | 121.7 | 126.3 |
| | as % of total | 10% | 13% | 15% | 15% |

**Source:** Derived from Table 2 in Butcher and Hart (1995: 216) reporting spring LFS results. Figures include unpaid overtime hours except in 1979 when the information was not collected.

are concentrated in clerical work (21%), retail sales (18%), personal service occupations (20%) and miscellaneous other unskilled occupations (18%); only 10% were in professional and managerial occupations compared to 27% of women full-time workers and 30% of male workers (Table 3.6). In general, part-time jobs are low skill jobs with few promotion prospects (Rubery et al, 1994: 210-214). Part-time employees have the lowest levels of trade union membership, one indication of a lesser involvement with the world of work. There is little difference in trade union membership rates among men and women working full-time. Trade union membership among part-timers is half that among full-timers: 21% versus 38%, and only among the self-employed are rates lower than this (Beatson and Butcher, 1993: 676; Corcoran, 1995: 192).

Part-time jobs are just as permanent and secure as full-time jobs (Hakim, 1990a: 185-197; Rubery et al, 1994: 214), but labour mobility remains consistently higher among part-timers than full-timers (Gregg and Wadsworth, 1995: 80; Hakim, 1996). For example annual job turnover among part-timers is twice as high as among full-timers, and very few part-timers stay in the same job for ten years or longer (see Table 5.5). Secondary earners, and hence

**Table 3.6** Occupations of part-time and full-time workers

|  | Men | Women working | Full time | Part time |
|---|---|---|---|---|
|  |  | Total |  |  |
| Managers and administrators | 19 | 11 | 16 | 5 |
| Professional occupations | 11 | 9 | 11 | 5 |
| Associate professional & technical occupations | 8 | 10 | 12 | 8 |
| Clerical and secretarial occupations | 7 | 26 | 30 | 21 |
| Craft and related occupations | 22 | 3 | 4 | 2 |
| Personal and protective service | 6 | 15 | 11 | 20 |
| Sales occupations | 5 | 12 | 6 | 18 |
| Plant and machine operatives | 14 | 4 | 6 | 3 |
| Other occupations | 9 | 10 | 3 | 18 |
| Base: all in employment (000s = 100%) | 13,301 | 10,617 | 5,910 | 4,604 |

**Source:** Winter 1992-93 LFS data for Great Britain reported in Sly (1993:489) Table E.

part-time workers, have qualitatively different work orientations (as shown in Chapter 4), leading to a lower investment in training and skills, or what economists term 'human capital'. The main consequence is that they are then typically restricted to low skill jobs with low earnings, which are also the jobs most readily organised as part-time jobs by employers (Beechey and Perkins, 1987; Rubery et al, 1994). Full-time work declines sharply from 65 per cent among professional and managerial women to 6 per cent among unskilled women. Part-time work rises from 16% to 57% as a woman's occupational grade declines and, to a lesser extent, so does economic inactivity, that is, full-time domestic work (Table 3.7). Most part-time jobs have similar or lower status than the housewife role (see Table 2.7), so that the opportunity cost of not working is low, in social and economic terms. This explains some contradictory research results on part-timers who are found in some studies to place greater importance on social relations at work or on the intrinsic interest of a job, and yet found in others to be instrumental workers, working only at times of particular financial need. Either way, part-time work seems to have little or no value for long-term careers (Corcoran, Duncan and Ponza, 1984: 184, 189).

People with part-time jobs may be just as attached to their jobs, for different reasons, as full-timers are attached to theirs (see Table 4.7). However secondary earners do not have a central self-identity

**Table 3.7** Patterns of work and inactivity among women of working age by occupational grade, 1991-93

| Socio-Economic Group | Full time work | Part time work | Unem- ployed | Econom- ically inactive | Total N = 100% |
|---|---|---|---|---|---|
| Professional & Managers/employers | 65 | 17 | 3 | 14 | 2245 |
| Intermediate & Junior non-manual | 42 | 29 | 5 | 23 | 10074 |
| Skilled manual & Own account | 37 | 30 | 5 | 26 | 1541 |
| Semi-skilled & Personal service | 26 | 29 | 7 | 36 | 4005 |
| Unskilled occupations | 8 | 55 | 6 | 31 | 1568 |
| All occupations* | 38 | 30 | 5 | 26 | 19433 |

* includes women in the Armed Forces, in inadequately described occupations, and women who have never worked.
**Source:** OPCS (1995: 67) Table 5.11 presenting combined data for 1991, 1992 and 1993 for Great Britain. The nine SEGs are combined into just five occupational groups in this table. Data are for women of working age (16-59 years) reporting occupation of current or last job. Percentages have been rounded.

as workers in the same way as primary earners. The great majority of women working part-time see themselves as housewives, whose primary responsibility is keeping home, with employment fitted around family life (see Tables 4.1 and 4.2). Despite their short hours, women part-timers are far more likely than full-timers to take unpaid time off work for domestic reasons (Rubery et al, 1994: 219). The secondary earner's distinctive priorities between family life and employment explains the paradox of part-time workers being equally, and often more satisfied with their typically low-status low-paid jobs than full-timers with their objectively superior and more attractive jobs. The disproportionate job satisfaction of part-timers has been observed in so many surveys in so many countries that the pattern is no longer disputed (Martin and Roberts, 1984: 41, 74; Hakim, 1991: 101-3; Curtice, 1993: 104-115). Although some of the 'excess' satisfaction is attributable to the fact that part-time jobs offer more convenient hours, produce less stress and exhaustion at the end of the day, and generally offer pleasant social relations at work, there seems to be an additional factor over and above these, which must be due to the different perspective of the secondary earner (Martin and Hanson, 1985; Curtice, 1993: 115).

It is sometimes argued that women are forced into part-time work by the need to combine employment with their childcare activities.

**Table 3.8** Reasons for working part-time, 1994

| Reason for taking part-time work | All 1984 | 1994 | Women Married | Other | Men Married | Other |
|---|---|---|---|---|---|---|
| Student/still at school | 7 | 11 | 1 | 30 | 3 | 57 |
| Ill/disabled | 1 | 1 | 1 | 2 | 4 | 2 |
| Could not find a full-time job | 10 | 13 | 9 | 20 | 33 | 25 |
| Did not want a full-time job | 68 | 74 | 89 | 48 | 59 | 16 |
| No reply/Other reasons | 14 | 1 | 1 | * | * | * |
| Base 000s = 100% | 4,913 | 6,121 | 4,144 | 1,179 | 449 | 547 |

**Source:** Table 2.4 in Beatson (1995: 16) reporting Spring 1994 LFS data, United Kingdom, plus Spring 1984 LFS data, UK, in the first column. In 1994 there was no 'Other reasons' reponse option. In 1984, this response was offered.

While plausible, the evidence does not support the idea. The vast majority of married women take a part-time job in preference to a full-time job; among unmarried men and women, many of the part-timers are still students (Table 3.8). Virtually all part-time work is voluntary, in the sense of being preferred over a full-time job, in Britain, Germany, Ireland, Denmark and the Netherlands, all countries with high levels of part-time work, apart from Ireland (Hakim, 1990a). Although childbirth may be the initial stimulus to taking up part-time work, most part-timers feel their combination of employment and domestic work gives them 'the best of both worlds' and continue with part-time work long after children have left home or their husband has retired (Watson and Fothergill, 1993). This choice is simply not available to primary earners, who are obliged to work full-time throughout the lifecycle. Part-time work is an option open only to people who have choices to make, such as secondary earners. For this reason, men only do part-time work during the transition from full-time education into the labour market, or during the transition out of employment into full-time retirement. Students often take holiday jobs or do seasonal part-time jobs (Table 3.8) and they are the ones most likely to work less than 10 hours a week (Naylor, 1994: 480). Men who have taken early retirement on an employer's pension sometimes take a part-time job in the years up to full retirement at normal pension age. Both these groups of men are secondary earners in that they have another main source of income: their occupational pension in the case of older men, their student grant or parental support in the case of young people.

Siltanen's case study of primary and secondary earners in the Post Office showed that married men were almost invariably primary earners, working unsocial and long overtime hours when necessary in order to support a dependent wife and children. The few men in sex-atypical secondary earner jobs were generally young single men still living with their parents. White women were typically secondary earners if they were married and primary earners if they were not supported by a husband. In contrast, black women behaved like primary earners throughout the lifecycle, choosing jobs that ensured their financial independence whether they were currently married or not, even when they had young children (Siltanen, 1994: 85-87). Black women demonstrate clearly that there is nothing inevitable about mothers becoming secondary earners, or financially dependent, as a result of childbirth; it is a choice white women feel they can safely make.

Siltanen's case study is also notable because many of the secondary earners were doing full-time jobs rather than part-time jobs. However the secondary earner jobs were distinguished by not having the unsocial hours, in particular nightwork, and long hours of regular overtime that characterised the primary earner jobs. Overtime hours averaged a 33 per cent addition to a basic 43 hour week, so the secondary earners were working much shorter weekly hours than the primary earners, even though both groups were classified as full-time workers. Primary and secondary earners also had quite different employment histories. None of the primary earners had ever worked part-time; either they worked continuously, or they had one short domestic break and returned to continuous full-time employment. None of the secondary earners had worked continuously full-time; the great majority worked intermittently in both part-time and full-time jobs (Siltanen, 1994: 33, 134).

It is because women part-time workers are secondary earners that their work roles and earnings do not produce significant changes in their primary role as housekeeper and have only a small impact, if any, on their relative power in family decision-making. Secondary earners often trivialise their earnings, emphasising that their earnings only pay for 'extras' or holidays, underlining that they are only 'helping out' and not usurping the primary earner's role as breadwinner (Zelizer, 1989). Some women do this even when they are working full-time and their earnings constitute more than half the couple's income. They may underline the fact that these earnings are temporary, and will cease when she stops work for childbearing. Or they emphasise that the wife's earnings are in fact lower than the husband's after deducting all childcare costs from her salary. The point of these family 'myths' about economic and domestic roles is not that they are objectively untrue in the immediate present, but that they are true within the longer-term horizon of a permanent relationship in which a normative sexual division of labour is accepted and over-rides short-term variations. Jobs can be changed or lost in a day. Partnerships have longer time horizons. When men cease to believe in the sexual division of labour, or have a wife who overturns sex role stereotypes by working continuously for years, they start to share more of the domestic work (Kiernan, 1992: 104; Gershuny et al, 1994: 170).

Household money management systems provide one indicator of relative power in family decision-making. Generally research shows that financial equality depends on a wife's full-time employment. Part-time employment simply reduces the pressures on the husband's wage without increasing wives' influence over finances (Kiernan, 1992: 103; Vogler, 1994b: 246). However money management systems are more strongly related to *normative* views on sex roles than to the actual division of labour within couples: male control over family finances is associated with a couple agreeing he should have ultimate responsibility for income-earning; couples who manage their finances jointly are more likely to agree that they should have joint responsibility for income-earning (Vogler, 1994b: 250-3).

Unlike women who work full-time, part-timers accept that they retain responsibility for housework (see Table 4.1). They do as many hours of domestic work as do full-time housewives, almost twice as many hours as done by women working full-time (122 hours and 74 hours a week respectively). However they spend far less time on childcare than full-time housewives: 27 hours a week compared to 74 (Horrell, 1994: 208-9). The only indication that their part-time job alters their position within the family is a slight increase in their sharing of financial management with their husband (Kiernan, 1992: 101-3).

One might expect part-timers to fall half-way between full-time workers and non-working women in terms of attitudes and behaviour. On some work-related attitudes they do. But more often than not part-timers are closer to full-time housewives than to women working full-time. Housewives and part-timers share financial dependence on their spouse and a primary role as homemaker because, as noted in Chapter 4, they accept differentiated sex roles. Secondary earners take jobs that are too small and too intermittent to significantly alter personal identities. Secondary earners earn too little for financial independence, and the independence of spirit that goes with it, to become a real option.

In the relatively unregulated British labour market, part-time work expanded quickly to provide the majority of jobs taken by secondary earners. In countries where part-time jobs are less widely available, secondary earners often work full-time after their children reach school age or leave home. In most countries, secondary earners also work full-time before they start child-bearing. Pringle (1989) and Hochschild (1990) describe secondary earners whose primary self-identity and commitment is the homemaker role, despite working full-time hours, usually in non-career jobs such as secretarial and clerical work. Sorensen and McLanahan (1987) estimate that the proportion of white wives who were 100% economically dependent on their spouse fell dramatically from 84% in 1940 to 31% in 1980 in the USA; however the proportion with earnings equal to or greater than their husband's rose only from 6% to 15%. As late as 1980, substantial financial dependence remained the norm for wives in the USA as well.

### The demasculinisation of work

The decline of manufacturing industry has not been completely balanced by the growth of service sector industries, so that full-time employment fell from 21 million in 1951 to 19 million in 1995 (Table 3.3). All of the net loss has been in male employment. Workforce projections predict further job losses in manufacturing and greater growth in female employment than in jobs typically held by men, all of it in part-time jobs and self-employment (IER, 1995). Clearly the nature of work has changed since 1951. The question is, has it changed to the detriment of men as well as to the advantage of women?

Most commentators, including women, emphasise that the workforce now consists of almost equal numbers of men and women: men are only 55% to women's 45% when part-timers are included. This is one source of the fear that work is being demasculinised. The other is the all too visible decline of mining and manufacturing industry in Britain, the location for huge numbers of male manual jobs, skilled and unskilled, which the Conservative government did nothing to prevent. The fear is expressed indirectly in Campbell's *Goliath*, pointing out that young working class men whose energies are not harnessed by jobs will express these energies in more destructive ways, rioting and fighting the police.

The change in the sex ratio in the full-time workforce is a small five percentage point decline from 72% male in 1951 to 67% male in 1995 – too small to conclude that the feminisation of the workforce has been at the expense of male jobs. The feminisation of the workforce has been limited to the creation of a separate part-time workforce recruiting secondary earners who are not competing with primary earners for jobs. Chapter 6 also demonstrates the segregation of the part-time and full-time workforces. Given that 2.4 part-timers are needed to replace one full-time employee (see Table 2.4), it could be argued that the 5.3 million new part-time jobs created since 1951 have effectively substituted for the 2 million full-time jobs lost since 1951 (just as the rise in self-employment is due to employers subcontracting work previously done by employees). The problem with this argument is that the full-time jobs lost and the part-time jobs gained are in completely different occupations and industries, so that quite different employers are involved. Sales assistant jobs in urban shops do not substitute directly for coalmining jobs. Although particular companies, such as Burtons, are known to have directly substituted part-time jobs for full-time jobs in retailing, these few well-publicised cases in the 1990s form a tiny element of the total growth in part-time jobs in retailing and other service sector industries over the past four decades. Surveys of employers show such strategies to be rare except among foreign-owned international firms. Most employers are traditionalists or opportunists in their use of part-time, temporary and self-employed workers (Hakim, 1990b), and increased use of non-standard employment contracts is found in heavily regulated European countries as well as in Britain (Hakim, 1987, 1990a), partly due to the impact of recessions and economic uncertainty and partly due to changing patterns of consumption.

Leaving aside the (hopefully short-term) impact of recession, the long-term trend is in fact for work to be demasculinised *and* defeminised. This seems to pose more problems for men than for women.

Occupations are becoming more skilled, technical and gender-neutral (Routh, 1987: 39, 67). Between 1911 and 1971, the proportion of the workforce employed in professional, managerial and clerical occupations doubled from 19% to 37% (Routh, 1980: 5). Between 1971 and 2001, people in professional, technical, managerial and clerical occupations will have increased from 40% to 53% of the workforce (IER, 1995: 41). Over the century, manual occupations shrank from 81% to 47% of the workforce. The stereotyping of jobs as 'suitable' for men or women can be more persuasive in relation to manual occupations with a substantial physical element. White-collar occupations, particularly those requiring skills or knowledge, training and education, rarely have any obvious sex-stereotyping. Men and women can both be teachers, accountants, librarians, dentists, lawyers, doctors, musicians, economists, systems analysts and information engineers. Local, social, economic and historical factors determine the actual pattern of jobs taken up by men or women at any one time. As we show in Chapter 6, work cultures are far more heavily gendered than occupations themselves are.

As the entire occupational structure shifts upwards over time, with lower grade jobs shrinking in number and more qualified jobs expanding, the occupational structure is gradually becoming gender-neutral. Since male jobs greatly outnumbered female jobs in the 1951 workforce, the scope for the demasculinisation of work was always greater than for the defeminisation of jobs. The shrinkage of male manual jobs that were physically hard, dirty and dangerous is illustrated by the decline of the mining and ship-building industries. On the other hand we have to remember that women and children were working in mining in Britain one hundred and fifty years ago, so the masculinity of such work is socially determined.

A quite different source of the demasculinisation of work is the impact of technological change in reducing, even eliminating the need for physical strength and risk-taking in many jobs, not just in manufacturing industry. Jobs in construction require far less brute force as machines are now used to lift and place materials. Power steering on buses and other large vehicles allows slender young women to drive and control vehicles that previously required strong male drivers. Even war has become more high-tech, intellectual rather than physical in many areas.

Anyone feels personally threatened and discouraged by the discovery that one's skills are no longer in demand, are even redundant, that there is no demand for one's occupation and experience. Working class men are the largest group affected by the long-term changes in the nature of work. Within the British working class culture, manual labour is valorised as an expression of masculinity through movement, action and assertion. The physical domination of the world is valorised over the 'effeminate' intellectual domination of the world represented by educational attainment and white-collar jobs. Willis (1977) offers this inverted snobbery as an explanation for working class young men's acceptance of manual occupations at the lower end of the social class structure. (Willis mistakenly equates these attitudes with *machismo*, an entirely different gender ideology with no link to manual labour, valorising force of personality rather than physical strength.) Reliance on a masculine work identity was closely tied to the 'lads' insistence on the sexual division of labour which restricted women to domesticity or to 'effeminate' white collar work and office jobs. Thus manual labour was associated with the social superiority of masculinity and mental labour with the social inferiority of femininity (Willis, 1977: 147-152). Unemployment for this group is thus doubly threatening: they are denied the psychological reassurance of doing masculine work in male work groups, and they are thrown into the feminine social environment of the domestic home, often on socially isolated housing estates, dominated by the quite different daily pursuits of mothers and children. Women exclude men from the domestic sphere just as effectively as men exclude women from the world of work. The tragedy of the sexual division of labour is that it makes men strangers and trespassers in their own homes, so that they cannot function effectively there, forcing them out into the streets, bars and clubs when not at work.

While it is understandable that men might seek to make women the scapegoats for their loss, in fact both groups have experienced the effects of structural and technological change at work. Men's loss of manual jobs and masculine work cultures has occurred in the same process as the defeminisation of women's jobs. In 1891 one-third of women were employed as indoor domestic servants and one-fifth worked in dressmaking and sewing; over half of all women worked in feminine jobs, often in private households rather than in industry. By 1991, the most typically female occupation of secretaries, typists, personal assistants, and word processing operators provided jobs for no more than 7.5% of women and childcare jobs provided work for only 3%. In 1991, the largest occupations employing women were simply low-skill jobs with no particular association with women's domestic skills, such as sales assistant, sales worker, check-out operator, clerk and cashier. The most important occupations for women are now gender-neutral rather than typically feminine work. They are also jobs carried out in highly public locations, involving interaction with a large and diverse clientele. The social seclusion of employment in domestic service has given way to low-skill jobs that are very much in the public eye (Hakim, 1994: 445).

The aristocracy of labour used to be in highly skilled craft occupations and trade unions used to express craft professional identities as well as class interests. Even less skilled men could take pride in work that was difficult and dangerous, as manual work generally required physical effort, skill and judgement. Today the aristocracy of labour is in professional and intellectual occupations; the most highly paid and risky occupations are in financial services; trade unions are in decline. Working class men have lost face and have lost courage. They cannot, like women, retreat into domestic life during recessions. Women had far less to lose in the decline of manufacturing and they have far more to gain from the expansion of white-collar work, which has only favoured women by being more gender-neutral, without the exclusively masculine character of manual jobs. White collar jobs require skills and qualifications plus the social skills required for providing a service to others, as exemplified by the teacher, police officer and management consultant. Service sector jobs can involve manual work too, albeit combined with social skills, as illustrated by nurses, hairdressers, waiters and cooks. These jobs are clearly as open to men as they are to women. If women have any advantage in the service sector it is in their greater willingness to service and care for others in contrast with men's more aggressive, self-centred or 'individualistic' achievement orientation. On the other hand, jobs as cooks, waiters, bartenders, sales and related work are held equally by men and women in Southern European countries whereas they tend to be female-dominated in Northern European countries (Rubery and Fagan, 1993: 46-47). Proof, once again, that it is work cultures that are gendered rather than occupations themselves, so that social change is far more open-ended than institutional sociologists admit.

## Conclusions

The feminisation of the workforce gave women great expectations, which have not materialised. Reviews of post-War trends repeatedly note the paradox of, on the one hand, an enormous growth of female labour force participation and, on the other hand, an intensified segregation of women into lower grade, low-paid jobs. Women's rising employment has brought them few 'good jobs' (Jenson, Hagen and Reddy, 1988: 4-9, 44). The paradox is of course the result of superficial analyses that fail to distinguish trends in full-time and part-time work. As noted in Chapter 2, the one hour a week minimalist definition of employment has not helped, as it produces inflated economic activity rates which are ultimately misleading. The only growth has been in part-time jobs, most of them half-time jobs but also many marginal jobs involving less than ten hours a week. The relatively unregulated British labour force may represent an extreme case, but most European countries are discovering that the apparent rise in female employment in recent decades is due mostly, or entirely, to the creation of a part-time workforce for secondary earners, with a substitution of part-time for full-time jobs in some periods (de Neubourg, 1985; Hakim, 1993a; Meulders et al, 1994: 3; OECD, 1994: 77).

The full-time work rate among women has not changed for about 150 years in Britain, since 1851 and possibly before then. The importance of this finding is difficult to overstate. It means that all the expectations of social and economic change, of greater equality between men and women in the workforce and in the home have rested, in practice, on the creation of a large part-time workforce. This is clearly nonsense. Even if part-time workers were identical to women working full-time in terms of qualifications, occupations and work experience, differing only in their shorter working hours, they would be poorly placed to provide the vanguard of change in the labour force and the catalysts for wider social and political change resulting from women's greater economic independence. The example of Sweden is instructive.

So-called 'part-time' workers in Sweden are in fact working *reduced* hours of 30 hours a week, which classifies them as full-timers by European Commission standards (1994: 116). Most commonly they continue to work in the same job when they transfer *temporarily* to reduced hours work, so there is no reason for the 'part-time' workforce to develop as a separate, segregated sector. Despite all this, and a vigorous policy of promoting equal opportunities, occupational segregation remains at a high level in Scandinavia. Women are concentrated in the public sector, in jobs where they are paid to do what women in other countries do unpaid much of the time: childcare, care of the elderly, health care and education services. Relatively few women work in the private sector and women are less likely to attain management positions than in the competitive hire-and-fire economies of North America. Rosenfeld and Kalleberg (1990) showed that women are less likely to achieve senior positions at work in Scandinavian countries than they are in North America: only 1.5 per cent of women working full-time had management jobs in Sweden compared to 11 per cent in the USA. Swedish women still fail to achieve the jobs with most power and authority in the workforce, even though they now hold 40 per cent of political representative posts compared with an average for European parliaments of 11 per cent (Statistics Sweden, 1995; Wright, Baxter and Birkelund, 1995).

In Britain, as in most European countries, the part-time workforce is a separate, segregated sector of jobs in the lower grades of manual and white-collar work, jobs which require relatively little training and are thus less affected by high turnover rates. Since there has been effectively no net change in female full-time employment, in absolute or relative terms, since 1950, it follows that the part-time workforce has drawn different and new groups of women into employment, women who previously remained full-time home-makers. With some rare exceptions of *in*voluntary part-time work, part-timers are secondary earners who are not interested in full-time jobs but seek supplementary income to that provided by someone else, parent or husband. This limited interest in, and contribution to the paid workforce provides a weak basis for consequential social change. As shown in Chapter 4, part-timers have fewer ambitions than full-timers, are more family-centred and accept sex role differentiation.

Our findings also have important theoretical implications. As noted in Chapter 1, Walby's theory that there has been a change from private to public patriarchy, and a change from exclusionary to segregationist strategies for maintaining women's subordination rests heavily on the premise that more women are in employment (Walby 1986, 1990: 48, 53-57). She also believes that women now work continuously apart from a five year break for having children

(1990: 9), which is also untrue, as shown in Chapter 5. Walby's thesis collapses in the face of the evidence. True, the part-time workforce is a segregated workforce, but its development owes little to trade union segregationist strategies in Britain or other European countries. Until the 1990s, the British Trades Union Congress and most trade unions simply ignored part-time workers as marginal workers who were not really part of the workforce. Employers do not care whether part-timers are male or female, which is why young men and older men also pass through part-time jobs at particular stages of the lifecycle. Part-time jobs are only of interest to secondary earners, who are not in competition for jobs with primary earners, so there was no need for a trade union strategy towards them. Furthermore, male employers resisted trade union attempts to exclude female workers, from clerical work for example, right from the start, so that exclusionary and segregationist strategies were pursued *in parallel* over this period by different trade unions. Employer resistance to trade union attempts to control and restrict the supply of labour warns us against generalising from specific trade union policies to a broad theory of patriarchal policies pursued by men generally against women generally. Milkman's (1987) analysis of trade union strategies in the USA reveals a similar diversity, denying the idea of consistent and hegemonic patriarchal policies restricting women's employment and wages.

Trade union campaigns for a family wage and protective legislation restricted women's wage work, forcing wives into economic dependency and full-time domestic work – arguably to the benefit of the women themselves, as well as their families, in the working class (Humphries, 1981). Unpaid domestic work in one's own home was usually preferable to paid domestic work as a servant in someone else's home, the occupation of one-third to one-half of women in the late nineteenth century (Grossman, 1980; Matthaei, 1982: 197-203, 284; Hakim, 1994). The clearest evidence of policies to exclude women from employment was the marriage bar introduced in the late nineteenth century, maintained in some British trade unions up to the 1960s (and not formally eliminated until the Sex Discrimination Act 1975), with similar policies applied by many USA employers (Cohn, 1985; Grint, 1988; Goldin, 1990: 160-179). But most women accepted the marriage bar. As late as 1930, a ballot among women in government employment found only 3% in favour of abolishing the marriage bar (Grint, 1988: 101). Furthermore, occupational segregation on the basis of sex was already well established by 1891 but then *declined* over the next century (Hakim, 1994). On closer examination, the trade union policy of maintaining unequal pay for women even when doing the same jobs as men was the most effective deterrent to women's employment and guarantee of their economic dependency. The more empirically grounded conclusion is that the twentieth century saw the demise of patriarchy as practised by the aristocracy of labour. By the 1990s the British system of industrial relations itself was in decline (Millward et al, 1992: 350; Purcell, 1993).

Since the rise of female employment cannot be the catalyst for recent social and economic change, we must explain any change that did occur with reference to other factors, such as the impact of sex discrimination legislation (Zabalza and Tzannatos, 1985a,b, 1988), wars (Milkman, 1987: 152), changes in attitudes or even in the sex ratio (Britton and Edison, 1986) – a much wider range of explanations than a simple focus on male policies for subordinating women.

The domestication of women (Rogers, 1981) lasted less than a century in Britain. However, as we show next, the sexual division of labour did not die but was simply regenerated in its modern form.

# 4
# Work orientations and work plans

By the early 1990s, it had become received opinion among social scientists that sex differentials in work orientations and work commitment had faded away. One after the other, research reports and literature reviews asserted confidently that any differences that may have existed in the past had now disappeared. This view was offered in Britain, in other European countries and in the USA. It was never challenged, and sometimes regarded as ideologically suspect to do so. Like many other myths about women's employment (Hakim, 1995a), the constant repetition of this claim has required selective and one-eyed presentation of the research evidence.

There is no doubt that in the 1950s most working women regarded their jobs in a substantially different light from men, attitudes that were reflected in rates of absenteeism that were two, three or four times higher than among men, even after disregarding absences due to pregnancies and confinements (Myrdal and Klein, 1956, 1968: 94-106). After reviewing the evidence for Britain, Sweden and the USA, Myrdal and Klein concluded that women had 'a less serious attitude to their work', displaying 'a certain laxity' and 'immaturity' in their tendency to stay off work for any domestic reason. However they pointed out that this behaviour occurred at a time when women were constantly reminded of their lower value and unequal position in the workforce by being paid at a lower rate than men for the same job (Myrdal and Klein, 1968: 98, 101, 105, 108). The Equal Pay Act 1970 removed this factor from the 1970s onwards, and absenteeism no longer displays any marked sex differential. It seems plausible that sex differences in work orientations have also disappeared, and most studies draw this conclusion.

Just one example is a report on a 1992 survey concluding that the difference in the significance of employment to men's and women's lives would appear to have largely evaporated (Gallie and White, 1993: 18). The explanation for this finding is of course that the study only reports data for employees, leaving five million non-working women out of the picture altogether. The Netherlands has long had the lowest female work rate in Northern Europe, with only half of women aged 16-65 currently in the workforce (Pott-Buter, 1993: 28; European Commission, 1994: 41), yet Tijdens still suggests that the work commitment and orientations of men and women do not differ because one-fifth of *working* women and men plan a career (Tijdens, 1993: 84). Reskin and Padavic simply dismiss sex differentials in work commitment and work effort as implausible or out of date ideas (1994: 39-41, 86, 112-3). Their evidence is a study by Bielby and Bielby (1988) which purported to test and reject Becker's thesis about some married women giving priority to family responsibilities over market work, thus seeking less demanding jobs. They used the 1977 and 1973 USA Quality of Employment Surveys, which collected data only on permanent jobs involving at least 20 hours a week, with the emphasis therefore on the full-time workforce, despite the fact that currently non-working wives, wives in part-time jobs of under 20 hours a week, and wives in temporary jobs were all crucially relevant to the theory being tested. The authors acknowledged that the dataset was not appropriate, but went ahead anyway. Within their selective group of workers, work effort was significantly lower among part-time and part-year workers, women with young children and in the lower occupational grades. Greater work effort was associated with all the features typical of men rather than women: longer education, greater work continuity, self-employment and, paradoxically, with being female. The results seem to confirm that women have to work harder than men in the same job, but they do not even address, let alone refute Becker's thesis. The majority of wives, who do no market work at all or work less than 20 hours a week, were excluded from the study, so that results are weakened by sample selection bias (see Chapter 5).

**Attitudes to the sexual division of labour**
Studies which investigate attitudes to the sexual division of labour, that is, *qualitative* differences between the roles of men and women, are surprisingly rare, compared with innumerable attitude surveys on whether mothers should stay at home or go out to work, and whether women are as capable as men of doing a job well. Early studies identified four theoretically distinct components of sex-role attitudes, and showed that male and female views converged on

some and diverged on other components (Osmond and Martin, 1975). Even among university students, both sexes accepted a sharp sexual division of labour in the family, with wives retaining primary responsibility for the home and childcare, and husbands responsible for income-earning. Disagreement was centred on the character of women's labour force participation, their role in public life and politics – with men being far more traditional than women in allocating political and other leadership roles and career commitment to men. Yet men were happy to accept a wife earning more money than they did, more than women believed they would be (Osmond and Martin, 1975: 755). The huge volume of research since then has been less sophisticated, addressing public attitude to women's employment, most of it showing women to be more 'modern' than men, much of it relying on multivariate analysis rather than on theory to identify components within sex role attitudes. However studies generally find little or no association between such attitude statements and respondents' own employment choices (Bielby and Bielby, 1984; Hakim, 1991: 105). There are three reasons for this.

First, attitudes are poor predictors of actual behaviour: very low associations are typically found (Wicker, 1969; Bielby and Bielby, 1984). Second, people can and do endorse mutually contradictory attitudes and incompatible stereotypes of male and female behaviour and sex-roles. This allows a researcher's perspective to influence the choice of questions included in, or excluded from, a survey and the key findings that result. Third, *general* attitudes on the desirability of women working or not tell us little about women's *personal preferences* and aims (Bielby and Bielby, 1984; Hakim, 1991: 105). Too many surveys fail to make the distinction between approval and choice, between personal goals and beliefs, between what is desired by the survey respondent and what is desirable in society in general (Hofstede, 1980: 21). If we want to understand the choices women make, research must focus on women's plans for their own life. There is thus a gulf between attitude surveys revealing steadily increasing public approval for working wives and mothers, and other research showing that only a minority of women plan long-term careers, aim at higher grade occupations and invest accordingly in appropriate educational qualifications (Sutherland 1978; Jacobs, 1989b: 77-84; Hakim, 1991). Even among college and university graduates, a minority of women have firm plans for employment careers; most expect to work

**Table 4.1** Attitudes to the sexual division of labour in Britain

|  | Women working | | | Working age | |
|---|---|---|---|---|---|
|  | FT | PT | All | women | men |
| 'The female partner should be ultimately responsible for housework'   % agreeing | 44 | 80 | 61 | 68 | 65 |
| 'The male partner should be ultimately responsible for breadwinning'   % agreeing | 29 | 60 | 44 | 50 | 56 |
| 'I'm not against women working but the man should still be the main breadwinner in the family' % agreeing or indifferent | 39 | 61 | 49 | 53 | 40 |

**Source:** 1986 and 1987 SCELI data reported in Tables 2.1 and 2.12 in C Vogler, 'Segregation, sexism and labour supply' pp 39-79 in *Gender Segregation and Social Change* (ed) A M Scott, Oxford: OUP, 1994, and 1986 LFS data on the structure of the labour force in Great Britain reported in Table 2 in Department of Employment, 'Women in the labour market', *Employment Gazette*, December 1990, pp 619-643. Data for all women of working age are based on Vogler results for working women, adjusted to take account of non-working women who are assumed to have the same attitudes as women working part-time. Data for men are based on the assumption that Vogler's data for working men are fully representative of all men of working age.

while giving priority to marriage and motherhood (Bielby and Bielby, 1984),

Clearly, there have been huge changes in sex role attitudes in recent decades, with few now insisting that women are defined entirely by their family role. However Vogler's (1994a) analysis of data from the SCELI surveys demonstrates that the sexual division of labour is still accepted by the majority of adults in Britain. Vogler's analysis concerns what she describes as 'sexist' attitudes, concluding that men are more 'sexist' than women. In fact the SCELI survey obtained the best data yet produced on modern sex role attitudes and acceptance of the 'bourgeois' domestic division of labour which allocates the breadwinner role to men and the housekeeping role to women. Commendably, the researchers did not confuse the issue with any reference to childcare tasks, which now constitute a small part of women's domestic work across the lifecycle, as noted in Chapter 2. The 1986 and 1987 surveys asked about housekeeping and income-earning roles, both of which are continuous rather than time-specific, and the questions were put to everyone aged 20-60 years, whether working or not (Table 4.1). The analysis thus excludes people aged over 60, who hold the most traditional views (Scott, 1990: 54). Unfortunately Vogler's report, like so many studies on this topic, excluded non-working women and men from the analysis of work orientations. In most studies, the relevant information is not collected from non-working women. In the SCELI study the data was collected for everyone and the researchers made a conscious decision to ignore the data for non-working women and men (Vogler, 1994a: 42). In 1986 40% of women of working age were out of the workforce, and their opinions on the sexual division of labour are more traditional than those of working women. On the conservative assumption that non-working women have the same attitudes as part-timers, we can adjust the results to provide information for all women of working age. After taking non-working women into account, we find that women are in fact equally or more 'sexist' than men, in the sense of supporting the domestic division of labour (Table 4.1). Since the majority (78%) of men of working age are in employment, their views can readily be taken as representative of all men in the age group, without adjustment.

Overall, two-thirds (68%) of women accept that the housework and homekeeping role takes priority for them, more than the 61% average for working women and 65% average for working men quoted by Vogler (1994a: 45). Women turn out to be more sexist than men in relegating themselves to domestic work. Slight differences in question-wording in two items on who should have ultimate responsibility for the income-earning 'breadwinner' role produce small differences in results. Men are slightly more likely to acknowledge *ultimate* responsibility for breadwinning: 56% compared to 50% of women who assign this role to them. Women are more likely to say that their own secondary-earner role does not eliminate men's *main* role as breadwinner: 53% compared to 40% of men. Surprisingly, the majority (60%) of men now believe that women's income-earning activities should have changed social norms about their own income-earning responsibilities, whereas the majority of women (53%) still insist that this remains men's primary role. Opinion is more unanimous on women's primary responsibility for domestic work than on men's primary responsibility for income-earning: female and male roles are allocated in the traditional manner by two-thirds and half of adults respectively.

So where does the idea come from that women are challenging the traditional sexual division of labour? From the minority of women working full-time (see Table 3.2), it would appear, the group most likely to include the media reporters, social scientists and other opinion-leaders who claim to know the trends. Among women working full-time, and *only* in this minority group, the majority reject the traditional household division of labour: less than half think that women should be responsible for housework, and only one-third allocate the primary income-earning responsibility to men (Table 4.1). Women working part-time emerge as an extremely conservative group, in contrast to men and women working full-time. The great majority of part-time workers regard themselves as housewives in the main, and almost two-thirds believe that women's contribution as secondary earners does not alter men's primary responsibility for income-earning. The contrast between women working full-time and part-time is far greater than the contrast between men and women (Table 4.1). Women part-time workers are twice as conservative as women full-timers in their 'sexist' acceptance of the sexual division of labour and research shows that non-working women hold even more traditional attitudes on the sexual division of labour and on sex role differentiation than do part-time workers (Hakim, 1991: 105, 1993b: 308-310). Vogler herself shows that women who were more sexist had longer breaks from employment (1994a: 53). The 1991 BSAS shows that the sexual division of labour is accepted by twice as many women working part-time and full-time housewives as by women working full-time: 55% and 60% compared to only 28% of full-timers accepted the statement 'A husband's job is to earn the money; a wife's job is to look after the home and family', and in each case husbands held similar views (Kiernan, 1992: 99). So the views of women full-time workers are seriously unrepresentative of the views of the majority of adult women. Women currently working full-time divide into two groups: the minority who work full-time throughout adult life, with or without breaks, and those who change to part-time work and, often, intermittent work after having children (see Chapter 5). It appears that the views of women working full-time and continuously are the least representative of women as a group - not surprising, since they constitute only one-tenth of adult women (see Table 5.2). This analysis also shows that the BSAS practice of reporting attitudes among all adult women is misleading, creating the profile of an 'average' British woman who does not exist. For example Table 4.3 shows that about half (42%) of all women accept sex role differentiation, but this result combines full-timers who *reject* the idea with part-timers and non-working women who *accept* the idea.

In general, actual practice reflects views on the appropriate division of labour. Half of all married couples aged 20-60 years agreed between them that the husband was in practice the main income-earner and 42% agreed that he *should be* ultimately responsible for income-earning. Three-quarters of married couples agreed between them that the wife was in practice the principal housekeeper, and 54% agreed she *should be* ultimately responsible for housework. Hardly any couples agreed they should both be responsible equally for the housework. Only one-quarter of couples agreed that in practice, and in principle they were both equally responsible for income earning (Vogler, 1994b: 251-3). Thus among couples of working age the majority still adhere to and agree on differentiated sex roles, with only a minority choosing a more egalitarian approach.

Men are notably more open to sharing the income-earning role than are women, a finding that does not accord with the theory that a key patriarchal strategy for keeping women under male control is to exclude them from wage work. The SCELI surveys did not employ nationally representative samples, but were a collection of surveys in six localities in Britain, so it is possible that the results in Table 4.1 are not truly representative of the national picture. However consistent results are found in national surveys.

The 1980 WES found that 60% of husbands of *non*-working wives did not object to their wife working, compared to 84% of husbands of working wives. Husbands of non-working wives are two to three times more likely to prefer their wife *not* to work, but even so, less than half raised objections (Table 4.2). In most cases the argument simply reflects the conventional sexual division of labour: the wife's main task is looking after the home, whether or not there are any children at home. When there are children at home, around half of all husbands believe that their wife should only work if her job fits in with family life; this view is widespread and does not vary across subgroups. However the husbands of non-working wives are in some sense more selfish than others in that a two-thirds majority, with little variation, simply want their wife to be at home when he is. The key point about all these results is that couples with a non-working wife differ significantly and systematically in their sex role attitudes from couples with a working wife, a difference that is not simply attributable to the presence of children in the home. Furthermore,

**Table 4.2** Husbands' views on their own wife's employment by age of any children

| | Childless wives | | Youngest <16 | | All children 16+ | | All working wives | | | All wives |
| --- | --- | --- | --- | --- | --- | --- | --- | --- | --- | --- |
| | Working | Not working | Working | Not working | Working | Not working | FT | PT | All working | Not working |
| Percentage of wives reporting each view as definitely true of their husband: | | | | | | | | | | |
| My husband feels my main job is to look after the home | 8 | 32 | 20 | 46 | 17 | 50 | 10 | 22 | 17 | 46 |
| My husband would prefer me not to work | 11 | 29 | 18 | 35 | 15 | 55 | 14 | 17 | 16 | 40 |
| My husband likes me to be at home when he is | 49 | 58 | 47 | 64 | 48 | 72 | 46 | 49 | 48 | 65 |
| My husband would only be happy for me to work if it fitted in with family life | 30 | 36 | 56 | 60 | 48 | 43 | 38 | 57 | 49 | 54 |
| Base | 443 | 103 | 1244 | 1125 | 748 | 397 | 1089 | 1346 | 2435 | 1625 |

**Source:** Derived from Tables 8.19 and A8.9 of Martin and Roberts (1984) reporting results of the 1980 Women and Employment Survey.

wives who work part-time only are twice as likely as full-timers to accept that her role is primarily as homemaker and most think that any work she does must fit around the demands of family life. These attitudes contribute to the pronounced social class differential in work rates (see Table 3.7).

It might be objected that these are the views of husbands rather than wives. However wives have a clear idea of their husband's views; inaccurate perceptions were rare (Martin and Roberts, 1984: 107-108), and since arranged marriages are rare in Western societies, we can assume that people choose partners with compatible views on the sexual division of labour and family life. Married couples generally hold consistent views on their roles within the relationship (Kiernan, 1992: 99).

It is often argued that women's role in childbearing and childcare is central to the sexual division of labour. Case studies of voluntarily childless couples contradict this assumption. The traditional division of labour is often maintained even among couples rejecting parenthood, with the wife's job treated as secondary to the husband's because he retains the primary income-earning role (Campbell, 1985: 68-79). Some feminists argue that the ideology of motherhood is part of patriarchal ideology, serving to keep women subordinate to and dependent on men. Women who reject motherhood are belittled as unwomanly (Morell, 1994). However all the evidence is that in modern industrial society the social pressures towards parenthood are equal for men and women, and that it is typically women who are the prime movers in seeking or rejecting childbearing within couples (Campbell, 1985; Marshall, 1993). Many women welcome motherhood as a confirmation of their sexual and social identities. Some gain an irreversible sense of achievement from childbearing, reducing the motivation to seek achievements in the labour market. But homemaking activities are also treated as an expression of femininity, so that the homemaking role can be actively retained, even in the absence of children, in competition with a paid job, as Matthaei (1982: 301-307) has most eloquently described.

### The modern sexual division of labour

Most surveys measure attitudes somewhat crudely in terms of acceptance or rejection of statements proposing a complete division of labour between wives and husbands, in the sense that

**Table 4.3** Western views on the roles of men and women

Percentage disagreeing with these two statements:
A  A husband's job is to earn the money; a wife's job is to look after the home and family
B  Being a housewife is just as fulfilling as working for pay

|  | Separate roles | | Housewife job | |
|---|---|---|---|---|
|  | Men | Women | Men | Women |
| Britain | 47 | 58 | 33 | 36 |
| USA | 47 | 52 | 22 | 21 |
| Irish Republic | 40 | 50 | 17 | 24 |
| West Germany | 33 | 35 | 29 | 32 |

**Source:** 1988 ISSP data reported in Scott, Braun and Alwin (1993: 30-31).

income-earning is presented as an *exclusively* male function and home-making as an *exclusively* female function. This approach is illustrated in the International Social Survey Programme's (ISSP) item 'A husband's job is to earn the money; a wife's job is to look after the home and family' which is often treated as a measure of 'modernity' in attitudes. Throughout the 1980s and into the 1990s this statement (or equivalents) attracted roughly 50% of men and women disagreeing and 50% agreeing or indifferent, in Britain, in other European countries, and in the USA, with attitudes fluctuating over time but broadly balanced (Matthaei, 1982: 317; Witherspoon, 1988: 189; Scott, 1990: 57; Kiernan, 1992: 97-99; Scott, Braun and Alwin, 1993: 34; Haller and Hoellinger, 1994: 102). In Germany, Italy, Austria and Hungary, support for the statement is stronger than disagreement. For example only one-third of German men and women reject the sexual division of labour compared to half in Britain (Table 4.3). Attitudes to the housewife role are less ambivalent and more positive, with a majority agreeing that it can be just as fulfilling as working for pay; only one-third in Britain and Germany and even fewer in the USA reject the idea (Table 4.3). However sex roles have been updated to accept wives going out to work as a secondary activity. Vogler's study (Table 4.1) is important because it shows that the domestic division of labour is now *relative* rather than absolute, and shows too that attitudes to income-earning can change at a different, faster pace than attitudes to the homemaker role.

One EC Eurobarometer survey is also unique in measuring support, across Europe, for the *modern* sexual division of labour, which falls half-way between separate roles and egalitarian sharing of income-earning and domestic functions (Table 4.4). Roughly one-third of the EC population supported each family model. The egalitarian model attracted most support in Greece, Denmark, Italy and France, followed closely by the Netherlands and UK. The complete separation of roles attracted most support in Luxembourg, Ireland and Belgium. But in all countries there was a wide spread of support for all three models of the family, none receiving majority support, with the single exception of Greece's majority support for the egalitarian model. This suggests that the 'modern' egalitarian family is really a reversion to a pre-industrial model. Overall, a two-thirds majority of European men and women favour the idea of the working wife, and a two-thirds majority also favour the wife retaining all or the major part of the domestic role. Within countries, differences by sex are negligible except in Greece, Italy and France where men are distinctly less favourable than women towards the egalitarian marriage (European Commission, 1984: 9). Age has by far the strongest influence on attitudes (Table 4.4) and in this case we can safely read the results as reflecting generational differences. The key advantage of this survey is that it shows, for all European countries, that people who reject completely separate roles for men and women do not necessarily accept egalitarian or symmetrical roles: at least half only go as far as supporting a secondary earner role for the wife, who retains the larger share of domestic and childcare work. Many attitude surveys have presented people with a false dichotomy which failed to recognise the *modern* version of the sexual division of labour, a compromise that stops a long way short of truly egalitarian attitudes.

There have been three important attempts to eliminate the sexual division of labour and create symmetrical sex roles: in the Israeli *kibbutzim*, in Sweden and in China. All three have been only partially successful, revealing that social engineering cannot eradicate sex role differentiation. Tables 4.5 and 4.6 display the relative success of Sweden compared with other European societies and of China compared with other Far Eastern societies. The attitude statement in Table 4.5 proposes the complete separation of roles; the statement in Table 4.6 does not completely exclude wage work for wives.

In 1993, one-quarter of women aged 20 and over in Britain, France, Germany and the USA agreed with the rigid separation of roles in the statement 'The husband should be the breadwinner,

**Table 4.4**  European views on the sexual division of labour

Percentage supporting each of three models of the sexual division of labour:

|  | Egalitarian | Compromise | Separate roles | Total |
|---|---|---|---|---|
| Greece | 53 | 23 | 25 | 100 |
| Denmark | 50 | 33 | 17 | 100 |
| Italy | 42 | 28 | 30 | 100 |
| France | 42 | 27 | 31 | 100 |
| Netherlands | 41 | 27 | 32 | 100 |
| United Kingdom | 39 | 37 | 24 | 100 |
| Belgium | 35 | 25 | 40 | 100 |
| Ireland | 32 | 26 | 42 | 100 |
| West Germany | 29 | 38 | 33 | 100 |
| Luxembourg | 27 | 23 | 50 | 100 |
| Men 15-24 years | 49 | 33 | 18 | 100 |
| 25-39 | 40 | 38 | 22 | 100 |
| 40-54 | 28 | 36 | 36 | 100 |
| 55 and over | 26 | 28 | 46 | 100 |
| Women 15-24 years | 60 | 25 | 15 | 100 |
| 25-39 | 45 | 32 | 23 | 100 |
| 40-54 | 36 | 34 | 30 | 100 |
| 55 and over | 31 | 29 | 40 | 100 |
| Total for EC of 10 | 38 | 32 | 30 | 100 |

**Notes:** The question asked: People talk about the changing roles of husband and wife in the family. Here are three kinds of family. Which of them corresponds most with your ideas about the family?

A family where the two partners each have an equally absorbing job and where housework and the care of the children are shared equally between them.

A family where the wife has a less demanding job than her husband and where she does the larger share of housework and caring for the children.

A family where only the husband has a job and the wife runs the home.

None of these three cases

Percentages have been adjusted to exclude the 3% not responding to the the question and the 3% choosing the last response.

**Source:** Derived from Eurobarometer report *European Women and Men 1983* (1984)

and the wife should stay at home' (Table 4.5). In Japan and the Philippines two-thirds accepted the complete sexual division of labour. A decade earlier, in 1982, acceptance of the idea was invariably higher, except in the Philippines, even though the earlier survey was limited to women aged 20-59, excluding older women who are usually more conservative in outlook. Sweden demonstrates that energetically 'egalitarian' policies, which in this

**Table 4.5** The sexual division of labour: cross-national comparisons

Percentage of women agreeing with or indifferent to the statement:
The husband should be the breadwinner, and the wife should stay at home

|  | 1993 | 1982 |
|---|---|---|
| Sweden | 13 | 16 |
| UK | 21 | 28 |
| France | 24 | .. |
| Germany | 29 | 38 |
| USA | 27 | 35 |
| Korea | 33 | .. |
| Japan | 62 | 76 |
| Philippines | 67 | 56 |

**Notes:** Results from nationally representative random samples of 1000 or more women aged 20 and over in 1993 for all countries except Japan where results are based on a nationally representative random sample of 2000 women aged 20 and over interviewed in November 1992. Data for 1982 relates to women aged 20-59 years. The survey covered West Germany only in 1982 but the whole of unified Germany (including East Germany) in 1993.

**Source:** Calculated from Figure 1-35 in Tokyo Metropolitan Government (1994: 78).

context means policies promoting symmetrical roles for men and women and supported by vigorous fiscal and social security rules to prevent backsliding, can substantially change social attitudes: the vast majority (around 85%) of women reject the complete separation of roles. However there remains a stubborn minority of women (16% in 1982 and 13% in 1993) who still accept this design for living, albeit a lower proportion than in the rest of Europe (Table 4.5). While these results show how malleable attitudes are at the aggregate level, they also point to small minorities of women across Europe whose perspective has not changed, for whom the complete separation of domestic roles remains entirely satisfactory. China demonstrates both these points even more sharply.

China implemented the most determined social engineering policy aimed at eradicating the sexual division of labour and associated attitudes. The Marriage Law of 1950 laid down the principles of equality between the sexes, monogamy, freedom to choose marital partners and the right to sue for divorce, marking a break away from Confucian patriarchal values which supported an essentialist conception of the difference between the sexes and sharply segregated roles for men and women (Stockman, Bonney and Sheng, 1995: 141-154). The successes and failures of this largest-ever real-world social experiment are immensely valuable to social scientists, particularly for the study of women's position in society. Success was greatest in eradicating centuries-old perceptions of sex differences in ability and in the practice of male dominance in the household. There was also substantial success in eradicating the sexual division of labour: a low-wage full-employment policy made it necessary for all adults to work and hence for couples to share domestic work as well. However in 1988, after the economic reform programme begun at the end of the 1970s had introduced a new climate of opinion, there was a major public debate over a new trend for women to withdraw from wage work and their reasons for doing so. A survey carried out in Beijing in November 1993 showed that one-quarter of all women, one-third of wives and two-fifths of men accepted the sexual division of labour as the ideal to aim for (Table 4.6).

The attitude statement here was worded sufficiently vaguely as not to completely exclude wage work (social labour in China), but the relatively large minorities of women (especially wives) agreeing with the sexual division of labour is still remarkable. Respondents to the survey were aged 20-69 years (typically 30-50 years) and resident in Beijing, thus including the most educated and most cosmopolitan groups in Chinese society, 40 per cent of them professionals and senior administrators, who had lived in a communist society for virtually all their adult lives. Half the wives had earnings similar to or higher than their husbands. The policy of one child per family meant that in 1993, and for the foreseeable future, the great majority of couples had only one child to raise, and they had access to good socialised childcare facilities staffed by professionals. Yet even in these most favourable circumstances, a consistent one-third of wives in all age groups (varying slightly 27%-40%) preferred to stay at home as a housewife if their husband earned enough money to permit it. Similarly, acceptance of the sexual division of labour as the ideal was found in all age groups, varying only from 20% for people in their 60s to 38% among people in their 30s.

It might be argued in this case that people were simply reverting to traditional patriarchal values which had been suppressed but not abandoned. This might have been so in some rural areas, but not in urban areas, let alone Beijing. The 1993 survey found strongly egalitarian attitudes on all aspects of family roles and relationships. For example over three-quarters of husbands and wives in all age groups stated that family decisions were made jointly, whereas

**Table 4.6** Far Eastern views on the roles of men and women

| Percentage agreeing with each statement | Beijing | | Seoul | | Bangkok | | Fukuoka | |
|---|---|---|---|---|---|---|---|---|
| | Men | Women | Men | Women | Men | Women | Men | Women |
| There are no significant differences of abilities between men and women | 70 | 77 | 62 | 67 | 87 | 90 | 55 | 54 |
| The ideal is for men to have a job and for women to take care of the family | 40 | 24 | 69 | 51 | 68 | 71 | 72 | 60 |
| If my husband earned enough money I would rather stay at home as a housewife (asked only of married women) | .. | 35 | .. | .. | .. | .. | .. | .. |

**Source:** Calculated from Figures II-5-1, II-5-20, III-6-1 and III-6-2 in Ma et al (1994: 122, 154, 344). The surveys were caried out in 1989 (Fukuoka), 1991 (Seoul), 1992 (Bangkok) and 1993 (Beijing), with representative samples of N=1736, N=1608, N=1570 and N=1920 respectively.

the husband dominated decision-making in Bangkok, Seoul and Fukuoka, the three other cities surveyed. Acceptance of the traditional family division of labour was lowest among people in their 20s, but also among people in their 50s and 60s. It was only among people aged 30-50 that acceptance rose to two-fifths, clearly linked to childcare concerns. Four-fifths of men and women in all age groups thought women should stay at home when a child is young (Ma *et al*, 122-133, 344-363). This is strong evidence to support Becker's argument that the sexual division of labour in the household can be accepted voluntarily as efficient and mutually advantageous rather than as something imposed on people by custom and patriarchy. The other side of the coin is that only one-third of wives (one-quarter of all women aged 20-69 years) would prefer this option; two-thirds of Chinese women rejected it firmly, despite the burden of combining wage work and domestic work, with consistent views on related topics (Ma *et al*, 1994; Stockman, Bonney and Sheng, 1995: 141-154).

The impact of social engineering in China is highlighted by comparisons with almost identical surveys in Bangkok, Seoul and Fukuoka (a large town in central Japan with attitudes closer to the national average than to those of Tokyo residents) carried out in 1989-1992 (Table 4.6). Acceptance of separate sex roles is much higher in Bangkok, Fukuoka and Seoul than in Beijing. The Thai case shows that this is not necessarily related to beliefs about sex differences in abilities, as the Thais do not believe there are any significant differences of ability between men and women, whereas in China this belief had to be eradicated. It appears that the complete separation of roles between men and women will continue to attract support, even if minority support, because it does, as Becker argues, offer certain concrete benefits to couples. The modern version of the sexual division of labour attracts even greater support.

**Work orientations**
There is a huge volume of research contributed by social psychologists as well as sociologists on what is variously called work orientations, work attitudes or work values (Hofstede, 1980, 1994; Macarov, 1982a; MOW, 1987; Furnham, 1990). Concern about the declining work ethic or concern to increase work effort and productivity have prompted much of this research, and the focus has generally been on the work orientations of men rather than on those of women and any sex differential in work attitudes. For example Kalleberg (1977) did not explore sex differences in work orientations although his dataset included women working full-time, and Furnham is more interested in the impact of age (misread as generational change) than sex on work attitudes (1990: 124-5).

Results have generally been inconclusive, contradictory or ethnocentric, if interesting (Macarov, 1982b: 178). The failure to deliver conclusive results is illustrated by a series of cross-national comparative studies carried out in the 1980s to see if there were important cultural differences between societies in the strength of the work ethic and in work attitudes more generally (Hofstede, 1980; Fogarty, 1985; Yankelovich, 1985; Harding, Phillips and Fogarty, 1986; MOW, 1987). Research on labour market behaviour is affected by the particular definitions, classifications and concepts applied, as noted in Chapter 3. However in the volatile area of attitudes and opinions, research results are hugely determined by the questions asked, or not asked, the wording used and the methods of analysis. Studies variously address attachment to the current employer or job, to the occupation, or to paid employment generally (Kalleberg, 1977; Warr, 1982; Mueller, Wallace and Price, 1992). Some studies focus on the *relative* importance of work as against family, leisure, community and religion as central life concerns (Dubin, 1956; Bielby and Bielby, 1984; MOW, 1987). Here again, researchers often rely on multivariate analysis to identify components within work orientations, with theory playing a limited role in focusing attention on particular aspects or themes. Even when research topics and questions are carefully focused, cross-national comparisons reveal the problem of non-equivalent meanings of apparently simple words like 'achievement'. Cross-national comparisons also reveal the ethnocentric and male-centred character of theory in this field (Hofstede, 1980, 1991: 159-174). Furthermore, studies in this field vary hugely in design and scope. Large nationally representative sample surveys are rare. Samples are typically small, restricted to particular groups even when 'national' in aim, and frequently restricted to highly selective social, industrial, occupational or age groups. It is sometimes difficult to ascertain whether studies of 'workers' or 'employees' included women, and if they did, how large and representative a subgroup they formed. However the over-riding problem is that research findings in this field are largely shaped by the particular topics addressed, the sample used, question-wording and analysis techniques. The comparative studies have found that the centrality of work as a life interest increases with age (MOW, 1987: 86-7) while work commitment declines with age (Warr, 1982; see also Table 4.5) or else rises with age (Harding *et al*, 1986: 167). They have found no sex differences in work orientations (Harding *et al*, 1986: 158), significant sex differences (Fogarty, 1985: 192-9; MOW, 1987: 87, 240) and even that women score higher than men on the work ethic (Yankelovich, 1985: 344-5). The volatility of research results is further illustrated by attempts to identify societies where the work ethic is strong or weak. If included in a study, Japan regularly emerges as having such a strong work ethic that it belongs in a category of its own, with a large sex differential in work orientations. However studies regularly show Germany to have the lowest levels of work commitment and work ethic (Fogarty, 1985: 175; Yankelovich, 1985: 398-9; Harding et al, 1986: 169; MOW, 1987: 275, 283; Furnham, 1990: 130-9), although one analysis classifies it in a category of its own with the strongest work ethic in Europe (de Vaus and McAllister, 1991: 84). Within a single study, the UK is shown to have the lowest work ethic and a high level of work commitment when compared with the USA, Sweden, West Germany and Israel (Yankelovich, 1985: 398-9; see also Harding et al, 1986: 169). It should be clear that judgements about the theoretical and methodological adequacy of any study will determine whether its findings and conclusions are regarded as admissible, useful or relevant. In the field of work orientations virtually any result can be manufactured, by accident or by design, and survey results can be implausible or perplexing.

Given widespread acceptance of the sexual division of labour, with only gradual change across generations, we would expect men and women to differ in work orientations. Indeed we would have to question research results that denied this. The most complete theory predicting a sex differential in work orientations and behaviour is Becker's thesis that married women economise on the effort expended on market work by seeking less demanding jobs, if they work at all (see Chapter 1). The evidence presented above on attitudes to sex role differentiation indicates that Becker's thesis remains valid for between two-thirds and three-quarters of couples of working age in Britain in the 1990s.

It is therefore surprising that studies of work orientations generally show small sex differentials. There are three reasons for this. First, there is the usual problem of a weak link between attitudes and behaviour (Wicker, 1969; Yankelovich, 1985: 16-17, 263) so that people can voice opinions that bear no relation to the work choices they actually make. Similarly, statements about what is valued in a job do not predict how hard people work, or their productivity. Second, more often than not there is the problem of sample selection bias (see Chapter 5), a common problem in studies of women's employment. Third, most studies adopt a high-tech quantitative approach focused on the male work perspective which is unlikely to reveal *qualitative* differences between men and women, and between different groups of women, in the meaning and value of work. For example quantitative studies ask about *intrinsic* job rewards (such as interesting work and the opportunity to use one's abilities) versus *extrinsic* job rewards (such as good pay and job security) and conclude that sex differentials in work orientations are small or non-existent (de Vaus and McAllister, 1991). Yet other studies reveal that paid work is rarely a central life interest for women and for most women takes second place to family concerns; that what women value in a job are convenient or flexible hours, the option of part-time work, pleasant colleagues and a friendly atmosphere – aspects of a job that are *qualitatively* different from the criteria relevant to men such as opportunities for promotion (Martin and Roberts, 1984: 71-74, 183, 191; Fogarty, 1985: 194-7; Hakim,

1991). Wives working part-time in Britain can regard work almost as a kind of social club, a place to meet people, to get out of the house while earning additional income (Rose, 1994).

Kalleberg used multivariate analysis of 1973 USA Quality of Employment Survey data for people working full-time (20 hours a week or more) to identify six dimensions in work orientations: features of the work situation that can be of greater or lesser importance to individuals and can be the source of greater or lesser satisfaction with a particular job or type of work. The *intrinsic* dimension refers to the work task itself, whether it is interesting, challenging, develops and utilises skills. The *convenience* dimension refers to practical characteristics that make a job 'comfortable' for a worker: convenient hours, convenient journey to work, pleasant workplace and so forth. The *financial* dimension combines rates of pay, fringe benefits offered by the employer and job security - the monetary value of a job. *Relations with co-workers* emerged as a separate dimension and refers to the social character of the work situation, whether it provides opportunities for friendly interactions. The *career* dimension refers to opportunities for promotion and advancement in a career. The sixth dimension, labelled *resource adequacy* refers to practical factors facilitating work performance, such as adequate equipment, authority and information required to do the job, helpful colleagues and supervision. The six dimensions combine features of paid work that may influence decisions to work, or not, with features affecting satisfaction with a particular job – the meaning that someone attaches to the work role as well as sources of satisfaction with the work role (Kalleberg, 1977: 129). While this classification is entirely reasonable within a Western cultural context, a very different classification was developed at the same time by Hofstede from a much larger cross-national dataset.

The most successful of the comparative studies was that by Hofstede (1980, 1991). Surveys of some 120,000 IBM employees around the world provided, in effect, carefully matched samples of occupations across 66 countries. This landmark study was the largest of its kind, and the analysis by far the most detailed and careful. In particular, Hofstede seeks cross-national validity in the dimensions of work orientations identified by the analysis; makes the crucial distinction between choice and approval, personal goals and beliefs; deals with the problem of acquiescence, the tendency to agree with everything, which is always greater among people with less education or in lower grade occupations; and offers a theoretically-informed analysis instead of relying exclusively on multivariate analysis to shape the results. Furthermore, Hofstede's multilevel analysis of differences between countries, occupations and individuals enables him to show, for example, how masculine cultures enlarge gender differences in work orientations while feminine cultures reduce them to insignificance (Hofstede, 1991: 83).

Hofstede's analyses identified four dimensions of work orientations across national cultures: the relationship with authority (sometimes termed authoritarianism); the relationship between the individual and the group (often labelled individualism); ways of dealing with uncertainty, relating to the control of aggression and the expression of emotions, which he labels uncertainty-avoidance; and a social-ego dimension which contrasted dominance, reward and challenge against good social relations and job comfort factors, and which he finally labelled the masculinity-femininity dimension because it reflected gender differences in work orientations. In addition to analyses focused on national cultural differences, Hofstede analysed work orientations at the occupational level, and then looked for any sex differences within occupations. At this level, only two of the four dimensions emerged as important. Authoritarianism emerged even more strongly than at the national level, but with no sex differential within occupations; education was the dominant correlate. The social-ego dimension was also most salient at occupational level and displayed sex differences so large that they provided the masculinity-femininity label. This dimension reflects apparently universal differences in the work orientations of men and women that echo Gilligan's account of personality differences between men and women (see Chapter 1) or else derive from sex role differentiation: the 'masculine' goals of high earnings, promotion opportunities, up-to-dateness and opportunities for training and updating contrast with the 'social' goals of greater importance to women: good relations with colleagues and managers, a friendly atmosphere and a pleasant workplace. As secondary earners, women can afford to discount the financial and career features of a job in favour of social and convenience factors. On the other hand in countries where more women hold jobs and more households have two earners, men too can afford to place less emphasis on the aggressive achievement-oriented features of work. The multi-level research design adopted by Hofstede, plus his huge research database, allowed him to reveal the variations across time, countries and occupational grades that cause so many contradictory findings across smaller and less sophisticated studies. For example Hofstede shows that sex differences are largest among the less educated in lower grade occupations and smallest among the more highly educated in higher grade jobs. Sex differentials can be eliminated or even reversed in professional and managerial grades, in part due to selection effects (1980: 276-281). He shows that work is more central in life within countries with high masculinity scores, such as Japan, Germany and Britain while work has a less central position in life in countries with high femininity scores such as Sweden, Norway, the Netherlands and Denmark (1980: 285, 1991: 81-86). These results tie in with the MOW International Research Team's finding that higher educational qualifications are associated among women *only* with higher work centrality and greater work commitment (1987: 191-2; see also Bielby and Bielby, 1988: 1047), and with the sex differences found in the European Value Systems study (Fogarty, 1985: 194-197). Men are usually the main income-earners and their work orientations (and behaviour) show less variation than those of women, for whom work is a matter of choice and may be either central or secondary. Hofstede's study is unique in identifying the sex differential in work orientations, the personal and cultural/social factors that increase or eliminate sex differences, and the sources of the polarisation in work orientations emerging within the female population.

**Work commitment**
Studies on the scale of Hofstede's are rare. Research on trends over time requires simple and robust measures, such as the indicator of work commitment used in Tables 4.7 and 4.8. This is the 'lottery win' question on what people would do if they won or inherited a lot of money, thus removing the purely financial incentive to work. This question has been asked in many surveys in Western countries with slightly different wordings (Morse and Weiss, 1955; Warr, 1982; MOW, 1987: 202; Rose, 1994). The question provides a simple measure of paid work as a key life interest without exploring exactly what it is about a job that makes it worth having. The measure has always shown a marked sex differential within the workforce in the USA and in Europe which has been falling gradually in recent

**Table 4.7** The sex differential in work commitment

|  | 1981 | 1984-5 | 1989 | 1992 |
|---|---|---|---|---|
| Proportion (%) saying they would continue to work in the absence of financial need | | | | |
| All workers | 66 | 70 | 74 | 68 |
| Women   all working | 58 | 66 | 76 | 67 |
| full-time | 65 | 71 | 77 | 69 |
| part-time | 54 | 56 | 74 | 64 |
| Men   all working | 69 | 74 | 72 | 68 |
| full-time | 69 | 75 | 72 | 69 |
| part-time | 55 | 45 | 80 | 58 |
| People who would continue to work as a percent of population of working age (16-59/64 years) | | | | |
| All persons | 61 | 54 | 59 | 53 |
| Women | 49 | 44 | 54 | 48 |
| Men | 67 | 65 | 63 | 58 |

**Notes:** In the 1981 survey the question wording was: 'Considering both kinds of work, that is not only being employed by someone else but also being self-employed, if you were to get enough money to live as comfortably as you would like for the rest of your life, would you continue to work (not necessarily in your present job) or would you stop working?' For non-working people the end of the question was modified to ask 'would you want to work somewhere or would you want to remain without a job?'.
Data for 1984-85 and 1989 are for all employees working 10+ hours a week, and the question was 'If without having to work you had what you would regard as a reasonable living income, would you still prefer to have a paid job, or wouldn't you bother?'.
In the 1992 survey the question wording was: 'If you were to get enough money to live as comfortably as you would like for the rest of your life, would you continue to work, not necessarily in your present job, or would you stop working?'.
**Source:** Derived form Tables 1 and 2 in Warr (1982), Table 9 in Hakim (1992) and Table 1.1 in Gallie and White (1993) plus unpublished tables supplied by the authors from the 1992 survey.

decades (Hakim, 1991: 106-7) and appears to have been eliminated, in Britain at least, by the early 1990s.

   Table 4.7 presents comparative information on work commitment from three nationally representative British surveys. Except for the 1981 survey, questions on work commitment were only addressed to people in work, so that results for the workforce have to be adjusted to take account of the non-working population in order to obtain the full picture on work commitment among all adults of working age (bottom part of Table 4.7). This adjustment invariably increases

**Table 4.8** Non-financial work commitment within the workforce by age

| Age in years: | 20-30 | 30-40 | 40-50 | 50-60 | Total | Base |
|---|---|---|---|---|---|---|
| Men working full-time | 75 | 72 | 64 | 55 | 69 | 1599 |
| Women working full-time | 77 | 69 | 65 | 54 | 69 | 873 |
| Women working part-time | 78 | 71 | 57 | 46 | 64 | 635 |
| Men working part-time | .. | .. | .. | .. | 58 | 48 |

**Note:** The question asked was 'If you were to get enough money to live as comfortably as you would like for the rest of your life, would you continue to work, not necessarily in your present job, or would you stop working?' The percentage choosing to continue working is shown for each age group.
**Source:** Derived from Table 1.1 in Gallie and White (1993) and unpublished tables supplied by the authors from the 1992 survey.

the sex differential, since by definition non-working women are choosing *not* to work given even a moderate income supplied by their husband. Furthermore, results for part-time workers in 1984-85 and 1989 are biased upwards by the BSAS definition of part-time jobs as those requiring 10-30 hours a week, excluding marginal workers working less than 10 hours a week who constitute almost 10% of the female workforce in Britain and over one-fifth of all part-time workers, as noted in Chapter 2. The most complete survey was carried out in 1981 by Warr (1982) based on a nationally representative sample of all adults aged 16 and over in Great Britain, including the retired who are excluded from Table 4.7. He put the same questions to non-working (and retired) people as well as to people in the labour market, so that the sex differentials for 1981 in Table 4.7 are survey results for people of working age without adjustment. Within the workforce, the sex differential seems small: 58% of working women and 69% of working men express strong work commitment in 1981. Within the complete population of working age, however, the sex differential is larger: just half of all women are committed to work compared to two-thirds of all men. The survey data for 1984 to 1989 is not exactly comparable with that for 1981 and 1992, due to differences in question-wording and to the exclusion of people working less than 10 hours a week who have the lowest levels of work commitment. However they indicate a small decline in male work commitment and a small increase in female work commitment, so that the gap between them shrinks appreciably over the decade. Results for 1992 indicate that the sex differential in work commitment had been eliminated *within the workforce*, a group that is always more strongly self-selective for women than for men, but which had become more selective generally after a decade of historically high levels of unemployment. In the adult population as a whole, however, the sex differential remained, although it seems to have shrunk markedly since 1981: half of all adult women (48%) were committed to work compared to just over half (58%) of all men by 1992. The reduced sex differential seems to be due partly to men becoming less committed to work and partly to women becoming more committed, a conclusion that is supported also by the results for 1984-89. One reason for the decline in the male work ethic might be the fact that the provider role is now more likely to be shared with a wife, at least in part, rather than because the welfare state reduces the will to work.

These changes could be due entirely to changes in the composition of the workforce rather than changes in attitudes, since the pattern of age differences in the 1992 survey (Table 4.8) is almost identical to Warr's results from the 1981 survey. Work commitment is highest among young people, who have yet to prove themselves, and declines sharply with age, despite the fact that voluntary early retirement and redundancy take many people with low work commitment out of the workforce. Work commitment is always highest in higher grade occupations which require longer years of education and training so that people with low work commitment drop out long before they start work, and also because these jobs offer greater rewards which reinforce and sustain work commitment over the years (Warr, 1982; Fiorentine, 1987). It is thus likely that part or all of the changes in work commitment in the male and female workforces is due to changes in their age structure and/or occupational structure. As shown in Chapter 6, women have been taking an increasing share of the top jobs in Britain and other European countries, and this trend implies some increase in work commitment in the female workforce. On the other hand, the expansion of a segregated part-time workforce noted in Chapters 3 and 6 should have the opposite effect.

The commitment of a part-time worker to their part-time job is not equal to the commitment of a full-time worker to their full-time job, and the difference is more than one of degree. Qualitative differences between the work orientations of full-timers and part-timers are not reflected in the simple measure of non-financial work commitment in Tables 4.7 and 4.8. As shown earlier, there are fundamental differences between women full-timers and part-timers in their self-identity as primary earners or as housewife secondary earners. Part-time workers are most likely to value the 'feminine' job characteristics identified by Hofstede (Hakim, 1991: 107-9). Few women regard themselves as following a career, but the proportion is consistently higher among full-timers than among part-timers: 24% and 7% respectively gave this as a reason for working in 1980, 7% and 2% respectively gave this as the main reason (Martin and Roberts, 1984: 68). A less representative 1986 survey found equally large differences: 68% of the self-employed, 61% of men working full-time, 56% of women working full-time and only 22% of women part-timers saw themselves as having a career (Rose, 1994: 321). Further analysis revealed two qualitatively different work orientations in the full-time workforce and in the female part-time workforce. Full-time workers (men and women) were most likely to endorse what Rose labels the *work ethic*, a normative commitment to work as a central life interest, with employment seen as a long-term career rather than as a short-term job. In contrast, female part-time workers (and working class groups generally) viewed employment in instrumental terms which Rose notes can be regarded as the *inverse* of the work ethic: work was not seen in terms of a career, nor as a primary breadwinning activity, nor as a means of exercising skill and ability, but rather as a social activity and secondary source of income. This group had very low commitment to paid work in the absence of financial need and endorsed the view that the welfare state erodes the will to work. Finally, the work orientations of housewives who intended to return to paid work at some point in the future were very similar to those of part-timers (Rose, 1994: 290-6, 308-13, 333-4). We can safely assume that housewives who did *not* intend ever returning to paid work would have even less positive views on employment than the anti-work ethic of the part-timers. A 1983 NOP national attitude survey in Britain found that half of all non-working women with children preferred not to work, even if they could made proper child care arrangements. Part-timers were similar to non-working women in giving priority to their role as wife and mother over any job, and in refusing to believe that a full-time job could be compatible with running a family (Table 4.9). This survey did not find any difference in work commitment between part-timers and

**Table 4.9** Contrasts between working and non-working women

| % endorsing each opinion | Women working FT | PT | No job in last 5 years | Stopped work 5+ years ago | All women 25-54 years |
|---|---|---|---|---|---|
| Would not work if not financially necessary | 21 | 27 | - | - | 24 |
| Would not work, even if had proper childcare | - | - | 51 | 52 | 51 |
| Married woman's first duty is to her marriage (rather than to her job or both equally) | 52 | 72 | 63 | 68 | 62 |
| A mother's first duty is to her children (rather than to her job or both equally) | 83 | 92 | 91 | 93 | 89 |
| A woman can successfully combine a FT job with running a family - % agreeing | 77 | 52 | 59 | 55 | 62 |
| Men make better bosses than women - % disagreeing | 66 | 70 | 68 | 61 | 67 |
| Prefers a male boss (of those expressing a preference, having had both) | 83 | 81 | 76 | 90 | 82 |
| Base = 100% | 309 | 261 | 237 | 176 | 983 |

**Source:** September 1983 NOP survey on women's issues. Representative sample of women aged 18-54 years in Britain. All % adjusted to exclude Don't Know and Undecided responses.

full-timers, but it showed that, in the absence of financial need, virtually all part-timers would work part-time, while roughly half of full-timers would continue to work full-time with the other half switching to part-time work. The preference to stop working, or stop working full-time, was determined by age more than childcare responsibilities. Similar results are found in the BSAS: the majority of full-time housewives and of part-time workers would only work part-time, or not at all, even if they had the childcare of their choice. There is no evidence that women looking after their children at home full-time are dissatisfied or that a majority would prefer to be working full-time (Witherspoon and Prior, 1991: 143, 148, 151).

Interest in promotion is another indicator of women's interest in their work as part of a career or as just a job. Surveys consistently reveal women to be less interested in promotion than men, with part-timers least interested of all. A 1980 British survey showed only half of all female employees aged 16-59 years to be interested in promotion, 60% of full-timers and 34% of part-timers. Family responsibilities and an unwillingness to take on more responsibility were the main reasons for not wanting promotion (Martin and Roberts, 1984: 53). Cross-national studies have also found a significant association between hours worked and work centrality (MOW, 1987: 90) and that women express less interest in promotion, partly due to competing family interests (Matthaei, 1982: 298; Fogarty, 1985: 196; Davidson and Cooper, 1993: 74, 142, 155, 193-5). Even in the highly selective group of working professional women, mothers of children work shorter hours and feel less job involvement (Carrier, 1995). The evidence is unanimous that part-timers invest less interest in their work, even if they work just as hard on the job. These qualitative differences cannot be picked up by the standard work commitment question.

Overall, we conclude that the sex differential in work commitment had disappeared from the workforce by the 1990s, even if it remained in the wider adult population. The conclusion is corroborated by a variety of behavioral indicators. There is no evidence that women work less hard than men, if anything they work harder. Part-time workers and homeworkers, for example, often have higher productivity because they are less likely to get tired than full-time workers who work much longer hours. The sex differential in absenteeism that concerned Myrdal and Klein in the 1950s has disappeared. Sickness absence rates stand at around 5% for all workers in Britain. International comparisons of absenteeism also find few differences between men and women, with the exception of countries like Sweden where long periods of state-funded parental leave are taken by women and seriously distort all labour force statistics (OECD, 1991; Jonung and Persson, 1993; Nyberg, 1994). So working women's work orientations and behaviour have grown closer to men's. However women's workplans continue to differ from men's, and this may explain continuing differences in attitudes to promotion.

**Work plans**
One problem for research on the links between work orientations and labour market behaviour is that, even when they find a connection, cross-sectional surveys cannot resolve the problem of

causality: which comes first, high work commitment or the stable career? The only adequate way of resolving the question of causal processes is the true prospective longitudinal study. There has so far been only one longitudinal study providing a rigorous test of the long-term influence of work orientations and work plans. The National Longitudinal Surveys (NLS) project initiated in the mid-1960s in the USA has provided a great wealth of longitudinal data on five age cohorts of young and mature women, young and older men. Of particular interest is the cohort of young women aged 14-24 in 1968 who were interviewed almost every year up to 1983 when aged 29-39 years. This cohort was asked in 1968, and at each interview over the next decade, what they would like to be doing when they were 35 years old, whether they planned to be working at age 35 or whether they planned to be keeping house or raising a family at age 35. This age was chosen as the peak age for competing work and family roles. Because it asked about personal preferences and choices, rather than general attitudes, the question turned out to have astonishing analytical and predictive power, and was used again in the second youth cohort study initiated in 1979.

Career planners constituted one-quarter of the 1968 young women cohort; another quarter consistently planned a homemaker career; the majority of the cohort were drifters with no fixed plans or had 'unplanned careers' (Table 4.10), as did women in the NLS mature women cohort aged 30-44 years at the start of the study in the late 1960s (Mott, 1978, 1982; Shaw, 1983). There are a number of independent analyses of the extent to which early workplans were fulfilled by age 35. They all show that women achieved their employment objectives for the most part, resulting in dramatic 'mark-ups' to career planners in terms of occupational grade and earnings (Mott, 1982; Rexroat and Shehan, 1984; Shaw and Shapiro, 1987). Furthermore, career planners were more likely to choose typically-male jobs and adapted their fertility behaviour to their workplans (Waite and Stolzenberg, 1976; Stolzenberg and Waite, 1977; Spitze and Waite, 1980). Workplans were a significant independent predictor of actual work behaviour. After controlling for other factors affecting labour force participation, a woman who consistently planned to work had a probability of working that was over 30 percentage points higher than did a woman who consistently planned not to work. Of the women who held consistently to their work plans, four-fifths were actually working in 1980, at age 35,

**Table 4.10** Long term workplans and outcomes among young women in the USA, 1970s

|  | Distribution of sample | % working at age 35 |
|---|---|---|
| **Homemaker career:** | | |
| consistently indicate no plans for work: aim is marriage, family and homemaking activities | 28% | 49% |
| **Drifters and unplanned careers:** | | |
| (a) highly variable responses over time, no clear pattern in plans for age 35 | 35% | |
| (b) switch to having future work expectations at some point in their twenties | 12% | 47% 64% |
| **Career planners:** | | |
| consistently anticipate working at age 35 throughout their twenties | 25% | 82% |

**Source:** Derived from Tables 2 and 3 in Shaw and Shapiro (1987: 8-9) reporting National Longitudinal Surveys data for the cohort of young women aged 14-24 years in 1968.

compared to only half of the women who consistently intended to devote themselves exclusively to home-maker activities. Women who planned to work at age 35 were likely to do so unless they had large families or a pre-school child. Women who planned a homemaker career nevertheless were obliged to work by economic factors in half the cases: their husband's low income, divorce, or the opportunity cost of not working led half to be in work at times. On balance, the homemaker career emerged as the least reliable. However most young women in this cohort were drifters with no fixed plans.

Planning to work yielded a significant wage advantage. Women who had consistently planned to work had wages 30 per cent higher than those of women who never planned to work. Those women who had aimed for the occupation they actually held at age 35 had even higher wages than women whose occupational plans were not realised. Women who make realistic plans and acquire necessary skills fare best in the labour market. Those who fare worst are women who aim for an exclusive homemaking career but end up working for economic reasons.

Perhaps most important of all, the NLS longitudinal analyses have finally disproven conclusions drawn from cross-sectional studies that women's work behaviour is heavily determined by the number and ages of any children, showing that the reverse process operates. Women who work only when their childcare responsibilities leave them free are in effect fulfilling a prior choice of emphasis on the homemaker career. Fertility expectations have only a small negative effect on young women's work-plans, whereas work-plans exert a powerful negative effect on young women's childbearing plans (Waite and Stolzenberg, 1976; Stolzenberg and Waite, 1977). Factors which have long been held to determine women's labour force participation, such as other family income, educational qualifications, marital status, and age of youngest child are revealed as being most important in relation to women with no commitment to employment careers, who have so far been in the majority. Women with definite career plans manifest a rather inelastic labour supply, similar to that of men (Shaw and Shapiro, 1987). An even bigger USA study, the National Longitudinal Study of the High School Class of 1972 has produced results that corroborate those of the NLS. It showed, for example, that young women who became mothers early, before the age of 25, differed significantly from those who remained childless: they were less work-oriented, more likely to plan to be homemakers at age 30, less likely to plan a professional career, and held more traditional sex role attitudes and aspirations *before* they gave birth. Parenthood strengthens pre-existing traditional attitudes in both young white men and women (Waite, Haggstrom and Kanouse, 1986; Morgan and Waite, 1987). European studies have also found that personal workplans are more strongly correlated with employment choices than general statements of work commitment as measured in Table 4.7 (Haller and Rosenmayr, 1971: 503).

The NLS surveys also suggest a faster pace of change in the USA than in Europe in recent decades. About one-third of the first NLS cohort of young women, aged 14-24 in 1968, planned to be working at age 35, in the 1980s (Rexroat and Shehan, 1984: 352). In contrast about two-thirds of the second NLS cohort of young women, aged 14-21 in 1979, planned to be working at age 35, in the 1990s, and barely one-third planned to be full-time homemakers (Desai and Waite, 1991: 553). Not all will hold to these plans consistently, but these single-time responses indicate a sea change in women's workplans during the 1980s. Unfortunately equivalent data are not available for Britain or other European countries. No relevant information was collected in the 1994 British Survey of Working

Lives, for example. An exploratory analysis of the 1986 SCELI data indicates that one-quarter of working women, compared to two-thirds of working men, had career-oriented employment in the primary sector (Burchell and Rubery, 1994), suggesting that sex differences in planned careers are much larger in Britain than the USA.

Surveys routinely collect information on educational qualifications, and human capital theorists pretend that career plans can be deduced from qualifications held. Separate information on career plans is rarely collected. It is as well to remember that even in the post-War period a minority of female college graduates in the USA and university graduates in Europe started work with plans for long-term employment careers (Goldin, 1990: 206-8). As noted in Chapter 5, qualifications can serve another purpose, achieving social status and economic rewards through the marriage career rather than through a personal career. In addition, we should distinguish between dual earner and dual career partnerships (Bonney, 1988).

## Male dominance and other work-related attitudes

The work ethic and work commitment attract the attention of researchers and policy-makers due to concern at increasing social welfare expenditure and welfare dependency in Western democracies. Less attention is paid to attitudes to male dominance and other work-related attitudes that impact on women's employment. The evidence suggests that attitudes to male dominance are just as important for understanding women's achievements *within* the workforce as 'work ethic' attitudes were for understanding decisions to work or not.

Sex-role stereotypes are closely intertwined with occupational segregation and social relations in the workplace (Hunt, 1975: 173-90; Hakim, 1979: 50-53; Witherspoon, 1988; Vogler, 1994a). This interdependence of ideology and practice is exposed most clearly when people take jobs considered sex-atypical in the society in question, such as female Marines in the USA, forcing colleagues to rethink and renegotiate self-concepts, occupational identities and social relations in the workplace (Williams, 1989). There is much variation between societies and across time in what jobs are considered suitable for men or women. But at any point in time in a particular society, certain job choices will be *felt* to be inappropriate for persons of one gender, prompting floods of arguments to justify the *status quo*. Female priests and members of the clergy and male homosexual members of the armed forces are just two recent hotly debated examples in Western Europe. But female office clerks also provoked strong reactions when first introduced (Cohn, 1985). Occupations confer public social identities as well as income, and many people find it more comfortable when these roles are congruent with, or at least not markedly incongruent with sexual identities (Matthaei, 1982: 187-203, 281-5). As noted in Chapter 1, Goldberg's male dominance theory goes further, to argue that men are more likely to do what is necessary to obtain the lion's share of top jobs in any society, and that women favour male dominance in public social relations, because it is congruent with private heterosexual relationships. In effect, sex roles enter the workplace to support vertical occupational segregation more strongly than horizontal segregation, as noted in Chapter 6.

It is sometimes claimed that women are by nature 'non-hierarchical' or egalitarian, and more inclined towards democratic processes and consultation in the workplace (Tijdens, 1993: 88-9). The idea seems to have emerged from within women-only groups, but whatever its origins it is without any foundation in reality (Kanter, 1977: 299-303). Psychologists argue that most women express and define themselves in terms of social relationships whereas most men focus on personal achievement within hierarchies (Chodorow, 1978; Gilligan, 1993; see also Beutel and Marini, 1995), but they do not deny that women recognise and accept social hierarchies – on the contrary they are clear that women routinely accept male dominance (Miller, 1976; Gilligan, 1993: 168). Women accept hierarchy so long as men are in positions of power and authority. Male dominance is accepted, as Goldberg argued; female dominance goes contrary to sex-role stereotypes and is unwelcome, uncomfortable and frequently rejected (Fogarty et al, 1971: 15, 191-207; Kanter, 1977: 69-126, 197-205, 230-7; Hennig and Jardim, 1978: 115).

Women systematically reject the idea that men make better bosses than women (Table 4.9). Two-thirds (67%) of women aged 25-54 years reject the idea, with relatively little variation across subgroups. Age is the main correlate. Rejection is highest among women aged 18-24 but declines steadily with age so that opinion is evenly balanced among women aged 45-54 years. At first sight, it seems that women accept male and female bosses equally. Not so. Women consistently prefer a *male* boss. They only reject the idea that men make *better* bosses. It appears that women prefer men as bosses even though they know that men do not perform better than women, the implication being that mediocre male managers are more acceptable than competent female managers.

The question on preferences was only put to women who had experience of both male and female superiors: three-quarters of the sample said they did. After excluding 'Don't know' responses, roughly half said they had no preference and half had a preference. Among those expressing a preference, preferences for a male boss outnumbered preferences for a female boss by 4 to 1 across all groups of women, working and non-working (Table 4.9). Reasons given for preferring a male boss were numerous, but all reflect common stereotypes of male superiors being easier to deal with, more fair, less emotional, less fault-finding than women and less inclined to have favourites. Reasons were consistent across subgroups, implying that these are fixed public stereotypes common to all women, working or not.

Consistent results are obtained from all surveys questioning women on the topic – whether in junior grades or in professional grades. Surveys of this sort have been carried out by employment agencies, who have been forced to confront this reverse sex discrimination among job *seekers* rather than recruiters. A 1991 survey of some 400 secretaries working for Alfred Marks, one of the biggest employment agencies in Britain, asked about preferences among women who had worked for both male and female bosses. Few were indifferent on the question. If the job was identical, two-thirds of secretaries preferred to work for a male boss and only 18% preferred a female boss. One fifth (18%) of secretaries who had worked for a female boss would not do so again. Exploration of the reasons for preferences did not reveal any important perceived differences in working style that could account for these marked preferences. However secretaries were significantly more likely to undertake additional duties, above and beyond everyday work tasks, for male bosses. Social sex roles become integrated with work roles, and relations between male bosses and female subordinates reflect familial and sexual relations outside the workplace. Pringle (1989) argues that this enables men to exercise authority in the workplace with less coercion and more mutual pleasure in relations with female subordinates than is possible for female bosses. Far from wanting to remove sexuality and 'private' sexual identities from the workplace, secretaries regard these as positive features of an otherwise monotonous job. Secretaries are also aware that universally men have higher status and more power than women (Kanter, 1977: 197-205; Molm, 1986) and seek to avoid being associated with a less powerful person in the organisation.

Similar results were obtained from a 1994 survey of some 600 people in accountancy, law and other professions who were registered with Hays, a specialist recruitment agency in Britain. Among those who expressed a preference, most women preferred to work with men rather than with other women. Men were less choosy than women about the sex of colleagues, but only 4% wanted to work for a female boss. Professional women were equally unenthusiastic about having a female boss, and one-quarter actively preferred to work for a man. The indications are that preference for a male boss is stronger among women than men, even among professionals.

Similar results are found across the world. Numerous USA studies show that no-one wants to work for a female boss (Kanter, 1977: 197). In a review of women in management in France, Laufer noted that there is much evidence that both men and women prefer to work for a male boss (1993: 115). In 1970 one-third of Dutch adults of working age agreed it would be unnatural for women to manage male subordinates; by 1987 the proportion had fallen to only 12% (Tijdens, 1993: 88). Blanket rejection of the woman manager had disappeared, but the social difficulties of the position had not been resolved. When asked who had the most difficult job, male and female workers agreed on the following ranking: male superior with male subordinates (easiest); male superior with female subordinates; female superior with male subordinates; and, most difficult of all, female superior with female subordinates (Tijdens, 1993: 89). Hofstede's cross-national study found that women, especially those in low grade occupations, had *less* preference for a consultative managerial style than did their male colleagues (1980: 108-9). However he held back from concluding that women were more authoritarian than men, after controlling for occupation, although other studies had drawn this conclusion. What he does admit is that there were marked differences in authoritarianism between occupations, largely due to the correlation with education. And of course women are concentrated disproportionately in lower grade jobs.

A complex experiment used by Molm (1986) to study sex differentials in the use of power can also be interpreted as showing degrees of cooperation between a boss and subordinate, as measured by the total amount of exchange between such dyads in different situations. Cooperation was at its lowest with a legitimated female superior and at its highest with a male superior, with or without legitimation. Males and females were equally good, or poor, power users. However the response of subordinates was crucial, and females responded differentially to male and female superiors. Female subordinates were twice as cooperative with a non-legitimated male boss as with a legitimated female boss. Overall the highest levels of cooperation were observed in male dyads and the lowest levels of cooperation were in female dyads, with cross-sex dyads in between, in line with the ranking of situations reported by Tijdens. Women are even more reluctant to acknowledge a female superior than are men.

It is commonplace to focus on the problems caused by a male work culture and by male colleagues being unhelpful and uncooperative towards women in management and supervisory posts (Fogarty et al, 1971; Hunt, 1975: 183-4; Kanter, 1977; Hennig and Jardim, 1978; Matthaei, 1982: 293-300; Davidson and Cooper, 1993; Reskin and Padavic, 1994: 91-99), with sexual harassment the most extreme mechanism for putting women in their place and excluding them from a male work culture (Crull, 1987; Husbands, 1992). This one-eyed view of the problem overlooks the equally important *active* contribution of women to maintaining a *status quo* that excludes women from the senior posts and management positions that give women authority. Women who succeed in getting top jobs create social and psychological problems for women in lower grade posts and non-working women as well as for male colleagues. Male resentment is understandable, as competent women increase competition for top jobs in what is seen as a zero-sum game. Women ought to be delighted, as successful women open doors for female successors. Goldberg's theory of male dominance is the only theory that can make sense of women's active role in maintaining women's exclusion from top jobs by refusing to cooperate with female managers as readily as they do with male managers. Kanter found no evidence of sex differences in leadership aptitude or style. She explains the negative stereotype of the female manager in terms of the more restricted power and promotion opportunities of women in organisations. But she has no adequate explanation for *women's* resentment of women who get promoted out of the female job ghetto (1977: 142-59, 199-205). Pringle explores the social and psychological problems that women experience in working for a female boss, noting that this situation provokes far more hostility than among men working for female superiors. Male authority is accepted as natural by women and male bosses are deferred to, even if disliked, because gender and sexuality are central to all workplace power relations, so that a streak of sexual excitement enlivens what is otherwise a master-slave relationship. The authority of female bosses is less 'natural' and more fragile, and women who have reached senior positions expose the subordination of secretarial and other lower grade jobs as chosen rather than inevitable or natural (Pringle, 1989: 28-85, 108, 130, 240). Women in senior positions provoke hostility among female subordinates because they expose female heterogeneity most acutely, whereas for men they represent women joining their game, choosing the same values and criteria of success.

## Conclusions

Ideas about male and female abilities and social roles have changed in the post-War decades: male intellectual superiority is rarely asserted; public attitude has become more favourable to working wives and mothers following the abolition of the marriage bar; fewer people regard men as taking priority over women for access to jobs in recession; complete sex role differentiation is rejected by the majority. However men and women still accept the modern sexual division of labour that allocates the primary income-earning role to men and the primary homemaking role to women. The working class holds on to these sex role 'stereotypes' more tightly than people with greater education in higher occupational grades. Work orientations and work commitment, workplans and interest in promotion are all determined by or consistent with acceptance of fundamental sex role differentiation.

The only group seriously challenging the *status quo* are career women working full-time, who seem also to provide the vanguard of change within the workforce. This minority group is not representative of all working women, let alone all adult women, yet its voice is the one most often heard. Once again, we find a polarisation among women that has not been recognised or addressed, a polarisation that reflects more fundamental conflicts of interest between career-oriented women and housewives or secondary earners, than between men and women working full-time.

Women are under-represented in senior grade jobs. Undoubtedly sex discrimination is one factor excluding women from access to well paid top jobs. Men prefer to reserve the best jobs for themselves, claiming women do not have the necessary skills. But this review points up two additional factors which are sometimes overlooked. First, women (as well as men) prefer to work for male bosses, even when they are not especially competent. Women in positions of authority and power present a serious challenge to sexual identities and sex roles for everyone, not only male colleagues. This response is consistent with, and supports Goldberg's theory of male dominance. No other theory has been offered which can explain women's rejection of females in authority. Second, employment careers are centrally important for only a minority of women, even today, even among university graduates. More than half of adult women accept the sexual division of labour and treat market work as an additional, secondary activity, to be fitted in with the demands of domestic life. Significantly, many childless couples maintain differentiated sex roles. Acceptance of sex role differentiation is independent of childbearing and childcare responsibilities and independent of views on women's abilities. These findings can be interpreted as supporting both Goldberg's and Becker's theories. Role specialisation can be a rational maximisation of efficiency, given socialisation processes in childhood and adolescence which create domesticated women and achievement-oriented men long before either spouse decides to reject parenthood as a major life activity. On the other hand, Becker's theory of comparative advantage predicts only specialisation, not which spouse will specialise in domestic work. If women specialise in homekeeping and men in competitive market work even in households that have intentionally avoided the constraints imposed by children, it is likely that fundamental psychological factors are operating, as Goldberg argues.

Most research on the labour market deals exclusively with behaviour, which is more easily reported in regular national surveys and censuses. Research on attitudes, motivations, preferences and plans is more difficult to do well, but is absolutely crucial if we are to obtain a complete understanding not only of *what* people are doing, but also *why*.

# 5
# Labour mobility and women's employment profiles

Is it true that women's attachment to work is increasing by leaps and bounds? This is certainly the impression given by virtually all recent research reports on women's employment. Work attachment refers to continuity of employment over a period of years, or across the lifecycle, and is measured at the individual level and longitudinally. It is thus quite different, and separate, from economic activity rates which are measured in aggregate data, usually at the national level and at a single point in time, using cross-sectional data (see Chapters 2 and 3). Most recent studies of individual work histories conclude that women's continuity of employment, or attachment to work, has been increasing in recent decades (Martin and Roberts, 1984: 187; Main, 1988a). I challenge this, as a one-sided and misleading reading of the evidence. The pattern of women's employment across the lifecycle has certainly been changing, but not as yet in the direction of greater work attachment in Britain, although this is certainly a trend in the USA and among the minority of childless women in industrial societies. Within Europe, the British pattern of change is more common than the USA model.

## Changing perspectives
Post-War writers on women's employment issues had no illusions about women's casual approach to market work. A comparative review of women's employment in the USA, Britain and other European countries by Myrdal and Klein (1956, 1968) acknowledged that women were the less stable workers, with substantially higher rates of absenteeism and turnover. Like others writing on what was then labelled the 'controversial phenomenon' of women's employment, they sought to defend women's right to work, demonstrating their physical and mental abilities for wage work, and suggesting novel

arrangements (such as part-time work) which could ease women's double burden of domestic duties and employment. Nonetheless, their espousal of this cause did not prevent a dispassionate data-based analysis of the issue. Under the heading of 'employers' problems' they addressed the sex differentials in work attitudes, behaviour and performance that were claimed by employers to justify their preference for male workers over female workers and to justify lower rates of pay for women doing the same job as men (Myrdal and Klein 1968: 91-115). Of these, the most important behavioral differences were women's higher rates of absenteeism, higher labour turnover and lower employment stability with an employer, all giving rise to additional costs. Employers' investment in on-the-job training offered a lower return in the case of female workers, who were less likely to stay with the firm, due to more job-hopping or to leaving the workforce for domestic reasons; there were also the extra recruitment costs of replacing workers who left. From the employer's view, the specific reason for a woman worker leaving a job is irrelevant. Whether she leaves to marry, have a baby, to take another job because her husband's job has been moved to another city, or to take another job because it is closer to home does not alter the employer's need to hire and retrain a replacement worker, with the associated costs (Chiplin and Sloane, 1974).

As late as 1971, a government report stated that the most widely accepted 'law' of absence behaviour was that women were absent more frequently, and more in total, than men; the evidence was absence rates twice as high among full-time women, and two to three times higher among part-time women, than among men in the period 1947-1949 (Jones, 1971: 18). Myrdal and Klein found that absenteeism was two to four times higher among women, even when absences associated with pregnancy were excluded. One study found that women lost about twice as much time as men, with married women losing up to three times as much as single women. They concluded that 'one of the major objections against the employment of women is based not merely on prejudice but on actual experience. The statistical data are undeniable evidence that, with all due variations as from one type of employment to another, the rate of absenteeism is higher among women than men in each occupational group' and they attributed this to a casual attitude to market work among women. Similarly, they found labour turnover to be very much larger among women than among men, on average

50%-60% higher, but reaching 100% per year in the textile industries despite their long tradition of female employment. Even here, they noted that most women lacked a sense of career and adopted a casual attitude towards continuity of employment, changing jobs for casual reasons (Myrdal and Klein, 1968: 94-107). A somewhat lower average annual turnover rate of 32% is quoted for women in the USA in 1957 (Blau and Ferber 1992: 79).

Twenty years later, Hunt's report on a 1973 national survey of management attitudes towards women at work was necessarily factual in its presentation of the survey results, but her interpretation was already excusing and downplaying sex differentials as unimportant, glossing over the inconvenient results on labour turnover and absenteeism to underline those showing women in a positive light, notably employers' view that women scored higher than men in patience with dull work! (Hunt, 1975: 101, 105, 107, 109). Nonetheless the sex differentials remained in evidence. Only a minority of employers thought there was no difference between men and women in their propensity to take days off for sickness or for other reasons, or in the likelihood of their working continuously for one firm. The dominant view was that men were preferable for their lower absenteeism and turnover rates. The perceived sex differential in behaviour was corroborated by analyses of actual absenteeism, job tenure and job mobility. The same pattern was found in management perceptions of full-time and part-time workers: the majority view was that full-time workers were markedly better than part-timers on low absenteeism, continuity with the firm and working hard. Again, employers' 'prejudices' were found to be supported by and clearly based on actual experience within the firm, with personal and family reasons dominating turnover rates among women (Hunt, 1975: 94-96, 105-6). It is also notable that absenteeism was higher among part-timers, who already had more time for domestic activities, indicating that the casual attitude to employment as an optional extra continued into the 1970s.

Another twenty years on and the issues of labour turnover and employment instability have disappeared from the social science research agenda. Studies routinely draw the conclusion that there is no evidence that women in general, and women working part-time in particular, show a lesser degree of attachment to work in terms of loyalty to a particular employer (Marsh, 1991: 57), that the employment stability of women part-time workers is no lower than among women full-time workers (Dex, 1987: 115), and that the evidence that part-time jobs are high-turnover jobs should not be taken at face value (Elias and White, 1991: 32-6, 58). When differences are noted, they are attributed to the occupations in question rather than to the incumbents, to labour market segmentation (Blossfeld and Mayer, 1988: 129; Elias and White, 1991: 5) or to age effects (Elias and White, 1991). Studies that reveal dramatic sex differentials in work orientations and employment patterns nonetheless emphasise the similarities between men and women (Pollert, 1981: 79-115; Elias and Main, 1982: 3-11; Dex, 1985: 20-46) or, *in extremis,* reject the differences as implausible, even when national surveys yield the same result year after year (European Commission, 1994: 87). Sensitive to the climate of opinion, economists often ignore persistent sex differentials in turnover and tenure as unworthy of emphasis in research reports (Burgess and Rees, 1994; Gregg and Wadsworth, 1995).

Turnover rates appear to have been lower in the USA throughout the century because of the marked heterogeneity of the female population: those wives who worked did so continuously while other women stopped work at marriage and never worked again (Goldin, 1990: 28-41). The post-War entry of women with lower work commitment and less work experience to the labour market may even have raised female turnover rates slightly. Even so, there is a sex differential in labour turnover in the USA as well, and a similar unwillingness to admit the differential runs through the USA social science literature (Reskin and Padavic, 1994: 39 41, 86, 112-3; Hakim, 1996). A popular USA textbook on labor economics and female employment (Blau and Ferber, 1992) does not include a chapter on patterns of labour mobility and women's work histories across the lifecycle, even though other chapters contain passing references to this topic, noting inadequacies in data on work histories and work experience. It is clear that economists as well as sociologists are suggesting that sex differentials in employment patterns are disappearing (Blau and Ferber, 1992: 80, 162).

### The sources of change
There are three reasons for expecting fundamental change in this area in most Western industrial societies. First, the abolition of the 'marriage bar', the prohibition on married women's employment, in

the post-War period through legislation making direct and indirect discrimination on grounds of sex or marital status unlawful. Second, equal opportunities legislation giving women the right to retain their jobs during pregnancy and return to work after childbirth, supported by European Union policy. Third, the advent of the contraceptive pill in the early 1960s giving women the means to control and plan their fertility behaviour if they wished, leading to the new phenomenon of sexually active but voluntarily childless women who were able to devote their lives to a career if they wished. These developments, especially the last, broke the link between women's domestic and reproductive work and the pattern of women's employment (Tilly and Scott, 1990: 7).

In the USA, Britain and other European countries, the marriage prohibition took the form of strong social norms against wives going out to work, especially in the middle classes; these norms were sometimes institutionalised in company rules and policies, especially for white-collar jobs such as teaching and clerical work (ILO, 1962; Oppenheimer, 1970: 39-55; Cohn, 1985: 99; Walby, 1986: 171-2, 180, 247; Grint, 1988: 96; Bradley, 1989: 211-3; Goldin, 1990: 160-79). Throughout history, the non-working wife, or concubine, has been a status symbol, proof of affluence and often essential to achieving high levels of consumption. In the second half of the nineteenth century, formal policies were invented to exclude wives from wage work. Historians and sociologists have shown how the 'bourgeois' ideal of marriage, with the wife devoted full-time to creating a haven of comfort and relaxation for the family was more often aspired to than achieved by working class families, as it relied on the husband having adequate and regular earnings (Holcombe, 1973; Roberts, 1984; Pollert, 1981). Marriage bars were often strengthened during the Depression (Walby, 1986: 180), with social norms sometimes reinforced by law. In the Netherlands, for example, a law introduced in 1935 prohibited wives from holding jobs in the civil service, thus reserving jobs for men during the 1930s recession. However the law was not repealed until 1957, long after the recession, and it encouraged private sector firms to apply similar rules, which lasted until 1979 (Pott-Buter, 1993: 246-251; Tijdens, 1993: 79, 87). In Britain the marriage bar was a legally enforceable rule, jointly imposed and policed by employers and trade unions in certain industries, mainly for white-collar occupations, that women left employment upon marriage. Resignation from work was 'sweetened' by giving the bride a lump sum payment which some have construed as a 'dowry' or bribe to promote turnover (Cohn, 1985: 102) but was often a refund of pension contributions paid so far, as wives were expected to rely on their husband's earnings and pension rights. There is some debate over the social impact of the marriage bar, its economic efficiency and profitability in the period 1870-1950 in the USA and Britain (Cohn, 1985; Walby, 1986: 247; Grint, 1988; Goldin: 1990: 160-79). It seems clear that its main effect was to support the sexual division of labour, and power, within marriage. The key motive was patriarchy rather than profit, benefiting all men rather than a few employers (Grint, 1988: 97). Marriage bars institutionalised the marriage career for women and discouraged young women from investing in qualifications and careers. After World War Two, the marriage bar was outlawed through equal opportunities and sex discrimination legislation, from 1971 onwards in Britain, from the 1960s in the USA and other European countries, but not until 1985 in Japan, for example. Direct and overt discrimination against women, or married women, became unlawful throughout Western industrial societies and in many other countries as well.

A less visible but profoundly important change is that reliable methods of birth control became readily available to the cohorts of women born after 1945 and entering the labour force in the 1960s. Having children ceased to be an uncontrollable hazard of women's lives, and became voluntary. Many women now sidestep childcare problems by simply not having children. In Britain, Australia and the USA about 20% of post-War cohorts of women are, or are predicted to remain childless. The rising trend of voluntary childlessness, reaching 20% of women born after 1955 in Britain, is strongly associated with increasing level of educational qualifications, that is, with an investment in their human capital and the employment career (Werner 1986; Werner and Chalk 1986). In the past, large proportions of certain cohorts of women have not had any children – for example 20% of those born in 1920 in Britain remained childless. But childlessness in the past has typically been associated with low marriage rates and shortages of men due to wars. Only in the case of women entering convents and other religious careers can we be sure that celibacy and childlessness were voluntary, in most cases at least. The current trend emerges among women who are sexually active from a young age, expect to marry at least once in their reproductive years and do not have to rely on a partner for reliable contraception. The World Fertility Survey shows that primary infertility affects only 2-3% of women aged 25-50 (Vaessen, 1984), so the new rising trend of childlessness is clearly socially determined and voluntary. Childlessness can emerge gradually from repeated postponement of childbearing, due to other activities taking priority, but some people make a firm choice early in life (Veevers, 1973; Campbell, 1985). Women in the lower social classes hold marriage and childbearing as their principal life objectives and reach these goals earlier in life than women in the higher social classes who are more likely to plan employment as well as marriage, so that social class remains the strongest and most enduring predictor of fertility patterns (Dunnell, 1979: 19-27; Campbell, 1985: 9). Women who choose to centre their lives on childbearing, with or without marriage, do not need to plan ahead in the same way as women choosing employment careers: they can rely on 'just letting things happen', which typically results in a greater number of children being born (Dunnell, 1979: 24-6). Finally, most women who do have children have no more than one or two, a huge reduction on the numbers common at the beginning of this century. Feminist debates on the value of domestic labour, women's reproductive role and the need for childcare services failed to take account of the dramatic decline in the childcare element within domestic labour, due to falling family size (Fine, 1992: 169-191). Contrary to popular stereotype, childlessness is acceptable to half of men and women in Britain, other European countries and the USA, although most people routinely confirm the joys of raising children. The acceptability of childlessness doubled among post-War generations (Scott, Braun and Alwin, 1993: 30-31). Declining fertility across Europe is slowly becoming a policy issue (European Commission, 1995: 59).

Researchers devote special attention to women's employment decisions around the time of childbirth (Martin and Roberts, 1984; Desai and Waite, 1991; Glass and Camarigg, 1992; Rexroat, 1992). The arrival of a new baby provides a strategic case study of the factors that influence women's choices, how these are weighed up, and how they have changed over time. In the 1950s, most women would drop out of the labour market around marriage or the first birth, although many resumed work, at least briefly, many years later. In the 1980s, many women returned to work within a year of a birth and worked between births, so that the bimodal pattern of employment flattened into what looked like more continuous employment in many European societies (Meulders, Plasman and Vander Stricht, 1993: 6-12; European Commission, 1994: 50-8; OECD, 1994: 55-61). Maternity rights legislation is widely believed to be a key factor in this process, giving women new rights not to be dismissed for pregnancy and to be reinstated in their job after a period of maternity absence. This is not true.

### The impact of childbirth on employment

There have been two national studies of the impact of the maternity rights legislation introduced in Britain in the mid-1970s; in each case both employers and new mothers were invited to report their experiences. Both surveys, in 1979 and 1988, showed that the statutory right to retain one's job was not a significant determinant of a woman's return to work soon after the birth (McRae, 1991: 183-4, 230-5). The 1988 survey is often quoted as showing an 'association' between the two, but it was not statistically significant. Having the legal right to keep one's job makes it easier to plan ahead, for women who have invested in training, qualifications and a career, but it does not become a motivating factor in its own right for other women. The determinants of a mother's return to work are the usual ones: better qualifications, higher earnings potential and higher occupational grade, all increasing the opportunity cost of not working.

Nonetheless, the maternity rights surveys give the impression that women's attachment to work is increasing. For example McRae emphasises her finding that the proportion of employees who gave formal notice to their employer of their intention of returning to work after the birth almost doubled between 1979 and 1988, from 26% to 47%. Almost three-quarters of women who qualified for the right to return gave formal notification during pregnancy of their intention to return compared with less than half in 1979 (1991: 170-4). These are indeed huge changes for such a short period, less than a decade, and testify to the impact of the maternity rights legislation on pregnant women's public statements. What she does not emphasise is the fact that the mothers' private attitudes and actual behaviour changed very little.

The right to reinstatement gives an employed pregnant woman in Britain the right to return to work with her former employer at any time before the end of twenty-nine weeks after the birth of her baby. On returning, a woman has the right to be employed on terms and conditions in line with those which would have been applicable if she had not been absent. Reinstatement rights are normally acquired after two years' service with an employer; with certain employers the qualifying period is shorter. Periods of absence can be longer in some countries and shorter in others (OECD, 1990, 1994: 182-5). The law requires women to signal an intention to return in order to retain the option of doing so. It does not penalise women who do not fulfil their commitment to return to work, although it would penalise an employer who refused to reinstate a woman in her job. Pregnant women thus have every incentive to notify an intention to return to work, and nothing to lose by doing so. Even today, the successful outcome of a pregnancy cannot be guaranteed. The level of notifications has understandably shot up, but says little about women's intentions of actually *using* their right to reinstatement. Among women who gave their employer notice of return, one-fifth (1988) and one-third (1979) of women had no intention or expectation of returning to work; another fifth (1979 and 1988) had hoped or planned to return but did not. Small numbers went back to work, but in a new job, typically part-time and closer to home, with a different employer. Altogether two-thirds (1979) and half (1988) of the women giving notice did not return to the job held open for them by their employer (McRae, 1991: 178). From the employers' point of view, notifications are not statements of real plans, as the likelihood of a woman returning to work was no better than chance by the end of the 1980s.

Understandably, maternity rights legislation does not affect women's private intentions: about two-thirds (60% in 1988 and 66% in 1979) of all women working during pregnancy had no intention of going back to work within nine months of childbirth, typically because they wanted to care for their child(ren) themselves. Many of those who intended to return to work still did not wish to return to their previous employer, preferring part-time jobs closer to home instead. This was especially common in relation to first births, which often prompt a switch from full-time to part-time work and to a less demanding occupation. Overall, women's private intentions predicted their actual behaviour more strongly than their formal notifications to employers. Four-fifths of those planning to stay at home after the birth did so. Two-thirds of the women planning to return to work did so. McRae correctly underlines a striking increase in the 1980s in the rate of return to work after childbirth: rising from one-quarter in 1979 to almost half by 1988, even though women often returned to part-time rather than full-time work. It does indeed appear that women's attachment to work is increasing, even if – a sore point with employers – they do not necessarily fulfil their notification of a return to work with the same employer within nine months of childbirth. Similar trends are observed in other European countries (Meulders ct al, 1993: 14) and the USA (Desai and Waite, 1991; Rexroat, 1992), even where there is no maternity rights legislation. One might conclude that women's employment continuity is thus driven by personal motivations, social and economic factors quite independent of employment rights.

### Sample selection bias

The key weakness in all these research results is sample selection bias – perhaps the most common error made in studies of women's work orientations and labour market behaviour. Sample selection bias, sometimes labelled 'selection effects', arises when research is based on a nonrandom subset of a wider population, typically because information is only available for cases that exceed a certain threshold. The systematic exclusion of cases with particular characteristics means that both the internal and external validity of research findings are in doubt (Berk, 1983). In the economics literature, the best known example is studies of wages earned by women. One can only observe wages for women who are employed and employed women are a nonrandom subset of all women: they have stronger non-financial work commitment, a larger investment in qualifications and a career, and have higher potential earnings than non-working women (see Table 3.7). Although there are techniques for the diagnosis of and correction for sample selection bias in quantitative studies (Berk, 1983) one cannot always eliminate it from research results. Many researchers do not even try.

Economists are more sensitive than sociologists to the heterogeneity of the female (working) population, are aware of the ensuing problems of sample selection bias and of the misleading notion of the 'representative' or 'average' woman, as illustrated by the contributors to Scott (1994) and by examples reviewed in Hakim (1996). American sociologists are generally more aware of the problem than are British sociologists, but they are also more likely to think that it is a purely technical problem with a statistical solution, thus ignoring the substantive and theoretically important heterogeneity of the adult female population (Hakim, 1996). Studies of the relationship between fertility and employment using event history analysis (such as Desai and Waite, 1991) are often assumed to overcome selection bias. However they routinely exclude the substantively important minority of women who remain childless and work continuously as well as women who were not working before the birth. In the maternity rights studies described above, only *half* the women surveyed in 1988 were in work when they became pregnant. The other half comprised 17% who had *never* worked before the birth, most of them with no qualifications at all, some of them women from Moslem ethnic minority groups and immigrants; 27% who had some work experience but were not working a year before the birth, most of whom already had at least one young child; and 3% who had been in work twelve months before the birth but stopped working before or soon after becoming pregnant, many of whom had been in temporary and part-time jobs. As the author herself notes, these three groups differed significantly in personal, family and employment history characteristics from the working women who were the focus of the maternity rights study, a group strongly biased towards the first births of younger, better educated women in full-time employment during pregnancy (McRae, 1991: 28-36). Taking the broader view, half of the women giving birth were in work during pregnancy, and only one-quarter were in work nine months after the birth (McRae, 1991: 196) – an entirely predictable sharp fall in work rates resulting from a birth.

Findings on the rising work attachment of women who were in work during pregnancy cannot be extrapolated to conclusions about all new mothers, let alone all women. Yet the inevitable process of simplifying and summarising research results in literature reviews means that this sort of misleading generalisation often emerges. Genuine facts about unrepresentative minorities of working women become generalisations about all women of working age, including those who have *never* held a job!

**Movement in and out of the labour force**
Women who have *never* worked are a rarity in most industrial societies. The 1980 Women and Employment Survey (WES) found that only 2% of a nationally representative sample of women aged

**Table 5.1** Rates of labour force entry and exit over the lifecycle in the USA

| Age | Entries to labour force as % of population | | Exits from labour force as % of population | | Exits from labour force as % of labour force | |
|---|---|---|---|---|---|---|
| | Men | Women | Men | Women | Men | Women |
| 16-19 | 21 | 21 | 12 | 13 | 25 | 29 |
| 20-24 | 14 | 16 | 9 | 14 | 13 | 23 |
| 25-29 | 5 | 11 | 4 | 12 | 4 | 18 |
| 30-34 | 2 | 9 | 2 | 8 | 2 | 13 |
| 35-39 | 2 | 8 | 2 | 7 | 2 | 11 |
| 40-44 | 2 | 7 | 2 | 7 | 2 | 11 |
| 45-49 | 2 | 6 | 3 | 7 | 3 | 11 |
| 50-54 | 2 | 5 | 4 | 6 | 4 | 11 |
| 55-59 | 2 | 4 | 6 | 7 | 7 | 14 |
| 60-64 | 3 | 3 | 11 | 8 | 21 | 25 |
| 65-69 | 4 | 3 | 9 | 5 | 38 | 37 |

**Note:** All percentages have been rounded.
**Source:** Derived from Smith (1982: 18-19) Tables 5 and 6 presenting mobility rates from worklife estimates.

16-59 years in Great Britain claimed never to have had a paid job (Martin and Roberts, 1984: 122). Given substantial Moslem and other ethnic minority groups in Britain who prefer to keep women at home, this percentage is unlikely to change. Thus the vast majority of women have some work experience, but women's patterns of work nonetheless differ greatly from those of men, because most women leave and reenter the workforce repeatedly across the lifecycle.

Among prime age workers (aged 25-50) in the USA, women are two to five times more likely than men to enter or leave the workforce (Table 5.1). Sex differentials are smallest among people retiring and among young workers aged under 25 years who have been the subject of intensive research in a series of longitudinal studies. But in the 35-39 year age group, women are five times more likely than men to leave the labour force (11% versus 2%) and they are four times more likely to (re)enter the workforce (8% compared to 2%). Similarly in Britain labour mobility differs little between men and women aged 16-25 during the labour market entry phase and in the retirement phase starting from age 50 onwards. But women are two to four times more likely than men to enter and leave the workforce during the prime age years, irrespective of the type of occupation they are in (Hakim, 1996).

**Table 5.2**  The decline in continuous employment and the marriage career

| Year of labour market entry | Proportion (%) of each cohort in each category 15 or 20 years after entering workforce: | | | | | | Base=100% | |
| | continuous employment | | discontinuous employment | | homemaker career | | | |
| | 15 | 20 | 15 | 20 | 15 | 20 | 15 | 20 |
|---|---|---|---|---|---|---|---|---|
| 1941-1945 | 20 | 13 | 36 | 51 | 44 | 36 | 511 | 502 |
| 1946-1950 | 18 | 13 | 39 | 56 | 43 | 31 | 449 | 433 |
| 1951-1955 | 15 | 10 | 47 | 67 | 38 | 23 | 523 | 510 |
| 1956-1960 | 11 | 8 | 53 | 73 | 36 | 19 | 609 | 574 |
| 1961-1965 | 13 | .. | 61 | .. | 26 | .. | 655 | .. |
| Total | 15 | 11 | 48 | 62 | 37 | 27 | 2747 | 2019 |

**Note:** .. sample too young for results at 20 years stage in 1980 survey
**Source:** 1980 Women and Employment Survey, Great Britain, data for women aged 16-59 in 1980. Continuous employment consists of continuous spells of paid work (whether full-time or part-time) without any breaks. The homemaker career is defined as a single employment spell early in adult life that ended in permanent non-work. Discontinuous employment consists of all other work histories combining spells of work and spells of non-work.

## Continuity of employment over the lifecycle: three employment profiles

If work attachment was really increasing among women, their work histories should resemble those of men more and more across generations. Analysis of the 1980 WES work history data identifying three employment profiles (Table 5.2) shows, on the contrary, a declining proportion of women in continuous work and a sharp increase in discontinuous employment.

*Continuous employment* is the stereotypical male employment profile, consisting of continuous employment throughout adult life, from the time of leaving full-time education to retirement. Strictly speaking, this should be labelled continuous economic activity, to allow for spells of unemployment. Given the practical difficulties of differentiating between unemployment and other non-working statuses among women in Britain (Cragg and Dawson, 1984; Martin and Roberts, 1984: 79-95), researchers usually measure periods of continuous employment (Elias and Main, 1982: 8; Main, 1988a: 24). On this basis, 80% of British men have had only one period of continuous employment, albeit it in different jobs. If periods of unemployment are ignored, virtually all men are economically active throughout their working age lives (Elias and Main, 1982: 10). The stereotype of the male employment profile is based on reality. Whether they choose it or not, this profile is imposed on men. A minority of women, about one-quarter, plan a career in market work irrespective of developments in their private life (see Table 4.10) and an exploratory analysis by Burchell and Rubery (1994: 96-7) found one-quarter of working women in continuous career employment in the primary sector. Long-term workplans over-ride marital status as a determinant of continuous employment (Rexroat, 1992). However there has been a systematic decline in continuous employment within successive cohorts of women (Table 5.2).

The *homemaker career* is the stereotypical female employment profile in Western industrial societies, consisting of a single period of continuous employment (if any) after leaving full-time education which ends in early adult life and is never resumed. Permanent cessation of employment may be prompted by marriage or by childbirth, but it is anticipated long before the event and involves a qualitatively different perspective on investment in educational qualifications, not necessarily a lower investment, as some human capital theorists argue. Higher educational qualifications may be acquired to ensure a girl marries a partner of at least equal status rather than with a view to acquiring marketable skills for long-term employment. The returns to education in this group consist of the husband's earning potential rather than personal earnings potential. Women in Europe can still achieve greater social mobility through marriage than through their own employment (Goldthorpe, 1987: 282-7). The popularity of apparently non-vocational degrees in the humanities among young women in Western societies is attributable to these subjects being appropriate for the homemaker career. In developing countries, a wider range of subjects serve the same 'intellectual dowry' purpose. For some women termination of market work acknowledges an efficient household division of labour along lines theorised by Becker (1991); for others, it also signifies their incorporation into their spouse's two-person career, a pattern especially common among the wives of politicians, professionals and managers (Pahl and Pahl, 1971; Papanek, 1973; Finch, 1983; Maret, 1983: 112, 115), at least up to the 1960s (Bonney, 1988: 100). The homemaker career is open to men, in principle, although it remains a rarity even among 'postmodern' men in Western industrial society. The homemaker career has long been the ideal held by the majority of girls, especially working class girls, in Britain and by a substantial proportion of one-third to two-thirds of women generally in industrial society (Matthaei, 1982; Pollert, 1981: 91-115; Hakim, 1991: 112) as shown in Chapter 4. In some European societies, such as West Germany, this model of the family division of labour provided the basis for social welfare and labour legislation; in other countries, such as Finland, this is not the case (Pfau-Effinger, 1993). Fiscal and social policies can sharply reduce the numbers adopting this career choice, as illustrated by Sweden (OECD, 1994: 61). This profile has been declining rapidly in recent decades (Table 5.2).

*Discontinuous or intermittent employment* is the residual category and consists of work histories with periods of employment broken by domestic breaks or other periods of non-work other than involuntary unemployment. This group includes the simplest M-shaped work profile of two long spells of continuous employment broken by a single long domestic break as well as 'marginal' and 'sporadic' workers whose employment is interrupted by several periods out of the labour market (Elias and Main, 1982: 11; Maret, 1983: 51). This group includes the drifters with no fixed objectives and unplanned employment careers identified in Chapter 4 (Table 4.10, see also Maret, 1983). Fragmented work histories are typical of secondary earners. Deregulation of the labour market and the expansion of 'flexibility' in the workforce in the 1980s has allowed this category to expand in size in recent years in Europe, among men and women (Rodgers and Rodgers, 1989; Hakim, 1990a,b). But this recent trend would not be important in Table 5.2, which presents employment profiles up to 1980.

It is notable that there is in practice only one 'choice' of work history for men, compared to three for women. Feminists who emphasise that women's choices are constrained and not 'completely free' overlook the fact that women have *more* choices than men.

Contrary to received opinion, there has been no increase in continuous employment among British women in the post-War period. The dominant trend is a massive increase in discontinuous employment. Perhaps most significant is that the simple three-phase broken work profile has declined in importance, replaced by an expanding marginal workforce of women with increasingly numerous breaks in employment, shorter periods of employment and more numerous job changes, often associated with part-time work. These results have been largely hidden in research reports which choose to emphasise women's increasing 'attachment' to the labour force across the lifecycle rather than the fact that participation in market work has become fragmented and is now even more likely to be contingent on and subordinate to non-market activities than in the past (Elias and Main, 1982; Stewart and Greenhalgh, 1984; Dex, 1987; Main, 1988a).

The relative importance of the three work profiles is best identified at age 40-49 when we obtain a picture close to completed work profiles and before the picture is clouded by early retirement after the age of 50. Analyses of the 1980 WES data in Figures 1 and 2 separate cohort effects from lifecycle effects to show women's employment profiles at about age 40 years. Figure 1 shows that only 3% of women aged 40 had been continuously employed by 1980, a smaller proportion than in previous cohorts. As Main (1988a: 51) notes, Martin and Roberts (1984) confounded cohort effects and lifecycle effects when they reported that 25% of the WES sample were 'always economically active' in Table 9.6 of their report on the 1980 survey. Main also showed that the frequency of breaks in employment has been increasing across age cohorts (Figure 2), so that the proportion of potential working life spent *out* of the labour force also increased across age cohorts (Main 1988a: 28-41). He concluded that the typical employed woman now has a *less intensive* record of employment than she did a few decades ago (Main, 1988a: 42), a finding consistent with the results of earlier studies (Hunt, 1968b: 121; Elias and Main, 1982: 30-31; Stewart and Greenhalgh 1984: 495-499). For example 15% of women aged 45-59 in 1965 had always worked (calculated from Table D4c in Hunt, 1968b: 121) compared to less than 10% in 1980 (Table 5.2). Both Main (1988b: 117-8) and Elias (1988) note an association between women's discontinuous employment patterns and part-time work in Britain, despite the fact that most part-time jobs are permanent, and Dex (1987: 84) notes an association between women holding traditional attitudes and downward occupational mobility, typically into part-time work.

As noted in Chapter 4, the *modern* version of the homemaker career permits employment after marriage if it is restricted to part-time and other jobs chosen to fit in with the domestic role, so that market work remains secondary to and contingent on a primary responsibility for home and family. Table 5.3 identifies the modern homemaker career by grouping together those who

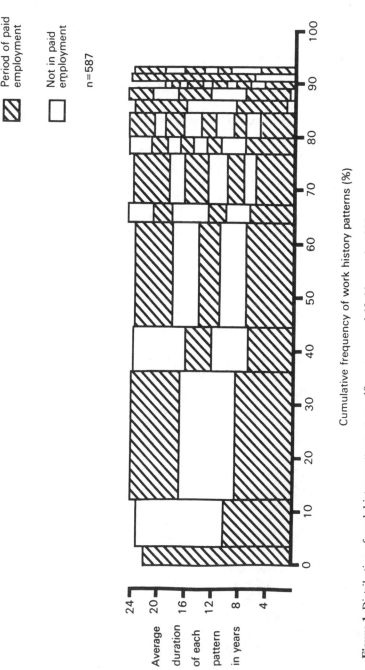

**Figure 1** Distribution of work history patterns at age 40, women aged 40-44 years in 1980

**Source:** Main (1988a). Figures 1 and 2 based on analyses of the 1980 Women and Employment Survey, data for women aged 16-59 in 1980 in Great Britain.

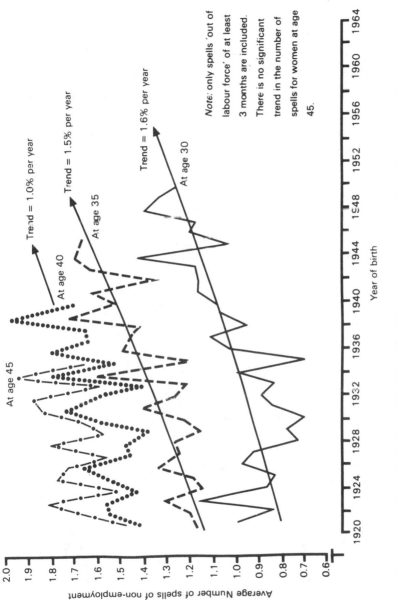

**Figure 2** Average number of spells 'out of the labour force' for respondents who are in employment at a given age, by year of birth

stop work early in adult life with women who return to part-time work after breaks in employment. This classification shows that there has been no change at all in the proportion of each cohort following the homemaker career broadly defined, about 60% of all cohorts entering the workforce after 1945. In effect the decline in the homemaker career narrowly defined in Table 5.2 is balanced out by women adopting the modern profile with intermittent part-time work after a domestic break. There is relatively little change in the other 40% of each cohort who work full-time in the twenty years following labour market entry, either continuously or, increasingly, with breaks in employment. This alternative classification of employment profiles indicates that there are essentially just two polarised employment profiles among women: the working woman and the homemaker (who may also be a secondary earner), with both profiles changing to include more employment discontinuity than before, so that the boundary between them becomes blurred. Whereas the classification in Table 5.2 suggested qualitative changes in patterns of employment, the classification in Table 5.3 shows continuity and stability. The homemaker career is still followed by some two-thirds of adult women, consonant with about two-thirds of adult women accepting the sexual division of labour as noted in Chapter 4.

Employment patterns in the USA are similar, but seem to be changing faster. Longitudinal studies show that the percentage of a married woman's life spent in employment is U-shaped, with high concentrations in the lowest and highest deciles, that is, in continuous employment and continuous non-work (Goldin, 1989: 25). In 1975, only one-quarter of *working* women aged 30-44 years had worked continuously since leaving full-time education; all the rest had worked intermittently (Corcoran, 1979: 241). Discontinuous employment accounts for the majority of women: around half of American women aged 30-44 years in 1967 (Stephan and Schroeder, 1979: 130; Maret, 1983: 54). The rise in full-time year-round employment among women in the USA (see Table 3.4) indicates a trend towards continuous employment among women, especially as women's work orientations seem to be changing at the same time, as noted in Chapter 4. Nonetheless discontinuous employment is clearly important, as illustrated by the fact that, on average, twice as many women have some work experience in a year as work full-time year-round: two-thirds versus one-third.

**Table 5.3** The rise of the new homemaker career

| Year of labour market entry | Proportion (%) of each cohort in each category 15 or 20 years after entering workforce: | | | | | | Base=100% | |
|---|---|---|---|---|---|---|---|---|
| | continuous employment | | discontinuous FT employment | | new homemaker career | | | |
| | 15 | 20 | 15 | 20 | 15 | 20 | 15 | 20 |
| 1941-1945 | 20 | 13 | 23 | 28 | 57 | 59 | 511 | 502 |
| 1946-1950 | 18 | 12 | 22 | 27 | 60 | 61 | 449 | 433 |
| 1951-1955 | 15 | 10 | 25 | 28 | 60 | 62 | 523 | 510 |
| 1956-1960 | 11 | 8 | 26 | 31 | 63 | 61 | 609 | 574 |
| 1961-1965 | 13 | .. | 24 | .. | 63 | .. | 655 | .. |
| Total | 15 | 11 | 24 | 28 | 61 | 61 | 2747 | 2019 |

**Note:** .. sample too young for results at 20 years stage in 1980 survey
**Source:** 1980 Women and Employment Survey, Great Britain, data for women aged 16-59 in 1980. Continuous employment consists of continuous spells of paid work (whether full-time or part-time) without any breaks. The new homemaker career is defined as a single employment spell early in adult life that ended in permanent non-work or in a transfer to part-time work. Discontinuous full-time employment consists of a career with breaks but continued with full-time work.

## The implications of intermittent employment

Does employment continuity matter? It does, in two ways. First, higher labour turnover rates mean that women build up shorter job tenures than men. Second, women accumulate less total work experience than men, due to spells out of the labour force. There is a wealth of evidence that continuing sex differentials in job tenure and in cumulative work experience explain a large part of the sex differential in earnings, and that women's relative earnings increase when their work experience and job tenure increase (Sandell and Shapiro, 1980; O'Neill, 1985; Zabalza and Arrufat, 1985; Goldin and Polachek, 1987; Main, 1988b: 118; Goldin, 1989, 1990: 73; Sorensen, 1989; Sloane, 1990: 150-5; O'Neill and Polachek, 1993; Wood, Corcoran and Courant, 1993; Kilbourne *et al*, 1994; Rubery and Fagan, 1994: 127-131; Wellington, 1994). Many employers offer workers small but regular annual increments on fixed pay scales, rewarding people who stay with them for many years and gain firm-specific experience. In other sectors, it is total years of work experience with different employers that attracts the highest salaries. Tenure in the current job and total work experience are important in achieving promotion up career ladders, with the same employer or with a change of job. The *increasing* number of spells out of the labour force shown in Figure 2 is important. A single long spell out of the labour force, in the traditional three-spell employment profile, is less detrimental to careers, given continuous full-time employment on return to the workforce. In sum, job tenure, continuity of employment and cumulative work experience are important determinants of earnings, and they contribute to women's lower representation in higher grade posts, the vertical occupational segregation discussed further in Chapter 6.

Job tenure, or enterprise tenure, is a worker's length of service with an employer or enterprise, disregarding any change of occupation. Job tenure is theoretically important as it provides a measure of the firm-specific skills and 'tacit knowledge' in the job that is accumulated over time but has no formal recognition in the shape of educational qualifications or certificates. Job tenure is important also in a policy context as it corresponds to the length of service criterion in labour law, which determines eligibility for key employment rights and benefits across much of Europe (Hakim, 1989a; Hepple and Hakim, 1996).

A sex differential in labour turnover and job tenure of about 50% has been the norm in Britain for the workforce as a whole for at least two decades (Elias and Gregory, 1994: 6-9; Burgess and Rees, 1994; Hakim, 1996). Britain's 50% sex differential in labour mobility is typical of the European Community as a whole, even though labour mobility in Britain is above the Community average, along with Spain, Denmark, the Netherlands, Ireland and France, in contrast with the lowest mobility rates found in Germany (European Commission, 1994: 86-87, 97-99). Periodic OECD reports on employment stability and job tenure (OECD, 1984, 1989, 1993) show substantial sex differentials in job tenure in all industrialised societies, with the exception of France, where the differential had almost disappeared by 1991. Women's high job turnover and hence lower job tenure is not limited to those with children (Table 5.4). Women without any children are more likely to have relatively long tenures of ten years or more with their employer: one-quarter compared to one in ten for women with children. But they still do not match the longer tenures of men: one-third have ten years' service or longer with their employer, and it is these long tenures that count most for promotion to management grades in the internal labour market of the organisation (Table 5.6).

**Table 5.4** The sex differential in job tenure

| % with stated length of time in present employment | all | Women youngest child aged <15 | no dependent children | Men |
|---|---|---|---|---|
| under 1 year | 27 | 30 | 25 | 19 |
| over 2 years | 59 | 54 | 62 | 70 |
| over 5 years | 37 | 27 | 42 | 52 |
| over 10 years | 20 | 11 | 25 | 35 |

**Source:** Derived from Department of Employment (1990) Table 8, reporting Spring 1989 Labour Force Survey, Great Britain, data for people of working age (16-59/64 years) in employment.

These differences are associated with and extended by women taking up part-time work in preference to the full-time employment typical of the male employment profile. In 1992 one-third of full-time employees had ten years' tenure or more compared to only 16% of part-time employees (Table 5.5). A comparison with 1986 shows that the gap between full-timers and part-timers is increasing. As the female-dominated part-time workforce grows in size, it is becoming more differentiated and distinctive in its labour market behaviour rather than more integrated into the mainstream workforce. A study by Gregg and Wadsworth (1995: 80) confirms that turnover levels are always higher for women than men, even in permanent jobs, whether full-time or part-time.

In general, higher grade occupations have low turnover rates and long job tenures and lower grade occupations have high turnover and low average job tenures. Clearly these differences are features of the occupations themselves, and the industries where they are concentrated (European Commission, 1994: 87-90). However the sex differential continues across all occupations, including managerial and professional occupations, so continuity of employment is also a characteristic brought to occupations by the people who self-select themselves into particular types of work. Careers in highly qualified fields have the lowest turnover and longest tenures because the long periods of education and training required automatically ensure that people with low work commitment drop out long before they enter formal employment (Fiorentine, 1987). However women have consistently lower average tenures and higher turnover, even

**Table 5.5** The decline in job tenure among full-time and part-time employees, 1986-92

| Proportion (%) with each length of service with the same employer | Full-time workers | | Part-time workers | |
|---|---|---|---|---|
| | 1986 | 1992 | 1986 | 1992 |
| under 1 year | .. | 13 | .. | 25 |
| over 2 years | 75 | 77 | 63 | 59 |
| over 5 years | 55 | 52 | 42 | 33 |
| over 10 years | 38 | 32 | 22 | 16 |

**Sources:** Spring 1986 and Spring 1992 Labour Force Survey, Great Britain.
The 1986 data are for employees only (excluding family workers, students and people on government employment schemes for the unemployed), and part-time jobs are those involving less than 30 hours a week. The 1992 data are for employees and the self-employed (excluding family workers and people on government employment schemes for the unemployed), and part-time jobs are self-defined by survey respondents.

in this group. The only exception is jobs in personal services, which recruit few men, where the sex differential is reversed (Table 5.6). Controlling for occupation tends to reduce the sex differential slightly below the average (Table 5.6), but it remains substantial in all occupational groups except for the female-dominated personal services group.

## Conclusions

Discontinuous employment has expanded in absolute and relative terms, at the expense of continuous employment and the home-making career. The result is a large substitution of fragmented employment for continuous employment in the female workforce in the post-War decades, in parallel with the massive substitution of part-time jobs for full-time jobs already documented by Hakim (1993a) for Britain and by Jonung and Persson (1993) for Sweden. This finding for Britain has certain similarities with Goldin's (1989, 1990) conclusion that the large post-War influx of women into the USA labour force resulted in a *lowering* of average years of work experience among working women, thus explaining the lack of change in women's relative earnings and the continuing sex differential in pay. We conclude that increasingly fragmented employment profiles explain continuing sex differentials in labour mobility and job tenure, and can contribute an important part of the

**Table 5.6** Mean elapsed job tenure in months by occupation 1975-1991

| Occupations | Men | | | Women | | | Average sex |
|---|---|---|---|---|---|---|---|
| | 1983 | 1990 | 1975-91 average | 1983 | 1990 | 1975-91 average | differential M/F |
| Managerial & Professional | 151 | 137 | 144 | 106 | 97 | 102 | 1.41 |
| Other white collar | 118 | 108 | 113 | 81 | 75 | 78 | 1.45 |
| Personal service | 81 | 47 | 64 | 78 | 73 | 76 | 0.84 |
| Skilled manual | 124 | 116 | 120 | 84 | 75 | 80 | 1.50 |
| Other manual | 105 | 94 | 100 | 79 | 65 | 72 | 1.39 |
| Total | 127 | 119 | 123 | 80 | 77 | 80 | 1.54 |

**Sources:** Derived from Burgess and Rees (1994) Table 4, plus unpublished tables, based on analyses of General Household Survey data for all years 1975 to 1991. Data for all in employment.

explanation for the slow decline in levels of vertical occupational segregation and in the sex differential in earnings (Polachek, 1979; Zabalza and Arrufat, 1985; Main, 1988b: 118; Hakim, 1992) – a topic discussed further in Chapter 6.

Recent USA studies claim that women's work experience averages three-quarters of men's work experience, measured in years (Reskin and Padavic 1994: 41). However this average conceals significant differences between working and non-working women and overlooks the fact that women are far less likely than men to work full-time throughout the year in any given year of employment (Smith, 1982; Maret, 1983: 54; Goldin, 1990: 31), as shown in Table 3.4. Estimates of annual hours in the USA reveal that women's average annual work hours are only *half* those of men despite the fact that women appear to contribute equally to the workforce on a headcount basis (calculated from Table 4 in Smith, 1983: 17). The sex differential is substantially larger in Britain, even ignoring the greater importance of years with only part-time and/or part-year employment.

In conclusion, the picture commonly painted of women's increasing 'attachment' to the labour force across the lifecycle could more accurately be described as a picture of increasingly fragmented, discontinuous, intermittent employment, much of it part-time. The total volume of market work done by women has been redistributed across the lifecycle and between women so that more women than before are now doing *some* market work, at different points in their lives. It is not obvious that employment has become a more salient priority in women's lives, rather than a more frequent interruption of their domestic activities, which clearly dominate choices and take precedence for most women. The male profile of continuous employment has become *less* rather than more common among women. This increasingly fragmented involvement in market work, along with the substitution of part-time for full-time employment noted in Chapter 3, further undermines the story of women's rising employment and expectations of social and economic change following from it. Employment stability is a key characteristic of the primary labour market (Chiplin and Sloane, 1974: 375), so women's increasingly fragmented employment patterns must increase the chances of their segregation in the secondary labour market, a topic to which we turn in the next chapter.

# 6
# Occupational segregation and the pay gap

Women are excluded from the top jobs, those with the highest status, authority and earnings. The gloomy view says this is a permanent situation that equal opportunities legislation has not changed to any significant degree. Pessimists point out that the majority of low paid workers are women, that the earnings gap between men and women has not visibly changed, that there is a glass ceiling preventing women from attaining the top jobs. This chapter looks at trends in the occupational segregation of men and women, in particular vertical job segregation, and in the sex differential in earnings, commonly called the pay gap. It shows that important changes started in the 1980s. These developments can only be identified if we take account of historical data showing the long-term trend, thus revealing a sharp increase in the pace of change after equal opportunities legislation was introduced in the 1970s.

## Job segregation and labour market segmentation

Segmentation and segregation are often confused and conflated, understandably, given that they are inter-related.

*Segregation* refers to social processes which result in certain individuals or social groups being kept apart with little interaction between them. The factors used to differentiate groups are normally personal, such as age, sex, race or religion, or they may be work-related factors such as occupational grade, as illustrated by separate canteens and trade unions for different grades of staff in an organisation. Occupational segregation on the basis of sex exists when men and women do different kinds of work, so that one can speak of two separate labour forces, one male and one female, which are not in competition with each other for the same jobs (Blaxall and Reagan, 1976; Hakim, 1979; Reskin, 1984; Reskin and Hartmann, 1986; Rubery and Fagan, 1993). To a much smaller extent race is an additional factor of occupational segregation, such that white and black women and men do not compete for the same types of job, although this is more pronounced in the USA than in Britain (Mayhew and Rosewell, 1978; Tomaskovic-Devey, 1993; Bhavnani, 1994; Owen, 1994). In some societies, jobs in government administration and all senior positions are reserved for members of the largest or dominant religious or ethnic group. For example Catholics were debarred from the professions and senior posts in Ireland until 1829, and substantially separate labour markets for Catholics and Protestants persist in Northern Ireland (O'Leary and McGarry, 1993: 81, 206, 262).

In the past, occupational segregation resulted from a combination of *de jure* or direct discrimination and *de facto* or indirect discrimination. For example before 1975 a relatively low quota of places in British medical schools (about 10%) were open to women applicants; this ensured that membership of the medical professions was reserved largely for men. Since 1975, when the Equal Pay Act 1970 and the Sex Discrimination Act 1975 took effect, *de jure* occupational segregation has almost disappeared, although entry to certain religious occupations is still reserved for men in Britain and in many other countries and cultures. However people with a common culture and interests tend to congregate together in social and geographical space, in neighbourhoods, occupations or clubs, producing varying degrees of natural, voluntary *de facto* segregation in areas of residence, in the labour market or leisure activities. The problem for the social scientist is to distinguish between natural, voluntary occupational segregation and that which occurs because people of one sex, race or religion are prevented from entering a particular occupation by a variety of subtle indirect exclusionary social processes, some of which will be lawful, some of which will be unlawful. The requirement that officers are transferrable from one posting to another in the Diplomatic Service produces a preponderance of men in this area of work. This mobility rule is not challenged, whereas mobility rules in other employment contracts have been challenged and judged to be discriminatory, as shown in Chapter 7. A person who is 'frozen out' of a work group by colleagues' silently hostile behaviour at present has no legal redress, whereas hostile behaviour which takes the form of sexual comment is now covered by sexual harassment regulations in most companies

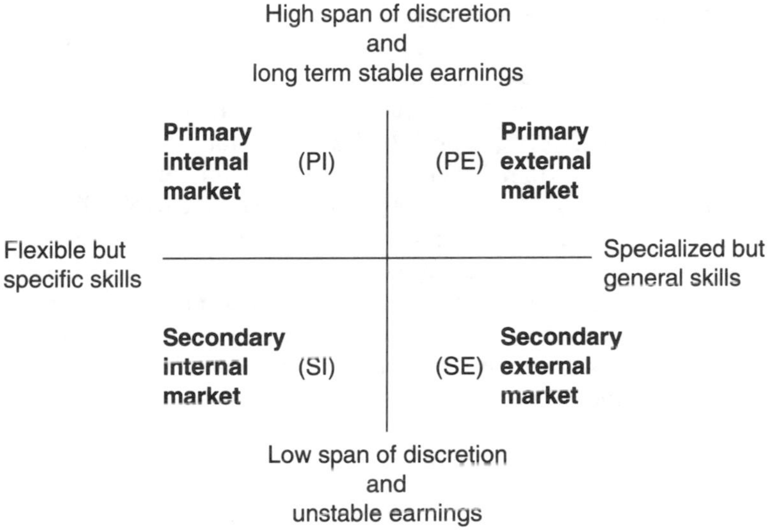

High span of discretion
and
long term stable earnings

|  |  |
|---|---|
| **Primary internal** (PI) **market** | (PE) **Primary external market** |

Flexible but specific skills _____ Specialized but general skills

|  |  |
|---|---|
| **Secondary internal** (SI) **market** | (SE) **Secondary external market** |

Low span of discretion
and
unstable earnings

**Figure 3** Labour market segmentation
**Source:** Loveridge (1983: 159)

and the victim may have redress under sex discrimination laws. What counts as indirect discrimination and indirectly exclusionary practices is being continuously re-assessed as this is socially defined rather than specified by an abstract logical principle.

*Segmentation* is the differentiation of the labour market into distinct firm-specific labour markets, each offering quite different conditions of employment, career patterns and rewards, as shown in Figure 3. The fourfold classification here was developed by Loveridge (1983: 159, 1987) from an earlier version by Mok and is often used in European research (Loveridge, 1983, 1987; Blossfeld and Mayer, 1988; Hakim, 1990a,b; Crompton and Sanderson, 1990: 39; see also Althauser and Kalleberg, 1981). It is obtained by cross-cutting internal and external labour markets with primary and secondary labour markets. The firm's core workforce would be in the primary internal sector offering full-time permanent jobs with career ladders, combining flexible but firm-specific skills with a high span of discretion and long-term stable earnings. Part-time jobs would typically fall in the secondary sector, either the internal market for permanent jobs or the external market for temporary jobs. Self-employed and sub-contractors would be in the external labour market which generally has higher rates of labour mobility. Professional and skilled craft work requiring occupation-specific skills rather than firm-specific skills may be supplied on a fixed-term contract or self-employed basis in the primary external market. Seasonal and casual jobs, homework and unskilled labouring jobs would be typical of the secondary external sector. At the minimum the segmentation perspective provides a useful description of qualitatively different sectors within the labour market. Some regard it as the basis for labour market theory which argues, for example, that there is little or no mobility between the four sectors: workers enter one sector, by design or by accident, and remain there permanently, unless there is a marked change in their characteristics. For example people may move up to the primary labour market as a result of returning to education to get a university qualification, or they may move down to the secondary labour market as a result of physical injury which limits the work they can do, or because their priorities change after they have children.

Barron and Norris (1976) argued that women are generally confined to the secondary labour market because employers perceive them to have little interest in training and careers, above-average turnover and little solidarity as reflected in low rates of trade union membership, features which equally well describe secondary earners, as they themselves note (see Chapter 3). This analysis was possibly valid for the 1960s and early 1970s, but is now dated. The proportion of women in full-time permanent employee jobs is declining, but still stands at about one-half compared to two-thirds of men (see Table 2.6). The winter 1994/95 LFS showed that 89% of all men in employment were in full-time permanent jobs compared to only 53% of women in employment. A full 39% of working women were in *permanent* part-time jobs and a further 8% were in a variety of temporary jobs. Thus by the mid-1990s, about half of all *working* women were in the primary labour market and about half were in the secondary labour market. Given that one-third of women of working age are not in the labour market at any one time (see Table 3.7), we can estimate that about two-thirds of all women of working age are confined to the secondary labour market today and about one-third are in the primary labour market at some stage in their life.

There is no necessary relationship between occupational segregation and labour market segmentation. In societies which insist on the physical segregation of men and women, there are good job opportunities for women in women-only schools, universities and hospitals; it can be easier for a woman to become the director of a girls' school in a Moslem country than of a mixed school in Western society where women have to compete directly with men for senior posts (Boserup, 1970: 119-138; Lewin-Epstein and Semyonov, 1992). Educational systems are universally perceived as non-discriminatory today, whereas labour markets are seen as discriminating against women, with the political arena seen as the most sexist and discriminatory of all (Sorensen, 1990: 158; Tokyo Metropolitan Government, 1994: 17-32). In the post-War period, similar proportions of men and women achieved tertiary-level qualifications (15-18%), although men were more likely to get university degrees and women were more likely to get nursing and teaching qualifications below degree level. The qualifications gap between men and women was until very recently most marked in relation to *secondary school* qualifications (Employment Department, 1992: Table A), which vindicated employers' stereotype of women generally being less interested in careers and less willing to invest in appropriate qualifications.

**Vertical job segregation and the pay gap**
Segregation can be both horizontal and vertical and no single measure can capture both these aspects. Most measures, in particular the popular Dissimilarity Index (DI), measure horizontal segregation, but vertical job segregation is far more important. Cross-national comparisons of the UK, USA, Canada, Sweden, Norway, Australia and Japan suggest that vertical job segregation is largely independent of horizontal occupational segregation (Wright *et al*, 1995).

Horizontal job segregation exists when men and women are most commonly working in different types of occupation – for example women are dressmakers and men are tailors, women are cooks and men are carpenters. Vertical job segregation exists when men dominate the higher grade and higher paid occupations and jobs, or when men are promoted further up career ladders within occupations – for example men are heads of schools while women are teachers. Occupational classifications vary from 6-9 broad occupational groups to 400-600 specific occupations, and they generally identify some combination of vertical and horizontal segregation. For example teachers are usually identified as a separate occupation group, which is staffed by a mixture of men and women, so it is integrated rather than segregated. More detailed classifications distinguish between primary school teachers (dominated by women in Britain and across Europe), secondary school teachers (with a mixture of men and women) and tertiary level teachers (dominated by men in Britain and across Europe). Even more detailed occupational classifications might distinguish head teachers and directors of educational establishments at each level (who are typically male) from ordinary teachers (who are either typically female or mixed). The more detailed the occupational classification, the greater the degree of occupational segregation identified, a point which is important for comparisons across time and across countries.

The degree of detail in the occupational classification is even more important for studies of earnings differentials. There is invariably a large difference in pay between primary school teachers and university teachers, between heads of educational establishments and ordinary teachers. If most primary school teachers are women and most university teachers are men, there will be a large sex differential in pay *within* the teaching profession that is attributable entirely to vertical occupational segregation which is hidden if an occupational classification groups teachers at all levels together. Similar problems occur with occupational classifications that do not separate school directors from teachers, a grading difference that has a large impact on earnings. These points may seem obvious, yet they are regularly overlooked in reports that claim to be surprised, even outraged, at the size of the difference in average earnings between men and women. Perhaps university teachers should be paid the same as primary school teachers. However this is a totally different argument from the idea that, within the current salary structure, the lower earnings of women reflect sex discrimination. Scandinavian countries have achieved greater income equality and reduced earnings differences between men and women without changing the high level of horizontal and vertical occupational segregation (Jensen, Hagen and Reddy, 1988: 181-5; Rosenfeld and Kalleberg, 1990; Wright et al, 1995), but in Britain periods of pay equalisation have always been followed by periods when differentials were reestablished and the earnings dispersion increased.

Studies of the pay gap between men and women within particular occupations indicate that vertical job segregation accounts for virtually all the difference, and national studies confirm this finding.

The impact of vertical segregation can be assessed easily in school teaching because of the formalised job grading absent from many other occupations. An analysis of data for 1973, some twelve years after equal pay was introduced in teaching, found that one-third of the earnings differential was explained by women being concentrated in the lower-paying primary sector and the remaining two-thirds by women being concentrated in posts with lower responsibility and grading (Employment Department, 1976: 965). Analyses of the New Earnings Survey (NES) invariably conclude that vertical job segregation *within* occupations explains more of the pay gap than horizontal occupational segregation. Chiplin and Sloane (1974, 1976) analysed NES data for 1974 while Sloane (1990) analysed NES panel data for 1970 to 1982, a period when average earnings of female full-time employees rose from 67 per cent to 75 per cent of male pay. Astonishingly, both studies gave the same result: vertical job segregation within occupations explained three-quarters of the difference in earnings and horizontal occupational segregation explained only 20 to 27 per cent. Sloane concluded that it is not the particular occupations that women enter that depress their pay, so much as their failure to advance up the occupational ladder, to gain promotion to better paid posts after entry to the occupational group (1990: 135-146). In the USA, horizontal occupational segregation, as measured by the national occupational classification, only explains one-quarter of the difference in earnings (Sorensen, 1989: 74) with vertical job segregation the main cause of the pay gap (Goldin, 1987). Sieling (1984) found the pay gap was virtually eliminated when comparisons were drawn between men and women in the same grade of specific white-collar occupations. For example the earnings of female chemists rose from 75 per cent to 96 per cent of male earnings after job grade was controlled. In virtually all the white-collar occupations studied, women were concentrated in the lowest grades. In general, white-collar occupations and jobs are more likely to have a variety of pay rates and grades and a larger wage spread than manual occupations which very often have only a single rate of pay in any establishment (Buckley, 1985). As a result, the earnings spread, and the sex differential in earnings are larger in white-collar occupations and jobs than in manual occupations and jobs (Buckley, 1985; Sloane, 1990: 134; Payne, 1995).

Studies at establishment level invariably identify far more segregation of *jobs* in individual workplaces than is found in national studies of segregation in the *occupational structure*: teachers may be all-male or all-female in particular schools while the teaching profession as a whole is mixed. Due to sex discrimination legislation there are now virtually no occupations which are 100% male or 100% female at the national level. Exclusively male or female jobs are still common at establishment level, however, and many establishments have no mixed occupations (Hunt, 1975: 173-9; Hakim, 1981: 527-8; Bielby and Baron, 1984: 35, 51). About half of all men and women report that they work with members of their own sex only in their workplace (Kiernan, 1992: 94). This had the effect of limiting the impact of equal pay laws to jobs that were integrated, or mixed, at company level, until equal pay for work of equal value legislation was introduced, at the insistence of the European Union, to allow pay comparisons between men and women doing different jobs of similar value to their employer. Generally, statistical analyses of the level and pattern of job segregation at company or workplace level are mainly of interest for internal practical purposes and rarely have theoretical value. From a social science perspective we are much more interested in knowing whether women have access to the teaching occupation, than in whether women are employed in every school across the country, large and small. It is useful to know that many people, men and women, work in single-sex work groups at their workplace, so that the workforce can appear to be totally segregated at the personal level. However this is not a public policy issue even if it is sociologically interesting. Most adults are aware of the world beyond their own workplace; they know that there are male as well as female teachers, that the occupation is mixed even if it is not part of their immediate experience. Case studies of particular industries or occupations that seek to establish causal processes are of course useful, as illustrated by Reskin and Roos (1990) and Rubery and Fagan (1993), but these are rare, and involve quite different research designs (Hakim, 1987a: 61-75).

## Recent trends in occupational segregation

The sex discrimination legislation that took effect in 1975 proved to be a turning point for patterns of occupational segregation and the pay gap in Britain. A study of occupational segregation over 1901-1971, the seventy years prior to the equal opportunities legislation, showed that at the aggregate level there was little overall change, the decline in horizontal segregation balanced by a marked increase in vertical segregation (Hakim, 1979: 23, 27-29, 1981: 521). The most notable change was that 'exclusive' occupations disappeared completely for women and were close to being eliminated among men. Occupations that were 100% female employed 11% of all working women in 1901; by 1961 they had disappeared. In 1901 half (47%) of the male workforce was employed in 100% male occupations; by 1971 the proportion had fallen to only 14% (Hakim, 1979: 24). Trends in the 1970s suggested that legislation had a dramatic and immediate impact in lowering the overall level of occupational segregation, but that these gains were partially reversed in the deepening recession at the end of the decade (Hakim, 1981). Since 1979, there has been a small but steady decline in horizontal occupational segregation (Hakim, 1992: 137-8). More important, the marked long-term increase in vertical segregation in both white collar and manual occupations was dramatically reversed after 1971 (Tables 6.1 and 6.2).

Occupations in which women were over-represented and under-represented are shown in Table 6.1. Coefficients of female representation are calculated for each of the major occupational groups by dividing the female share of employment in the occupation by the female share of total employment. Coefficients above one indicate female over-representation in the occupation; coefficients below one indicate female under-representation. The measure facilitates comparisons across occupational groups which vary substantially in size, and across years. Over the decade, women's dominance in lower-grade and lower paid occupations was reduced and their representation in all grades of professional and managerial occupations increased. The smallest increase, from the lowest starting point, was in professional and related occupations in science, engineering and technology, but here too there was an improvement, as also in literary, artistic and sports jobs. Women with the very highest earnings in Britain are writers (especially fiction writers), actresses and sportswomen, although earnings in these fields are also the most variable. Some types of work remained almost exclusively male throughout the decade: construction, mining, materials moving, transport operating, and production work involving metal and electrical goods remained virtually unaltered, with negligible or tiny female representation even by 1990 (Table 6.1). As noted in Chapter 3, there is no evidence of feminisation of the most stereotypically masculine

**Table 6.1** Women's representation in the major occupational groups 1979-1990

| | Coefficient of female representation in major occupational groups | | | |
|---|---|---|---|---|
| | 1979 | 81Cen | 1985 | 1990 |
| 1 Professional and related supporting management and administration | 0.52 | 0.54 | 0.57 | 0.66 |
| 2 Professional and related in education, welfare, and health | 1.62 | 1.67 | 1.59 | 1.56 |
| 3 Literary, artistic and sport | 0.84 | 0.92 | 0.90 | 0.94 |
| 4 Professional and related in science, engineering and technology | 0.23 | 0.23 | 0.16 | 0.29 |
| 5 Managerial - large and small establishments | 0.53 | 0.59 | 0.61 | 0.65 |
| 6 Clerical and related | 1.85 | 1.90 | 1.88 | 1.79 |
| 7 Selling | 1.53 | 1.51 | 1.47 | 1.38 |
| 8 Security and protective service | 0.25 | 0.26 | 0.23 | 0.27 |
| 9 Catering, cleaning, hairdressing and other personal service | 2.07 | 2.00 | 1.91 | 1.84 |
| 10 Farming, fishing and related | 0.34 | 0.38 | 0.40 | 0.51 |
| 11 Processing, making, repairing & related (not metal and electrical) | 0.87 | 0.82 | 0.73 | 0.68 |
| 12 Processing, making, repairing & related (metal and electrical) | 0.13 | 0.13 | 0.09 | 0.12 |
| 13 Painting, repetitive assembly, product inspection, packaging etc | 1.17 | 1.08 | 1.03 | 0.93 |
| 14 Construction, mining and related | 0.01 | 0.03 | 0.01 | 0.02 |
| 15 Transport operating, materials moving, storing, and related | 0.14 | 0.15 | 0.09 | 0.15 |
| 16 Miscellaneous | 0.19 | 0.23 | 0.20 | 0.18 |
| 17 Not stated or occupation unclear | 1.42 | 1.10 | 0.96 | 0.28 |
| Female share (%) of total employment | 39 | 39 | 41 | 43 |

**Source:** Extracted from Hakim (1992: 135) Table 3 based on 1981 Population Census and Labour Force Survey 1979-1990, Great Britain. Data for the economically active population 1979-1985, and for the employed workforce in 1990.

occupations. Overall, in most occupational groups, the coefficient of female representation moved towards one, indicating that women were more evenly distributed across occupations by 1990.

Women's share of top jobs increased sharply after 1971. Table 6.2 shows trends in vertical segregation over the two decades 1971-1990 by examining women's share of the most senior occupations which play the major part in running the country. The occupational classification does not allow us to identify parliamentary

**Table 6.2** Women in top jobs 1971, 1981, 1990

| Percentage of women in each of the following occupations | 1971 | 1981 | 1990 |
|---|---|---|---|
| Judges, barristers, advocates, solicitors | 4 | 14 | 27 |
| General administrators - national government | 12 | 19 | 29 |
| Local government officers - administrative and executive functions | 20 | 31 | 51 |
| Statutory and other inspectors | 2 | 10 | 18 |
| Senior officers - police, prison, fire services | 2 | 2 | * |
| Officers - UK armed forces | 5 | 4 | 3 |
| Accountants, valuers, finance specialists, underwriters, brokers | 4 | 10 | 19 |
| Personnel and industrial relations managers, O&M, work study officers | 12 | 29 | 46 |
| Economists, statisticians, systems analysts, computer programmers | 15 | 19 | 19 |
| Marketing, sales, advertising, public relations, purchasing managers | 11 | 16 | 24 |
| Other professional and related supporting management | 34 | 43 | 52 |
| Teachers in higher education - university, further & higher education | 25 | 27 | 37 |
| Medical and dental practitioners | 18 | 23 | 30 |
| Biologists, chemists, physicists, mathematicians, other scientists | 7 | 20 | 26 |
| Engineers  civil, municipal, structural, mining, quarrying | * | * | 2 |
| Engineers - mechanical, aeronautical | 1 | 1 | 2 |
| Engineers - electrical, electronic | 1 | 2 | 7 |
| Architects, town planners, quantity building and land surveyors | 1 | 4 | 6 |
| Managers - large and small establishments | 21 | 23 | 28 |
| Women's share of total employment | 36 | 39 | 43 |
| Women's share of full-time employment | 27 | 30 | 32 |
| Women's share of full-time permanent employment | .. | 30 | 35 |

* less than 0.5%

**Sources:** 1981 Census *Economic Activity*, Table A, 10% sample data for England & Wales 1981 and 1% sample data for 1971 recoded to 1980 classification; Spring 1990 Labour Force Survey results for Great Britain, data for all persons in employment. Women's share of full-time, and full-time permanent employment are derived from Tables 3.3 and 21.6 respectively in this volume.

representatives. Equally invisible are the 'captains of industry', the managing directors and chief executives of large companies in the private sector, who are men almost without exception. Women's exclusion from these upper echelons of the top jobs was underlined in a 1990 Hansard Society report showing women to be 6.3 per cent of parliamentary representatives (the lowest figure in Europe), 1 per cent of High Court judges, 3 per cent of university professors, and 0.5 per cent of directors of the Confederation of British Industry's top 140 firms. Managers of large and small establishments in the various sectors of industry are grouped together in the occupational classification used in the

1980s and are shown as a single group in Table 6.2. At this aggregate level, women's share was relatively high at one-fifth in 1971 rising to over one-quarter by 1990, which still left them under-represented.

Other professional and managerial grades are identified relatively well, and reveal sharp increases in women's share of these jobs, with a few exceptions. Women are barely visible with less than 5 per cent of senior posts in engineering professions, the armed forces, the police and the prison and fire services. Despite the fact that the expanding 'new' computing professions have no established 'traditional' entry barriers and sex stereotypes, there was virtually no change over the two decades in women's share of economist, statistician, systems analyst and computer programmer jobs. Apart from these areas of stability, women made significant gains in the decades after the legislation was introduced. Perhaps appropriately, the legal professions were among the first to open up, with women's share of jobs rising from a meagre 4 per cent in 1971 to 27 per cent by 1990, followed closely by national government management, with an increase from 12 to 29 per cent. By 1990, women's share of top jobs in certain sectors was broadly level with their share of total employment: local government administration and management, personnel and industrial relations managers, organisation and management and work study professionals, and the miscellaneous category of other professionals supporting management which includes company secretaries, management consultants, librarians, information officers, trade union officials, property and estate managers, officers of trade and professional associations, and officers of charities.

The vast majority of professional and managerial jobs are full-time permanent posts. Arguably the more appropriate comparison is with women's share of full-time permanent jobs, or at least their share of full-time jobs, rather than their share of total employment. These other two measures are shown in Table 6.2, where available. The percentages are lower and display a slower increase over the two decades than the more commonly quoted share of total employment, reaching about one-third by 1990. Using these alternative comparisons, and accepting that there will be some variation around the mean, the majority of top jobs listed in Table 6.2 had already achieved a proportionate share of women by the 1990s. The exceptions were those with hardly any women, which would be outliers whatever measure was used: the engineering professions and security services. Using the new comparison points, two occupational groups are now identified as having disproportionately *high* female shares: local government officers (51%) and professional and related supporting management (52%). Apart from women's exclusion from the upper echelons of the top jobs, as noted earlier, vertical job segregation seems to have been largely eliminated in the very short period of two decades after the introduction of equal opportunities legislation.

This analysis also demonstrates all too clearly how inadequate the standard occupational classifications are, even at the most detailed level, for identifying the extent of vertical segregation *within* occupational groups. Within the legal profession, judges rank far higher than lawyers in status and earnings, yet all grades are grouped together in the occupational classification used for Table 6.2, even though it is a relatively detailed one with 162 occupational groups which are further subdivided into 550 occupations. It is often remarked that occupational classifications identify male occupations in far more detail than female occupations. The more general point is that occupational classifications in Britain have excelled at differentiating types of manual work, which may not attract very differentiated earnings, but classify white-collar occupations into broad groups, even though these may incorporate substantial skill and earnings differentials between grades. This is a fundamentally important point for studies that try to explain earnings differences between men and women on the basis of only broad classifications of white-collar jobs.

The most widely used measure of occupational segregation is the Duncan and Duncan (1955) Dissimilarity Index (DI). Originally developed in the USA for studies of racial segregation in cities, neighbourhoods and schools, its use was extended to trend analyses of the sex segregation of occupations as well (Williams, 1976; England, 1981; Reskin, 1984; James and Taeuber, 1985; Reskin and Hartmann, 1986; Jacobs, 1989a; Charles and Grusky, 1995). The DI is used in European research on social mobility, where it is well suited to measuring the dissimilarity of social classes of origin and destination (Goldthorpe, 1987; Erikson and Goldthorpe, 1993: 231-277) as well as in research on occupational segregation (Blossfeld, 1987; Rubery, 1988; OECD, 1988; Hakim, 1993b; Rubery and Fagan, 1993). However as soon as research moves beyond the analysis of long-term trends in one country, the limitations of the DI become serious (Hakim, 1993b,c, 1995c), especially for cross-national comparisons (OECD, 1988; Jacobs and Lim, 1992; Wright *et al*, 1995: 429). Perhaps the most important practical limitation is that the DI requires comparisons of pairs, and only permits comparisons of pairs. This becomes an impossible constraint as soon as one moves beyond analyses of national trends to comparisons of subgroups within the workforce. The point is illustrated by King's (1992) attempt to compare occupational segregation on the basis of both sex and race in the USA workforce, which required no less than six sets of paired comparisons, and by Hakim's (1993b) attempt to compare the degree of occupational segregation within the full-time and part-time workforces in Britain. As Goldthorpe has argued in relation to studies of social mobility, the single number index cannot adequately describe the pattern of change and movement within the occupational structure (Goldthorpe, 1990: 416; see also James and Taeuber, 1985: 26). The alternative is an analytical framework which distinguishes integrated and segregated occupations and measures their relative importance across groups and across time. This approach allows some variation in the definition of integrated occupations; can be adapted to cross-national comparisons; allows comparisons between any number of labour market subgroups; is not excessively sensitive to the degree of detail in the occupational classification available in the data source; and is useful in policy research as well as theoretical research. Perhaps most important of all, it facilitates theoretical linkages between macro-level studies and case studies of changes within particular industries, occupations, regions or labour market subgroups (Hakim, 1993b). This approach is applied in Tables 6.3 to 6.7. In each case mixed or integrated occupations are identified as those falling in a narrow band (±15% or ±20%) around the average female share of total employment for the period in question.

Another approach to analysing vertical segregation is to use the social class classification. As Goldthorpe (1987) pointed out, occupational segregation and social stratification are theoretically distinct facets of the distribution of occupations, status and rewards, so that research on the two topics has legitimately proceeded separately and in parallel. More recently, Goldthorpe and Erikson (1993: 277) concluded from a cross-national comparative study of women's class mobility in Europe that an explanation of the gender inequalities that are a common feature of modern industrial societies

**Table 6.3** Social Class composition of integrated and segregated occupations

| | Male | Mixed | Female | Total |
|---|---|---|---|---|
| | \multicolumn{4}{c}{Distribution of workforce in 1991 in each type of occupation} | | | |
| I Professional | 8 | 8 | * | 5 |
| II Managerial & Technical | 20 | 65 | 18 | 27 |
| IIIN Skilled white-collar | 5 | 7 | 48 | 24 |
| IIIM Skilled blue collar | 42 | 7 | 7 | 21 |
| IV Semi-skilled | 18 | 13 | 18 | 17 |
| V Unskilled | 7 | 0 | 9 | 6 |
| Base 000s=100% | 114 | 48 | 128 | 289 |

* less than 0.5%

Integrated occupations are those 25-55% female (40% ±15%) using an occupational classification with 371 occupational groups. The classification of occupational groups is based on 10% sample data from the 1991 Population Census.

**Source:** 1991 Census 1% Household SAR, Great Britain, which is Crown Copyright. Data for current and last jobs of people aged 16-64 years, excluding people in the Armed Forces and those with occupation not stated or inadequately described.

needed to be developed outside the scope of class analysis. Our analysis of the relationship between occupational segregation and social stratification (Table 6.3) points in the same direction. The classification of occupations into segregated and integrated categories is based on 10% sample data from the 1991 Census, that is, on data for 2.5 million workers who are coded to 371 occupations (OPCS, 1994: Table 4) and we use the standard Social Class classification (OPCS, 1991). The dataset is the new 1% Sample of Anonymised Records (SAR) from the 1991 Census of Population for Great Britain which is available for research analysis under strictly controlled conditions and has opened up both expected and unexpected avenues of labour market analysis (Hakim, 1982a: 54, 1995b).

Integrated occupations are the smallest group, and they are the most highly qualified as well, with no jobs in the lowest unskilled Class V and almost three-quarters of all workers in Classes I and II, as Scott and Burchell (1994) also found with a much smaller dataset. Male-dominated occupations include some professional occupations, which are virtually non-existent within the female-intensive sector (Table 6.3). Otherwise, male-dominated and female-dominated occupations are almost identical in their Social Class composition, apart from the well-known tendency for men to be concentrated in skilled blue collar work while women are concentrated in skilled white-collar work – Social Classes III Manual and III Non-Manual respectively. Contrary to expectation, it is not male occupations which have the highest proportion of higher status and higher paid occupations, but the small category of mixed occupations, which constitute one-fifth of 371 separately identified occupations and one-fifth of the total workforce. Integrated occupations are the most highly qualified and, partly associated with this, have the highest proportion of self-employed people, which suggests that they fall in the primary internal and primary external segments of the labour market. Table 6.3 shows that the middle group of desegregated or mixed occupations on the boundary line between the male-dominated and female-dominated sectors is not a random category with no distinguishing features, but a qualitatively different sector of the labour market. In the integrated sector certificated skills seem to create a uniquely egalitarian and open labour market which overcomes the need to rely on sex stereotyping and statistical discrimination to allocate people to jobs (Phelps, 1972; Cain, 1986: 724-9). Looking at it another way, there is less segregation in the higher grade occupations than in lower grade occupations. The two groups of segregated occupations, male and female, are characterised by horizontal segregation rather than vertical segregation. However in terms of absolute numbers, there are more men than women in Social Class I and II occupations. Table 6.3 provides an explanation for contradictory results from studies that dichotomise occupations into male and female, or that use a single continuous variable of % male (or % female) to characterise occupations (Rosenfeld, 1983; England, 1984; Kilbourne et al, 1994). Two-thirds of male occupations are skilled and unskilled manual work and two-thirds of female occupations are skilled and unskilled white-collar work, so there is no strong variation in occupational sex ratios, status and earnings except in the top two classes, where integrated occupations are dominant. The occupational structure is dominated by horizontal occupational segregation except in the top grades of highly paid professional, technical and managerial occupations.

A unique analysis by Blossfeld (1987) studied the pattern of occupational segregation across the lifecycle using the richly detailed 1981-83 West German Life History Study. His analysis took account of the qualitatively different employment profiles of men and women to show that women with discontinuous employment were more likely to be in typically-female occupations than those who worked continuously. In addition, Blossfeld found a surprising cross-sectional rising trend in occupational segregation across age cohorts, a result that was confirmed after separating cohort and lifecycle effects. He concluded that occupational segregation rides at successively higher levels within each younger age cohort in Germany, despite an impressive equalisation of educational attainment, reflected in a sharp fall in sex segregation scores across age cohorts in educational levels, albeit with increasing segregation of educational subjects. The puzzle he was unable to solve is why declining segregation in educational attainment was not matched by declining segregation in occupational attainment. One possible explanation is explored below: a tendency for people to prefer sex-typical occupations and work cultures, which seems to apply equally to men and women and has to be regarded as benign rather than noxious. However there is no obvious reason for expecting this preference to intensify in younger age cohorts; indeed quite the contrary is true. A second explanation may be that, in practice, many women use their educational qualifications to improve their prospects in the marriage market rather than the labour market, as noted in Chapter 5. The third possible explanation, which is consistent with the second, is that the creation of a segmented part-time workforce tends to increase occupational segregation, given that all of the increase in female employment is due to the expansion of part-time work in successive cohorts (OECD, 1988: 139). The impact of part-time work on occupational segregation is explored below with reference to the British labour market, which has one of the largest part-time workforces in Europe.

In the USA (Power, 1988: 145) and across Europe as a whole, female employment is polarising, with women increasing their share of professional, technical and managerial occupations at the same time as they increase their share of lower level service and clerical work. As Rubery and Fagan point out (1993: xxi, 1995) trends over the 1970s and 1980s have been pulling in opposite directions, so that overall measures of occupational segregation at the national level generally reveal little or no change; any change that is found may be upward or downward (OECD, 1988; Rubery and Fagan, 1993, 1995). Comparisons across Europe reveal a large degree of convergence in the occupations in which women are concentrated, but also puzzling diversity. Women's share of computer professionals varies from just 13% in the Netherlands to 31% in Greece, with Denmark, Portugal and Ireland following closely at 27%-28% (Rubery and Fagan, 1995a: 224). As this is a new profession, the historical and institutional factors that shape women's access to other jobs have little force here. In Spain, women's share of economists and legal professionals jumped from 9%-16% in 1980 to 33%-36% by 1991 in the private sector. In Germany, women's share of lawyers, judges and scientists increased by 50% in the period 1977-90, whereas there was relatively little change over the decade in France (Rubery and Fagan, 1993: 19, 1995). There is a haphazard element in the allocation of jobs to men and women which emerges most clearly in cross-national comparisons (Hakim, 1979: 37-43).

### Masculine and feminine work cultures

All our results show women entering previously male-dominated professional and managerial occupations in substantial numbers. On the face of it, this trend is inconsistent with Jacobs' 'revolving doors' thesis. Jacobs' social exclusion or social control thesis was that male colleagues refuse to provide the informal job induction process, the camaraderie and cooperative teamwork that new female entrants need to succeed, that male colleagues regularly ignore, harass and undermine female colleagues, forcing them to leave male occupations (1989b: 181-2). In effect he described the informal and invisible 'freezing out' mechanisms that complement the formal exclusionary policies of patriarchal trade unions described in Chapter 1. The thesis was plausible, resting as it did on patriarchy theory without ever using the term. However, by restricting his analysis to women, Jacobs fell into the sample selection bias trap noted in Chapter 5.

Fuller analyses comparing men and women, full-timers and part-timers reveal that there is a *general* tendency for people to leave sex-atypical occupations and move towards sex-typical occupations (Table 6.4). This process occurs among men and women to fairly equal degree, so any explanation must apply equally to men and women. It is notable that men and women who leave mixed occupations each move to sex-typical occupations most often. The most likely explanation is simply that working life is more psychologically and socially comfortable, or unproblematic, for many people when work colleagues are of the same sex, so that there is a natural tendency to drift back towards sex-typical occupations. The reversal to sex-typical occupations is 'natural' in the sense of being voluntary rather than forced on people by social institutions and work colleagues. Alternatively, men and women are equally hostile or unwelcoming to people of the opposite sex who 'invade' predominantly single-sex occupations. The 'revolving doors' process is not an exclusive feature of male occupations, as Jacobs argued, nor even stronger there. Among full-time workers, women are more likely to remain in male jobs than men to remain in female jobs. Waite and Berryman (1986) review reasons for women leaving male-dominated jobs in the military, an unsupportive social environment being only one of many. Finally, occupational stability outweighs the tendency to revert to sex-typical occupations. The analysis in Table 6.4 uses the same definition of integrated occupations as in Jacobs' analyses for the USA, namely occupations that are 30%-70% female (50% ±20%). The correlation coefficient between occupation type in 1971 and 1981 is around .40 for all subgroups shown in Table 6.4, varying only slightly or not at all between men and women, consistent with the results of other studies (Rosenfeld and Spenner, 1992: 429). Another replication by S. Jacobs (1995) also found that occupational changes over 15 years and 25 years, for men and for women, were largely stable within the three categories of male-dominated, female-dominated and integrated occupations.

Research is documenting the way that jobs are constructed by employers as female or male jobs, even in times of labour shortage during wars (Milkman, 1987; Bradley, 1989; Strom, 1989). But one reason for this is that women often prefer to work with women, men with men, partly as a demonstration of and confirmation of sexual identities (Matthaei, 1982: 194; Bradley, 1989: 229). Workers play a more important role in gendering jobs than employers do. Workplace cultures are often heavily coloured by job incumbents: women regularly celebrate their private relationships and private lives at work; men celebrate their sexual exploits and leisure interests (Pringle, 1989: 95, 120, 225, 243; Reskin and Padavic, 1994: 134-141). Both feminine and masculine work cultures and associated institutions, such as clubs, can be experienced as exclusionary by men and women. For example women can ostracise a female colleague who refuses to discuss private lives at work, while men can look down on a man who has no interest in cars or sport. As yet we have little solid evidence on the informal 'freezing out' exclusionary processes,

**Table 6.4** Occupational change 1971-1981 among people in continuous employment

| | Type of occupation in 1971 | Proportion (%) in each type of occupation in 1981 | | | | Distribution of occupations in 1981 + Base |
|---|---|---|---|---|---|---|
| | | Male | Mixed | Female | Total | |
| All persons | Male | 84 | 11 | 4 | 100 | 57 |
| | Mixed | 30 | 55 | 15 | 100 | 26 |
| | Female | 13 | 21 | 66 | 100 | 17 |
| | Total | 58 | 24 | 18 | 100 | 100 |
| | Base for this group | | | | | 131,600 |
| All women | Male | 37 | 29 | 34 | 100 | 11 |
| | Mixed | 10 | 61 | 29 | 100 | 39 |
| | Female | 7 | 21 | 72 | 100 | 50 |
| | Total | 12 | 38 | 51 | 100 | 100 |
| | Base for this group | | | | | 39,200 |
| All men | Male | 87 | 10 | 2 | 100 | 76 |
| | Mixed | 47 | 49 | 4 | 100 | 20 |
| | Female | 44 | 22 | 34 | 100 | 4 |
| | Total | 78 | 18 | 4 | 100 | 100 |
| | Base for this group | | | | | 92,400 |
| Women working full-time only | Male | 48 | 31 | 21 | 100 | 14 |
| | Mixed | 13 | 67 | 20 | 100 | 44 |
| | Female | 9 | 26 | 65 | 100 | 42 |
| | Total | 16 | 45 | 39 | 100 | 100 |
| | Base for this group | | | | | 17,700 |
| Men working full-time only | Male | 88 | 10 | 2 | 100 | 76 |
| | Mixed | 48 | 48 | 4 | 100 | 20 |
| | Female | 46 | 22 | 32 | 100 | 4 |
| | Total | 79 | 18 | 3 | 100 | 100 |
| | Base for this group | | | | | 88,500 |
| All working full-time only | Male | 86 | 11 | 3 | 100 | 66 |
| | Mixed | 37 | 54 | 9 | 100 | 24 |
| | Female | 20 | 25 | 55 | 100 | 10 |
| | Total | 68 | 22 | 9 | 100 | 100 |
| | Base for this group | | | | | 106,200 |
| All with any part-time work | Male | 49 | 22 | 29 | 100 | 17 |
| | Mixed | 10 | 56 | 34 | 100 | 34 |
| | Female | 6 | 18 | 76 | 100 | 49 |
| | Total | 15 | 32 | 53 | 100 | 100 |
| | Base for this group | | | | | 25,400 |

Integrated occupations are those 30-70% female (50% ±20%) using occupational classifications with 223 groups (1971) and 350 groups (1981). The classification of occupational groups is based on 10% sample data from the 1971 and 1981 Population Censuses.

**Source:** Analyses of the 1% Longitudinal Study (OPCS, 1988), data for people working in 1971 and 1981 aged 16 and over in England and Wales.

conscious or unconscious, applied by men and women to people in sex-atypical positions, and more generally to people who do not conform to gender stereotypes. As noted in Chapter 4, this can include female colleagues, even secretaries, as well as men, refusing to cooperate with, or even work for, a female boss or manager. Most of the time, masculine and feminine workplace cultures are unrelated to the nature of the work task; they are a gratuitous add-on. Quite often, it is the work culture that defines an occupation as male or female rather than the work task itself.

All this is demonstrated in Cockburn's (1983) case study of male newspaper printers in Britain which complements the broader, more analytical case study of printing in the USA by Reskin and Roos (1990: 275-298). Printers are the quintessential craft workers, the aristocracy of the manual workforce, democratic within their elite organisations (Lipset, Trow and Coleman, 1956). Between 1970 and 1990, printing feminised. In Britain, the percentage of compositors who were female rose from 3% in 1971 to 24% in 1991 (13% for printers by 1991). In the USA, the percentage of typesetters and compositors who were female increased from 17% in 1970 to 74% in 1988, as electronic composition and 'desktop publishing' computer programs changed the labour process, so that relatively dirty, noisy and heavy skilled blue-collar jobs were transformed into clean, quiet, skilled white-collar jobs – to the dismay of the male-dominated trade unions, who had long opposed women's entry to this well-paid work and did their best to resist the changes. Cockburn's case study of the masculine workplace culture in printing covers the trade unions' long-standing policy of excluding women from the skilled grades of printing work; the links between regular wage work, skill, status, physical strength, endurance, masculinity and patriarchal attitudes; and men's need to create supportive all-male work groups to bolster fragile sexual egos and to hide from women's gaze their regular failures in the rat-race for success and power. Cockburn describes the many arguments developed by working class men to justify the exclusion of women from skilled work, ranging from natural, physical, intellectual and temperamental inadequacies which meant women could not do the work, to economic and social reasons why women should not compete with men for skilled work (1983: 132-140, 151-190). Virtually all the arguments and concepts had to do with men's ideology of sexual difference; preserving the sexual division of labour at home and at work; and avoiding competition between men and women in the workplace because this would affect the way they related to women in their private lives. If women have been kept out of printing far more successfully in Britain than in the USA, it is due to trade union organisation and exclusionary male solidarity rather than anything to do with the nature of the work tasks. Explaining the much faster pace of feminisation in the USA, Reskin and Roos point out (1990: 279, 295) that technological change is the most visible factor but not in itself the main cause of social and economic change – as proven by contrasting developments in the USA and Britain.

### A segregated part-time workforce

A study of patterns of segregation in Britain over the two decades 1971-91 shows that the overall level of occupational segregation is the sum of two opposite trends which largely cancel out: declining segregation in the full-time workforce is hidden by higher and rising segregation in the expanding part-time workforce (Hakim, 1993b). Up to 1961, part-time workers were a tiny and almost invisible element of the workforce, just 9 per cent nationally (see Table 3.3). A study of occupational segregation in 1971 concluded that part-time work had no substantial effects on the overall level of occupational segregation at that time (Hakim, 1979: 29-31). So the emergence of a segregated part-time workforce is a new development, occurring only after the part-time workforce became large enough to become a separate and distinct sector of the workforce, consistent with labour market segmentation theory described earlier; consistent with the distinctive secondary earner characteristics of almost all part-time workers, as noted in Chapters 3 and 4; and consistent with the fact that part-time work is a key feature of the *modern* homemaker career, as noted in Chapter 5.

Using the DI to compare the full-time workforce as a whole with the part-time workforce as a whole yields a score of 49 for 1971 rising to 54 in 1991, within the possible range of 0-100. The two workforces differ markedly. More important, they are diverging rather than converging: as the part-time workforce grows in size it is becoming more differentiated rather than integrated into the mainstream; the peculiarities of a minority sector are becoming more, rather than less extreme. The occupational structure of the part-time workforce is in sharp contrast

**Table 6.5** Divergent trends in a polarised workforce 1971-1991

| | Type of occupation | % of all occupations | Complete workforce | | | Full-time workforce | | | Part-time workforce | | |
|---|---|---|---|---|---|---|---|---|---|---|---|
| | | | % of all | % of men | % of women | % of all | % of men | % of women | % of all | % of men | % of women |
| 1971 Census | Male | 66 | 49 | 72 | 9 | 54 | 72 | 10 | 15 | 61 | 8 |
| | Mixed | 18 | 15 | 16 | 15 | 16 | 16 | 17 | 12 | 17 | 11 |
| | Female | 16 | 36 | 12 | 76 | 30 | 12 | 73 | 73 | 22 | 81 |
| 1991 LFS | Male | 53 | 41 | 66 | 9 | 50 | 68 | 12 | 9 | 36 | 5 |
| | Mixed | 25 | 19 | 20 | 17 | 21 | 20 | 22 | 13 | 24 | 11 |
| | Female | 22 | 40 | 14 | 74 | 29 | 12 | 66 | 78 | 40 | 84 |

**Note:** Occupational groups are based on an implicit 40% average female share of the workforce, with mixed jobs defined as 40% ±15% as follows:

*Male* occupations are those with <25% female workers in each year;

*Integrated* occupations are those with 25%-55% female workers in each year;

*Female* occupations are those with >55% female workers in each year.

This typology was applied separately to the two datasets, which employed slightly different definitions of part-time work and different occupational classifications, identifying 223 and 371 occupations respectively in 1971 and 1991.

**Source:** Hakim (1993b: 297) Table 2 reporting 1971 Census 10% sample and 1991 Labour Force Survey data for people in employment.

to that of the full-time workforce (Table 6.5, see also Table 3.6).

The decline in horizontal occupational segregation 1971-91 is reflected in the increasing importance of mixed occupations, rising from 18 per cent to 25 per cent of the occupations listed in the classification and from 15 per cent to 19 per cent of the workforce, while male occupations shrank in size (Table 6.5). In both 1971 and 1991 the occupational structures of the male and female full-time workforces are shown to be virtual mirror images of each other. In 1971, three-quarters of men and women were in occupations dominated by their own sex, with a bare 10 per cent in what can be termed sex-atypical occupations dominated by the opposite sex. By 1991 this had changed markedly, although the mirror image pattern remained: two-thirds of full-time male and female workers were in occupations dominated by their own sex, and a good fifth were working in mixed occupations. In contrast the part-time workforce is completely dominated by female occupations, which contribute three-quarters or more of the sector, and it became more segregated after 1971. As the part-time workforce grew over the period, from 16% to 22% of the workforce, it had an increasing impact on the national pattern of occupational segregation. The trend towards integration in the full-time workforce is thus concealed and cancelled by the trend towards a more segregated part-time workforce (Table 6.5).

These conclusions are reinforced by the contrasting trends of feminisation and polarisation shown in Table 6.6. Over the two

**Table 6.6** Feminisation and polarisation of the workforce 1971-1991

|  |  | Occupational group: | | | |
|  |  | Male | Mixed | Female | All |
| % female | 1971 | 7 | 36 | 78 | 37 |
|  | 1981 | 7 | 36 | 80 | 40 |
|  | 1991 | 9 | 40 | 81 | 44 |
| % part-time | 1971 | 3 | 11 | 30 | 15 |
|  | 1981 | 3 | 11 | 36 | 18 |
|  | 1991 | 5 | 15 | 43 | 22 |

**Source:** Hakim (1993b: 298) Table 3 reporting 1971 Census 10% sample data for Britain for 223 occupations; 1981 Census 10% sample data for Britain aggregated to 350 occupations from 550; and 1991 LFS data for Britain for 371 occupations.

decades up to 1991, the workforce feminised, and this trend was found to an equal degree in all three types of occupation. In contrast, the expansion of part-time jobs was concentrated almost exclusively in female occupations, which changed from being one-third part-time in 1971 to half part-time by the early 1990s. The workforce has polarised into a female-dominated secondary labour market with part-time jobs and high turnover rates, while the primary labour market consists of male-dominated and mixed occupations, full-time jobs and low turnover rates, confirming Barron and Norris' (1976) earlier analysis. Table 6.5 suggests the female-dominated secondary labour market accounted for 40% of the workforce in 1991; the primary labour market accounted for 60%.

These results are consistent with Humphries and Rubery's (1992: 251) findings on trends in women's employment and earnings in the 1980s. They too concluded that the female workforce was polarising so that by the end of the 1980s it had become almost essential to distinguish between groups of women workers, for example between managerial and professional women and women in other occupations, or between full-time and part-time workers in analyses of women's evolving position in the labour market.

The location of part-time work on the periphery of the workforce is further demonstrated by an analysis of the jobs taken by students and schoolchildren in full-time education and by the last jobs of the retired, again based on the 1% SAR from the 1991 Census (Hakim, 1995b: Table 5). The current and last jobs of students are concentrated among female occupations, even for male students. When the current or last job was part-time, the overwhelming majority of such jobs were in the female sector. The last jobs of the retired were also concentrated among female-dominated occupations if they were part-time jobs, even for men. In contrast, the majority of men who moved from their last (probably usual) full-time job to full-time retirement had been in typically-male work in their last employment. Female occupations provide a source of short-term employment on the edge of the labour market for the very young who are still in the transition from school to employment and for older workers who are withdrawing gradually from the labour market. The similarity of male and female occupations in terms of Social Class composition is completely overturned as regards location in the primary and secondary sectors within a labour market segmentation perspective.

## Long term trends 1891-1991

These findings overturn the idea of female occupations as stereo-typically *feminine*. Closer examination of the nature of female occupations today confirms that their dominant feature now is low skill. This contrasts sharply with the distinctively domestic and feminine characteristics of female occupations a century ago. Even if the overall *level* of occupational segregation changes little over time, the character and social functions of occupational segregation have been rewritten. In effect, the pattern of occupational segregation is being constantly recreated and reinvented by men and women at work in a process sometimes called 'resegregation'.

Economic and social historians agree that the late nineteenth century was a key period for the study of occupational segregation, as it was in this period that the sexual division of labour and the sex-typing of jobs were socially constructed. Humphries (1987) states that the period after 1850 was crucial, with a *rising* trend in occupational segregation as gainful work was transferred from the home to separate workplaces and jobs were rearranged so as to physically segregate unrelated men and women in the workplace. The concern with the moral propriety of men and women working together, beyond the social controls of the family environment, was illustrated by the Gangs Act of 1867 which prohibited the employment of women or girls in gangs in which men worked, and required a gang-mistress wherever females were employed. This explanation for the creation and development of occupational segregation in the late nineteenth century emphasises the physical and social segregation of men and women at work, especially unmarried young women and men, far more than attempts to specify the particular jobs done by women or a concern with economic segregation. This meant all occupations could be open to both sexes so long as they were employed in separate offices or workplaces or on different shifts, as illustrated by Post Office policy (Grint, 1988: 88). This also explains large regional variations in the jobs done by men or women (Hakim, 1980: 567-8; Matthaei, 1982: 189). In contrast, social historians claim that contemporary accounts reveal a desire to construct separate, 'feminine' jobs for girls and women, if they worked at all, as well as to restrict contact between men and women at work. Holcombe (1973) describes the patriarchal ideas which, whether believed or not, were used to legitimate restrictions on women's work after marriage and restrictions on the types of occupation considered suitable for middle class ladies. Bradley (1989: 223-4) emphasises continuities in the social definitions of men's and women's jobs which were designed into the division of labour within mechanised mass production systems developed in America in the 1880s and subsequently exported to Britain and the rest of the world. Matthaei (1982: 194) asserts that the sex-typing of jobs in the late nineteenth century in the USA was prompted by the desires of men and women to assert their sexual identities by undertaking work reserved for their sex alone, that occupational segregation was actively sought as a means of asserting and reaffirming manhood and womanhood; she also notes that this sex-typing is now breaking down.

In 1891, the most common female occupation (employing 35 per cent of all women) was the domestic servant working in a private household and subject to the employing family's supervision of her private life as well as her work, and dressmaking and sewing, often carried out in homes or in all-female contexts, employing 17 per cent of women. Thus the two most important female occupations, employing half of all working women, combined feminine activity and relative seclusion. Similarly half of all working women in the USA and one-third in France were in domestic service in 1870 (Grossman, 1980; Matthaei, 1982: 197-203, 281-5; Fine, 1992: 124). Women's much commented-on concentration in service sector industries and occupations is not as new as changes in classifications imply. The key change is that service jobs have been transferred out of households into public commercial locations (Hakim, 1994: 444, 450).

By 1991 the link to women's non-market domestic work had totally disappeared. The most important female-dominated occupations are now gender-neutral white-collar jobs rather than feminine in character. Half of all working women are employed in a variety of clerical and sales occupations, as secretaries (8%), sales assistants (9%), clerks (5%), cashiers (7%), miscellaneous occupations in sales and services (9%) and miscellaneous other secretarial, clerical and sales jobs (9%), greatly outnumbering women's employment in childcare (3%), catering (3%) and teaching (5%). The social factors which shape occupational choices and notions of what is 'appropriate' work for women have changed radically over the century. Female occupations are now typically gender-neutral and low-skill rather than typically-female and drawing on undervalued feminine skills (Hakim 1994: 445). This finding undermines the feminist idea that the *main* reason for women's low earnings is the low value placed on feminine skills (Phillips and Taylor, 1980) which would be remedied by equal value policies (Treiman and Hartmann, 1981); it is consistent with Kilbourne et al (1994: 706) finding that a devaluation of nurturant feminine skills was only a tiny factor in female low earnings. A similar observation is made by Blitz (1974) who argues we are wrong to regard the contemporary situation as a major advance on the past: women's high share of schoolteaching professions was just as important in its time as a source of status and prestige as the newer professions are today. He goes further to argue that in the USA women's representation in professional occupations peaked in the 1920s and 1930s, at the same time as the proportion of college and university degrees earned by women, so that recent 'advances' pale in comparison with achievements prior to World War Two. We can conclude that the dominant feature of female occupations has become relatively low skill work which can easily be organised on a part-time basis (see Chapter 3) and allows the short-term work horizons found in intermittent employment profiles (see Chapter 5). Thus occupational segregation has been restructured in the late twentieth century to provide separate occupations and jobs for women who anticipate a homemaker career, but may work intermittently, taking jobs which remain subordinate to, conditional and contingent on wives' non-market activities. The search for universal economic explanations for trends and changes in occupational segregation (as illustrated by Reskin and Roos, 1990) is far too narrow. Occupational segregation is marked even in contexts where employers' prejudices are eliminated, such as crime, so supply side factors and self-selection are clearly equally, if not more important (Chiplin, 1976).

Another notable finding from this historical comparison is that this fundamental restructuring of work took place without any major changes in the relative female share of total employment. Over the one hundred years 1891-1991, the female contribution to the workforce changed very little (Table 6.7), especially when a Full-Time Equivalent (FTE) measure is used for 1991. (The FTE measure takes account of the hours worked to count two part-time jobs as equivalent to one full-time job, thus measuring the volume of female employment in 1991 on the same basis as in 1891.) The DI suggests a large fall in horizontal segregation over the period,

**Table 6.7** Changes in occupational segregation 1891-1991

|  | 1891 | 1991 | 1991b |
|---|---|---|---|
| Women's share of the workforce: |  |  |  |
| % of all working aged 15 and over | 31% | - |  |
| % of economically active aged 16 and over | - | 43% |  |
| "      "      "    FTE measure | - | 39% |  |
| Number of occupations in classification | 93 | 78 |  |
| Dissimilarity Index | 74 | 58 |  |
| Percent of all occupations that are: |  |  |  |
|      Male occupations | 62 | 46 | 31 |
|      Mixed occupations | 18 | 28 | 36 |
|      Female occupations | 19 | 26 | 33 |
| Percent of all workforce in: |  |  |  |
|      Male occupations | 53 | 40 | 29 |
|      Mixed occupations | 13 | 22 | 27 |
|      Female occupations | 34 | 38 | 44 |
| Percent of men working in: |  |  |  |
|      Male occupations | 75 | 63 | 48 |
|      Mixed occupations | 13 | 23 | 33 |
|      Female occupations | 12 | 14 | 19 |
| Percent of women working in: |  |  |  |
|      Male occupations | 5 | 9 | 4 |
|      Mixed occupations | 11 | 21 | 19 |
|      Female occupations | 84 | 70 | 77 |

FTE is Full-Time Equivalent measure based on counting two part-time jobs as equivalent to one full-time job, given the hours worked in each case.
Mixed occupations are those 15-45% female (30% ±15%) in 1891 and 1991b.
Mixed occupations are those 25-55% female (40% ±15%) in 1991.
**Source:** Hakim (1994: 440) Table 2, using 100% census counts from the 1891 Census of Population for England and Wales and 10% sample data from the 1991 Census of Population for Great Britain.

and substantial change is indicated also by the re-distribution of workers across segregated and mixed occupations. Between 1891 and 1991, the proportion of the workforce in mixed occupations rose from 13 per cent to 27 per cent if a consistent definition is applied (Table 6.7). Clearly, there was too little change in women's share of total employment for this to be an important driving force for consequential changes in the degree or pattern of occupational segregation, so other social factors must provide the main explanation. Similarly cross-national comparisons have found that there appears to be no association between the female labour force participation rate or the female share of employment and the level of occupational segregation, which is shaped by other factors (Boserup, 1970; Lane, 1983; Nuss and Majka, 1983; OECD, 1985: 44, 1988: 148; Charles, 1992; Jacobs and Lim, 1992; Lewin-Epstein and Semyonov, 1992; Sorensen and Trappe, 1995).

## The sex differential in earnings

While the pattern of occupational segregation changed fundamentally over the last century, the sex differential in earnings remained stable and unvarying for a century, until the Equal Pay Act 1970 which took effect in 1975, at the same time as the Sex Discrimination Act. This contrast alone argues against any association between occupational segregation and the pay gap, let alone a close connection.

The sex differential in earnings, or pay gap, is the difference between *average* female and male hourly earnings. In practice most studies quote average female earnings as a percentage of male earnings, the obverse of the pay gap. The measure is not weighted to account for changes in the occupational or industrial structure, nor for the different occupations of men and women. This is a simple measure which can meaningfully be applied to large and small populations, time series and cross-national studies, and to comparisons of the full-time and part-time workforces. However precisely because it is so simple, it is important to ensure that we compare like with like. Normally, comparisons are drawn between the *hourly* earnings of men and women working full-time whose pay is not affected by absence from work (on sick leave for example) and usually excluding any extra pay for overtime hours. Among full-time workers, male manual workers did an average of six hours overtime per week in the period 1971-1994, compared to three hours a week for female manual workers. Non-manual men did an average of one hour overtime compared to less than half an hour for women. Thus overtime pay is an important boost to male earnings, particularly in manual jobs (Beatson, 1995: 40), and comparisons of weekly earnings are misleading. One of the most misleading comparisons is between male full-time weekly earnings and female part-time weekly pay; this is often used to 'prove' the shocking degree of pay discrimination women suffer. Trends in earnings in Britain have been monitored since 1968 through the well designed New

**Table 6.8** The declining sex differential in earnings 1886-1995

| | Female earnings as % of male earnings | | | | |
| | Adult FT workers: hourly earnings excluding overtime | | | Adult manual workers | |
| | All | Non manual | Manual | hourly earnings | weekly earnings |
|---|---|---|---|---|---|
| 1886 | | | | | 52 |
| 1960 | | | | 61 | 51 |
| 1970 | 64 | 53 | 62 | 60 | 50 |
| 1976 | 74 | 63 | 71 | 71 | 61 |
| 1984 | 74 | 62 | 69 | 70 | 61 |
| 1987 | 74 | 62 | 71 | 70 | 61 |
| 1989 | 77 | 63 | 70 | | |
| 1991 | 78 | 67 | 71 | | |
| 1993 | 79 | 68 | 71 | | |
| 1995 | 80 | 68 | 73 | | |

**Source:** Zabalza and Tzannatos (1988: 841) Table 2 updated with annual New Earnings Survey data.

Earnings Survey (NES) which provides nationally representative annual data and panel data on pay rates and earnings for the entire workforce, apart from marginal workers, and is the basis for detailed analyses of the pattern and determinants of earnings (Gregory and Thomson, 1990). The NES replaced a variety of surveys of employers providing data for earlier periods (Routh, 1980). Some other industrial societies rely on household surveys instead, such as the LFS; these provide less detailed and less accurate data on rates of pay and earnings, often with substantial non-response affecting representativeness. Others provide pay data for the manufacturing sector or the private sector only. Britain is one of the few countries with detailed information about pay in every part of the economy (Saunders and Marsden, 1981; Rubery and Fagan, 1994).

Weekly earnings are quoted for the nineteenth century because full-time work was the norm, typically with far longer hours than are worked today. From 1886 to 1970, female earnings stood at half male earnings for manual work (Table 6.8). From the mid-nineteenth century, and long before that (Middleton, 1988: 36-39), men were paid twice as much as women, even for identical work. A more detailed analysis for the period 1913-1978 reveals small fluctuations over time, but women's average pay was half men's average pay in 1913 and 1970 (Routh, 1980: 123).

The first major change in the sex differential in earnings was forced by equal pay legislation, which pushed women's earnings up very suddenly by 10 percentage points, from 64% of male earnings in 1970 to 74% by 1976 (Tzannatos and Zabalza, 1984; Zabalza and Tzannatos, 1985a,b, 1988; IRRR, 1991; Spence, 1992: 581-2). Women's earnings remained at this level for over a decade, then started to rise slowly but steadily in the late 1980s – to 77% of male earnings by 1989, to 78% in 1991, to 79% by 1993 and to 80% in 1995 (Table 6.8). Seen in the context of the long-term stability in the relative pay of men and women, this second narrowing of the pay gap is exceptional and requires explanation.

The long-term stability in the sex differential in earnings over a period when there were considerable changes in the pattern of women's employment and in job segregation undermines Hartmann's and Walby's theory outlined in Chapter 1 that job segregation has been, or is now, the key mechanism for ensuring women's subordination and economic dependence on men; it suggests instead that unequal pay was always the principal mechanism for keeping women low paid. Despite the TUC's nominal support for equal pay from 1888 onwards, trade unions were content to allow men to be paid twice as much as women for their work, right up to the mid-1970s when there were sudden and huge pay increases for women (IRRR, 1991: 3). Patriarchal theory's emphasis on job segregation can be seen as a variant of the economic theory that the concentration of women into a small number of occupations produces an oversupply of labour that reduces their wage rates (Fawcett, 1918; Edgeworth, 1922). While this is plausible, the evidence goes against it. Scholars have repeatedly noted the absence of any link between the sex differential in earnings and the pattern of job segregation (Chiplin and Sloane, 1974; Joseph, 1983: 175; Grint, 1988: 89-92). Employers colluded with male trade unions to maintain earning differences directly, with or without job segregation.

The argument from economic theory that raising women's wages relative to men's through equal pay laws would result in fewer jobs for women, all other things being equal, was similarly proven wrong by events. Clearly, all other things are not equal quite a lot of the time. In this case, job segregation ensured that demand for female labour continued to *rise* despite the rise in women's pay rates – in Britain (Joshi et al, 1985: S170-2; Zabalza and Tzannatos, 1985a,b, 1988), in Europe (Saunders and Marsden, 1981: 222) and in industrial societies generally (OECD, 1985: 72), to the discomfiture of some economists.

The sex differential in pay was larger in the USA and shrank more slowly than it did in Britain, despite the introduction of equal pay legislation a decade earlier, in 1963. Goldin (1989: 62) reports female earnings 30% to 50% of male earnings in the nineteenth century, rising to 60% by 1960, where they stayed until 1978. Female relative earnings only began to rise systematically in the 1980s, at the same time as the second rise in Britain. The pay gap is larger in male occupations and lowest in female occupations (Rytina, 1981), no doubt due to the absence of higher grade jobs in the female sector. Within Europe, Britain has remained a low pay country and women's pay relative to men's has consistently been higher in France, Germany and the Netherlands, especially after controlling for occupation. Throughout Europe, women's concentration in lower-paid occupations, and within the lower grades of each occupation, is the main cause of their lower relative earnings at the national level, but the pay gap has been narrowing (Saunders and Marsden, 1981: 232; OECD, 1985: 69-91, 1987, 1993; Rubery and Fagan, 1994).

**Explanations for the pay gap**
As noted above, vertical job segregation *within* specific occupations can account for all, or almost all of the sex difference in earnings after equal pay rules have been implemented. The clearest example was the study of teachers' pay (Employment Department, 1976). So the best way to interpret studies that explain earnings and the reasons for the differences between men and women, is to read them as analyses of the social processes that enable men to attain jobs with higher status and pay more often than women. In effect, the analyses are explaining occupational attainment or career progression, with earnings used as economists' favoured indicator of status or grade. The key issue is whether sex discrimination is one factor in the whole process – which is not quite the same thing as saying sex is a factor in the process. One common way of measuring sex discrimination is to see if occupations with a lot of women in them have lower pay, after controlling for all the key determinants of earnings. This is especially relevant to the issue of equal pay for jobs of equal value (comparable worth in the USA). Some studies treat the

simple correlation between occupational segregation and earnings as a measure of discrimination (Treiman and Hartmann, 1981). More often it is assumed that any difference in earnings not attributable to factors such as qualifications, work experience and tenure must be due to discrimination (Sorensen, 1989). Results are in practice inconclusive, partly due to problems of data quality, partly due to a failure to differentiate between subgroups of women which, as noted in Chapters 4 and 5, has become essential.

The enormous number of papers in this field are reviewed by Treiman and Hartmann (1981), Cain (1986: 749-59) and Sorensen (1989). Most studies claim to be theory-driven. In practice, they are data-driven: the independent variables used to predict earnings are determined by data availability; hypotheses are constructed primarily with a view to their being testable rather than their being meaningful and worthwhile; quite often poor proxy measures are used, such as *potential* work experience as measured by age, rather than *actual* work experience as measured in work history information; quite often key variables such as educational qualifications and occupational grade are measured only in the broadest manner. This last factor is important: analyses routinely fail to discriminate between the various levels and types of higher education qualification, grouping *all* post-secondary school education and qualifications into a single category, which is hopelessly crude for explaining variations in access to high earning occupations. For example, most analyses do not distinguish between the qualifications of a nurse and a medical specialist or hospital consultant, between the qualifications of a primary school teacher and a university professor, so it is not surprising that analyses fail to explain the difference in earnings between these occupations. The white-collar workforce is not only the largest, at two-thirds of all workers, it is also very heterogeneous, comprising a huge variety of skills and skill levels which ought to be taken into account in studies. Excuses are the norm throughout, on the grounds that weak results are better than none at all. This is doubtful, especially when weak results are subsequently treated as conclusive. Because the PSID and NLS datasets provide better data for the USA on earnings linked to work histories than is available for Britain from any source, the bulk of the literature on this topic is North American, with some notable exceptions (Zabalza and Tzannatos, 1985a,b; Main, 1988b; Sloane, 1990). The problem is to control for *all* the variables that directly determine occupational attainment and earnings, that is qualifications, occupational tenure or tenure with the employer (a measure of firm-specific experience), total years of work experience, hours worked per week and occupational grade, plus a host of less important contextual correlates of earnings such as trade union coverage, region, company or establishment size, public/private sector location and industry, which produce variations in earnings within a given occupational grade at the national level (Gregory and Thomson, 1990). Given the important differences between internal and external labour markets noted earlier (Figure 3), we should also differentiate between them. Tenure with a particular employer and the number of promotions are especially important in internal labour markets; total work experience and qualifications are more important in external labour markets. However most analyses treat the labour market as single and homogeneous, for simplicity, and treat male and female workers as two homogeneous groups. Given the heterogeneity of female labour market behaviour observed in Chapter 5, this undifferentiated approach to explaining female earnings is bound to produce weak results.

With men and women treated as homogeneous groups, it would seem to be a simple matter to assess the relative importance of the main determinants of occupational attainment and earnings, controlling for all relevant contextual variables. In practice this is never achieved in national studies. Some studies include work experience and tenure variables; others include occupational grade; others include a range of contextual variables. No national dataset offers *all* the relevant variables in combination, so all studies give only a partial view. Yet researchers regularly conclude that the proportion of the pay gap not explained by their partial analysis is an adequate measure of sex discrimination rather than an indication of how partial and incomplete their analysis has been. Of the available studies, Sorensen (1989) includes the widest range of detailed variables, including work experience, tenure, part-time work, years of education, qualifications (crudely classified) and a range of contextual variables, as well as occupational sex ratios. She finds that education and experience explain one-quarter of the pay gap; industry and other contextual variables explain another quarter; the % female variable another quarter; leaving one quarter of the pay gap explained by omitted variables such as job grade, motivation and workplans. Occupational segregation variables are often interpreted as measuring discrimination, or the devaluation of women's occupations. But this is not yet proven. Given the pattern of occupational segregation shown in Table 6.3, this result could arise because of the absence of any female-dominated occupations at professional level.

Female heterogeneity cannot be treated as an optional extra in research analyses because it is *only* among employment career planners that earnings is an appropriate measure of occupational achievement. As noted in Chapters 4 and 5, women's workplans are not just different from men's, they are divergent among themselves. There are more fundamental qualitative differences between the minority of women who plan a homemaker career but end up working at times of financial need and the minority of women who plan continuous employment and almost achieve their aims, than between male and female career planners. The large middle group of undecided drifters are more appropriately classified as having modern homemaker careers than with the minority determined to pursue employment careers. As noted in Chapter 4, it is only those who plan continuous employment careers who achieve higher occupational grades and earnings. Aiming for a good job is a necessary and essential first step towards getting one; high earnings rarely happen by chance. The analyses in Chapter 5 suggest that in the absence of information on career plans, the best alternative operational definition might be continuous full-time year-round employment with only one or no domestic breaks. However analyses of earnings and so-called tests of human capital theory never draw such distinctions between subgroups of women, even when they have the necessary information. It is hardly surprising that Rosenfeld and Spenner (1992) found relatively chaotic unplanned employment careers in their sample of young women aged up to 30 years, since they overlook the fact that the vast majority of these women planned (modern) homemaker careers with work a subsidiary activity! Some use marital status as a proxy for career plans and work commitment, a weak proxy as most single people anticipate marriage and some wives pursue careers (Roos, 1983).

Because economists always analyse earnings, and have no alternative and additional measures of the rewards, value or utility of a job, they are obliged to treat earnings as the only measure of 'success' even for women planning the homemaker career in either its traditional or modern variants. Research shows that in this group convenience factors and good social relations at work are more important than the desire to maximise earnings at the expense of all else. It is hardly surprising that studies relying on earnings as the sole characteristic of jobs and occupations to be measured do not always yield meaningful results. For example Polachek's (1979) thesis that women's choice of occupation and concentration in non-professional occupations could be explained by their intermittent employment was quickly converted into hypotheses about maximising earnings or minimising wage depreciation from interrupted employment in typically-female occupations generally, with mixed or negative results in this reformulation (Beller, 1982; England, 1982, 1984; Corcoran, Duncan and Ponza, 1984). Polachek's thesis is consistent with the broad pattern of occupational segregation, in particular the development of a segregated part-time workforce in Britain and many other European societies, as noted above. There is a strong association between discontinuous employment patterns and part-time work, despite the fact that most part-time jobs are permanent, and intermittent employment reduces earnings as much as or more than part-time work (Corcoran, Duncan and Ponza, 1984; Elias, 1988; Main, 1988b: 117-8). It is also generally true that interrupted employment produces some wage depreciation on return to the labour market, although this may be repaired fairly quickly (Mincer and Ofek, 1982; Corcoran, Duncan and Ponza, 1984; Zabalza and Arrufat, 1985). Polachek's thesis fails as a general and complete explanation for occupational segregation, when pushed to the extreme of explaining job choices for all women and without making distinctions between women planning a career (who have few or no interruptions) and women *not* planning to work long-term, who are most likely to have a change of occupation and discontinuous work histories, if they return to the labour market after a long domestic break (Dex, 1987). However the failure to provide a full explanation for occupational segregation does not invalidate the usefulness of human capital theory in pointing up the importance of work experience, job tenure, hours worked and continuity of employment as major determinants of occupational grade and earnings (Department of Employment, 1976; Corcoran, 1979; Corcoran and Duncan, 1979; Corcoran, Duncan and Ponza, 1984: 184-5; Zabalza and Arrufat, 1985; Goldin and Polachek, 1987; Goldin, 1990: 73; Sloane, 1990: 150-5; Wellington, 1994). The theory is also useful in underlining the importance of plans and worklife expectations on behaviour, such as investment in work-related training and attitudes to promotion, the main problem being that these are never actually measured directly! O'Neill (1985) and O'Neill and Polachek (1993) explain the narrowing of the sex differential in wages in the USA from 1976 onwards into the 1980s as due to measurable gains in women's job tenure, work experience and qualifications, an increase in employment in integrated occupations and a small decline in female labour turnover. Similarly Hakim (1992) found that earnings differences between men and women fell in the late 1980s, in a period of rising full-time work rates among women, rising work commitment among women working full-time and part-time, the expansion of integrated occupations and sharp increases in women's share of professional occupations. So human capital theory can explain recent changes in the pay gap.

Four recent studies testify to the importance of employment profiles and to the frustratingly haphazard nature of analyses of earnings. An analysis of NLS data on earnings among young people in their 20s and 30s in full-time employment showed work experience to be the only important explanation of the pay gap, accounting for one-quarter in this age group, two to four times larger than the impact of the % female in occupations and dwarfing the impact of the authors' favoured thesis of a significant bias against occupations employing nurturant feminine skills which are devalued in the market economy (Kilbourne *et al*, 1994). An analysis of earnings among adult employees aged 25 to 62 years in 1985 based on PSID data failed to control for occupation or industry and found work experience prior to working for the current employer to have a *negative* impact on earnings! However other work history and tenure variables were important, in particular total years employed full-time, years out of the labour force and years of training in the current position, which together explained 38 per cent and 31 per cent of the pay gap in 1976 and 1985 respectively (Wellington, 1994). Interestingly, tenure with the current employer, a measure of firm-specific skills, was more important in 1985 than in 1976, favouring men who always had tenures at least twice as long as those of women. These results are probably due to differences between men and women in their propensity to enter career-track occupations rather than short-term jobs. An analysis of the work histories and earnings of law school graduates 15 years after graduation, at age 40 and over, showed that hours worked and employment history variables – in particular working part-time for a short period to care for children

(3 years on average) and frequent job changes – accounted for over half the wage gap between men and women. If differences in the types of job held are treated as personal choices, three-quarters of the earnings gap was explained. Most important variables were already controlled by comparing the graduates of a single law school, so this study provides strong evidence that earnings differences observed 15 years later are due partly to preferences for particular types of work or career, partly due to women choosing to take time out to care for small children, and partly to work history characteristics such as number of years practising as a lawyer and annual hours worked. Men chose private practice more often, which involved extremely long hours as well as rapid salary growth. Women more often chose public sector employment, with shorter hours and lower earnings. Having children did not, of itself, affect a woman's earnings, only if she took time out to care for them herself despite the fact that she could clearly afford quality child care. However 40 per cent of the female graduates remained childless by age 40. Wood, Corcoran and Courant (1993) note that some of these outcomes may reflect discrimination rather than choice, especially for the childless women. On the other hand these women earned enough for them to make real choices between higher earnings and more time for other activities. Finally, a study of MBA graduates showed that earnings differences were fully explained by human capital factors plus an allowance for performance-related pay additions which pushed up male earnings. Women tended to choose jobs with fixed or predictable earnings, whereas men more often chose jobs with a substantial element of pay contingent on performance, consistent with research showing sex differences in risk aversion (Chauvin and Ash, 1994). On the other hand, employers may choose men for certain jobs because they believe men to be more highly motivated to succeed than are women. Without personal interview information on motives and plans, the interpretation of multivariate analyses is pure speculation, whether theory-driven or not.

Some of the most important processes that contribute to greater career success among men than women are invisible, not just unmeasured but unmeasurable. One example is the 'freezing out' process employed by men and women, consciously or otherwise, to people in sex-atypical jobs. This matters most in senior positions, and management and professional occupations are often male-dominated. Another problem is the unstated, and perhaps unconscious, assumptions about what a manager looks like, as the following example demonstrates.

Statistical analyses of routine administrative records in British national government administration revealed that when promotion boards included a female member, the proportion of female applicants accepted as suitable for promotion was significantly higher than with all-male promotion boards. Because of the size of national government administration, promotion boards were normally held at regular intervals, nationwide, with standardised and transparent procedures for shortlisting candidates, interviewing and grading the promotability of candidates to the next grade up without reference to any particular job, on the basis of general criteria of proven competence and future potential. Candidates who were passed as 'fitted for promotion' would subsequently have informal interviews with people whose job vacancies appealed to them, to match promotees to particular jobs. However the main promotions procedures were as impersonal and free from gender bias as anyone could make them, unconnected from particular job vacancies and any personal preferences of managers seeking to fill vacancies in their sections. Nonetheless, statistical analyses carried out by the personnel department showed that the sex composition of the promotion board that interviewed candidates made a significant difference to the outcome. Promotion boards were then required to include at least one female member. The proportion of women sweeping through the barriers into senior levels started to rise sharply, to the discomfiture of men of average talent who previously benefitted from the sex-role stereotyping that profiled managers in masculine terms. No study is available to explain exactly what was changed by the presence of a single female member. We only know that a single female on every board made a difference to outcomes. We also know that survey datasets never contain information on these hidden social processes that have profound effects on women's career success.

Some women escape the restrictions of large organisations, where other people (usually men) define their abilities and potential (usually narrowly), by becoming self-employed consultants, an option that is especially accessible to professionals and technical experts, and was given moral support (but little else) by government policy in the 1980s. They escape the sex stereotyping of colleagues for that of customers, as illustrated by F International, a home-based company set up to employ homeworking computing specialists, especially programmers. F International started small and stayed small until its owner changed her name from Stephanie Shirley (a recognisably female name) to Steve Shirley (a recognisably male name), after which work flowed in and business boomed. The greater success of male self-employed entrepreneurs is due in part to this hidden discrimination which always gives men the benefit of the doubt and almost never gives women an even chance.

It is obvious that analyses of earnings and of the pay gap can offer few pointers for action and policy innovations, as well as being routinely partial and inconclusive. Case studies seem to offer a far more promising method for explanatory research in this field. Economists hardly ever use this research design; it is popular among sociologists who rarely study quantitative topics such as earnings. Once again, the failure of research is due to disciplinary divisions within the social sciences that impede worthwhile multidisciplinary studies, in this case in economic sociology.

## Conclusions

The pattern of occupational segregation is more complex than has been assumed. It is not a simple case of men being concentrated in the higher grade and higher paid occupations while women are concentrated in lower grade and low paid occupations. The occupational structure is dominated by horizontal occupational segregation except for the very top grades of highly paid professional and managerial occupations. This picture only emerges when we separate integrated occupations from the segregated sector, and it explains the variable results obtained from attempts to measure the association between the % female in an occupation and earnings: much depends on the degree of detail in the occupational classification used, especially for the higher grades. The sex differential in earnings is not distributed evenly throughout the workforce, as is often assumed, but increases as one moves up the occupational structure in Britain (Sloane, 1990: 134) and generally in Europe (Rubery and Fagan, 1994: xxix, 191). Our analysis has also clarified that it is mainly in the higher grades of professional and managerial occupations that women lose out. Lower earnings are otherwise due more to part-time jobs and intermittent employment than to job segregation. This is probably why comparable worth (equal value) policies implemented by employers in the USA and in Australia have generally raised women's earnings by only 5-6 per cent, after allowance is made for contemporary pay upratings, and rarely exceed 10 per cent (Steinberg, 1988: 207; Ehrenberg, 1989; Willborn, 1989: 140, 147; Killingsworth, 1990: 277; Kahn and Meehan, 1992: 13; Gunderson, 1994). Patriarchy cannot yet be ruled out as part of any explanation for women's position in society, but occupational segregation does not appear to be quite so important an economic weapon as Hartmann and Walby believed it to be. Human capital theory provides a more powerful explanation of changes in earnings and earnings differences between men and women.

Attempts to explain the pay gap are numerous but invariably partial. The best studies still fail to incorporate all relevant variables and to measure key variables in sufficient detail. The results leave room for continuing disagreement over causal processes. Almost all the pay gap can be explained by women's failure to attain the higher grades within occupations. The question is, why does this happen? The general drift of research results is that the main explanation for this outcome is that men are more likely to put in the longer hours, the more continuous employment and the longer tenures that lead to the top jobs. However a subsidiary factor, accounting for maybe one-quarter to one-third of the pay gap seems to be discrimination, unconscious as well as invisible, that excludes women from the top jobs and the highest earnings. Much clearer and more differentiated explanations are obtained by analyses that take account of female heterogeneity, as noted in Chapter 5. It appears that this approach is needed here too. The unit of analysis in social science is whole people and their careers (Dex, 1987), not the job changes, transitions and employment flows that have become the focus of so many data analyses that can only speculate blindly about the meaning and causal processes behind the results obtained for variables rather than people (Rosenfeld and Spenner, 1992). The polarisation of the female workforce is too pronounced for us to ignore it any longer in research and requires different analytical approaches.

One policy response to these results is to assume women will never move into the top jobs and hence focus on comparable worth (USA) or equal value (UK) initiatives to raise women's pay in lower grade jobs. The other response is to find ways of breaking down the barriers to women's promotion into higher grade and better paid jobs. As shown in Chapter 7, European Union employment law and policy encourages both approaches (Rubery and Fagan, 1994).

# 7
# Social engineering:
# the role of law

Social policies, such as those designed to rewrite sex roles and redistribute paid and unpaid work between adults can use four mechanisms of social engineering: ideological reform and moral exhortation; legislation; fiscal policy; and institutional change. Most commonly, some combination of these tools is used. In pluralist societies like Britain, where competing interests and ideologies have to be accommodated, there can be contradictions between the implicit policies of the four tools of social engineering, so that social change is slow and uneven.

The power of moral exhortation and ideology is illustrated by the effectiveness of government campaigns to pull women into the workforce during World War Two, to do manual jobs in factories that had previously been classified as men's work. The ideology of domesticity was then revived after the war to reinstate the pre-War sexual division of labour, against some resistance from women (Summerfield, 1984; Milkman, 1987: 99-152). In China, where the strong tradition of collective adherence to the common ideology of Confucianism was transferred to communism, ideology and moral exhortation constitute a powerful tool of social engineering, as illustrated in Chapter 4 by the relatively successful transformation of sex roles after 1950, and by the success of the one-child per couple policy in a country where it had traditionally been regarded as imperative to have at least one son. By 1993, four-fifths of men and women in Beijing said a son or daughter were equally acceptable as their only child (Ma et al, 1994: 248).

In Europe, legislation prohibiting sex discrimination and promoting equal treatment of men and women in the labour force is the main tool of social engineering. It is the only mechanism common to all member states of the European Community, although most countries, like Britain, introduced national legislation at some point in the post-War period and have linked positive action programmes. Legislation promoting equality between men and women in the labour market, health and safety regulations and proposals for minimum standards for employment contracts have in practice been the principal integrationist measures of European social policy. Apart from these exceptions, there is as yet no common European social policy because nation states have so far not wanted it. In particular there is no agreement to harmonise direct taxation on earnings and state social welfare systems that are not employment-related (McCrudden, 1987: 20-22, 119-121, 186; Tsoukalis, 1993: 148-174). European sex discrimination legislation is having a major impact in Britain and the rest of Europe, over-riding national legislation.

Fiscal policy influences the employment decisions of secondary earners and, to a lesser extent, the hours worked by primary earners, by changing income tax rules and social welfare benefit rules to alter the net benefits from different quantities of wage work by one or both persons in a couple (Kay and King, 1978: 37). For example, husband and wife may be taxed separately as individuals or jointly as a couple; tax allowances and benefits may be transferrable or not. At present, home production of goods and services by a non-working wife is untaxed, but that too is a policy by default. Eligibility for key welfare benefits, such as pensions, may be dependent on a person's own employment record and contributions, or wives may be allowed to benefit from their husband's work record, or full-time housewives may be credited with pension rights despite not working. In Sweden, for example, fiscal policy proved an effective mechanism for virtually eliminating the housewife with no market work and financially dependent on her husband. Benefit rules also push women into full-time jobs as important benefits are dependent on a record of full-time work.

Social institutions are influential everywhere but almost never decisive factors in social change. Just one example is the relative importance of childcare services in facilitating women's employment. As Humphries and Rubery noted (1992: 253), female employment, in particular full-time female employment, rose in the late 1980s in Britain despite no change at all in the relative absence of childcare services. In the USA, universal no-cost childcare is estimated to increase women's labour force participation rate by just 10 percentage points (Connelly, 1991: 110). Social institutions change relatively slowly – except in small city states like Singapore, where social policy can shift sharply and quickly in response to changing needs. The choices made by individuals and couples can change much faster than social institutions, and thus need to be explained by other factors.

There is a fifth factor which affects female employment rates: the choice between a low-wage full employment policy and a high wage, high productivity and low employment policy, as illustrated by the contrast between Britain and Germany or between China and Japan. In low wage economies, families usually need two incomes to attain an adequate and secure income. However this is a general, long-term choice of economic policy which is not aimed specifically at women, although it has an impact on the number of women entering the workforce (Fine, 1992: 152).

This chapter examines the role of law in helping to redefine women's position in the labour market. It does not provide a general review of recent developments in labour law, sex discrimination law and their implications for women, which are discussed more fully by other writers (Davies and Freedland, 1984, 1993; Lewis, 1986; McCrudden, 1987; Prechal and Burrows, 1990; Ellis, 1991; Nielsen and Szyszczak, 1991; Pitt, 1992). The focus here is on the impact of equal opportunities legislation on the sexual division of labour in the workplace; its role in creating a more 'level playing field', that is, fairer competition, between male and female workers as well as between member states of the EU; and on the contribution of social science evidence to the analysis of indirect discrimination issues.

## European and national law
Sex and race discrimination are often discussed together by labour lawyers, but they pose quite different problems from a social engineering perspective. Women are a fully integrated majority in society as a whole, and differential treatment of women in the labour market derives primarily from widely accepted norms on the sexual division of labour and sex roles that are now being challenged and rewritten. Racial and ethnic minorities are small groups; they are sometimes better integrated in the labour market than in society as a whole, but exclusion is the main problem so that policies have a general aim of social inclusion by prohibiting what is most often overt prejudice and direct discrimination. In the European Union, ethnic minorities may be migrant workers who are not EU nationals and citizens, as illustrated (at present) by Turkish workers

in Germany, or they may be nationals and citizens, as illustrated by the Asian, black and Chinese minorities in Britain. European Union law prohibiting discrimination on grounds of nationality and sex discrimination developed into two of the foundation stones of the European Union, whereas there is no prohibition on discrimination against non-EU nationals. Racial discrimination is dealt with only by national law (McCrudden, Smith and Brown, 1991; Hepple, 1996).

The Treaty of Rome signed by 'the Six' (Germany, France, Italy, Belgium, the Netherlands and Luxembourg) in 1957 laid the foundation stone for the development of the current European Union, setting out aims and objectives, creating the legislation and key institutions of the EU, including the European Court of Justice (ECJ). Under the title of Social Policy, Article 119 of the Treaty of Rome laid down the principle that men and women should receive equal pay for equal work, an adaptation of ILO Convention No. 100 of 1951 which declared the principle of equal remuneration for men and women workers for work of equal value (which the UK ratified only in 1971). It is clear that the original intention of Article 119 was to specify equal pay for people doing the same job, narrowly defined. As European Community policy developed over time, the intention was clarified and broadened to include work of equal value, as set out in the Equal Pay Directive (EEC Council Directive 75/117 of 1975), and this wider interpretation was confirmed by the ECJ in 1982 (Davies and Freedland, 1984: 381, 1993: 217). The EU 'principle of equal pay' means, for the same work or work to which equal value is attributed, the elimination of all discrimination on grounds of sex with regard to all aspects and conditions of remuneration. This was followed by the Equal Treatment Directive (EEC Council Directive 76/207 of 1976) which laid down the 'principle of non-discrimination' as regards access to employment, promotion, vocational training, working conditions, termination of employment and employment-related social security benefits. The European courts (like the USA courts before them) interpreted this to encompass indirect discrimination, and the principle of equal treatment is now read as excluding all discrimination in the labour market on grounds of sex, either directly or indirectly, by reference in particular to marital or family status. The Social Security Directive (No. 79/7 of December 1978) further clarified the progressive implementation of the principle of equal treatment for men and women in matters of employment-related social security; it allowed member states to treat favourably persons with family responsibilities but it did not oblige them to do so. Two further Council Directives on Equal Treatment in Pension Schemes (Nos. 79/7 and 86/378) and a series of ECJ decisions on pension issues following on from the 1990 decision on the *Barber v. Guardian Royal Exchange Assurance Group* case (262/88 [1990] ICR 616) clarified the application of the principles of equal pay and non-discrimination to pensions. For example, the widespread practice in state and employer pension schemes of allowing women to retire with a pension at a younger age than men (typically 60 versus 65 in Britain) was ruled to discriminate in favour of women and must be abandoned.

When the UK joined the European Community in 1973, along with Denmark and Ireland, it became bound by the Treaty of Rome and the principles of equal pay and equal treatment, along with other EC legislation, given that European legislation overrides conflicting national law. In 1982, the ECJ ruled that the British government's Equal Pay Act 1970 was deficient in not making provision for equal value claims. As a result the UK was obliged to amend national legislation through the Equal Pay (Amendment) Regulations 1983 which allow claims for equal pay between men and women for work which can be shown to be of equal value carried out within the same workplace or for the same employer (Davies and Freedland, 1993: 211-218, 581-3). This case was of enormous importance in making people aware of the force of European legislation prohibiting sex discrimination in all its forms, both direct and indirect, and that national legislation would have to implement the equal pay principle. This first ECJ decision against the British government was followed by a second in 1983 which ruled that the UK Sex Discrimination Act 1975 failed to comply with the European Equal Treatment Directive, firstly in that the Act's exemption for small firms was not permissible, secondly in failing to declare void discriminatory provisions in collective agreements. This led to the Sex Discrimination Act 1986 which combined necessary amendments to sex discrimination legislation; the repeal of legislation dating back to the 1930s which imposed restrictions on women's working hours, especially nightwork; and the equalisation of retirement ages (Davies and Freedland, 1993: 583-5).

It may appear from these two cases that Britain has had difficulty in establishing the general principles of equal pay and non-discrimination in national legislation. There is no doubt that the Conservative Government's enthusiasm for European law in the 1980s in this, and other areas was minimalist. But it is inappropriate to present the problem in party political terms, as academics often do (Fredman, 1992: 119; Davies and Freedland, 1993: 583), given that the original legislation was passed by a Labour government, and the European Commission sued not only Britain but also Belgium, Denmark, France, West Germany, Luxembourg and the Netherlands for violating Article 119. The problem is rather that all member states of the EU experience genuine difficulty in implementing the simple but broad principles of equal pay and non-discrimination, since the differential treatment of men and women has long been written into most labour market practices, norms and labour law, often linked to assumptions about the sexual division of labour in the home. Implementation of the two principles thus involves a continuing process of re-examining existing practices and norms, with the courts providing a public forum for debate as to their fairness or discriminatory effects, whether intended or not. For example in the 1970s and early 1980s, the courts in Britain (also in the USA and Canada) decided it could in some cases be lawful to dismiss a pregnant woman; following ECJ rulings, such dismissals have invariably been judged discriminatory and unlawful in recent cases (Fredman, 1992: 121-2; Sohrab, 1993: 146-7), with substantial compensation paid to women dismissed from careers in the British armed services due to pregnancy (as high as £350,000 in one case). Discriminatory practices may be ruled lawful, if the employer can provide objective justification for them in national courts. One difficulty is that proof of *indirect* discrimination requires assessment of social scientific and statistical evidence which goes contrary to British law's traditional focus on the circumstances of individual cases. There are also major practical problems in rewriting rules and redesigning practices so as to pass the non-discrimination tests. These are illustrated by a series of ECJ rulings in the 1990s on pensions which, as a form of deferred pay, are subject to the equal pay principle. Redesigning pension schemes that have been running for decades on the basis of differential treatment is no easy matter, and while the courts can decide what is unlawful, they rarely offer constructive advice on the design of new arrangements.

It is also not true that European non-discrimination principles invariably benefit women. For example the ECJ approved the abolition of unequal pension ages in Europe by raising women's pension age to that of men without compensation to those affected, and some commentators objected to the repeal of 'protective' laws controlling women's work hours in Britain. The principle of non-discrimination means that women become subject to the same competitive market forces as men, and it does not permit any reverse discrimination at all. For example in the 1987 decision on the *Bilka* case (*Bilka-Kaufhaus v. Weber von Hartz*, 170/84 [1987] ICR 110), and in several other cases, the ECJ has rejected arguments that employers should take into account women's family responsibilities and be obliged to make special arrangements for them, such as providing childcare facilities, special working hours or special pension arrangements. Employers only have an obligation not to discriminate. Similarly special advantages granted to working mothers by the French state, including leave when a child is ill and an allowance for childcare costs, were ruled discriminatory and unlawful by the ECJ in 1988 (Commission v. France 312/86 [1988] ECR 6315). Positive discrimination (for example preferring a woman in job recruitment) is ruled out by European law; affirmative action is allowed in British race relations and sex discrimination law, for example in relation to training. It is the function of the Commission for Racial Equality and the Equal Opportunities Commission to promote equality of opportunity through positive action *inter alia* (Pitt, 1992: 31). In any event, the effectiveness of positive discrimination is doubtful (Hepple and Szyszczak, 1992). Finally, European 'social policy' was prompted initially by concern with fair competition and deals exclusively with the labour market and workers (Bercusson, 1990; Hepple, 1990; Nielsen and Szyszczak, 1991; Tsoukalis, 1993: 151; Hepple, 1996); it does not extend to other areas or other social groups, which remain subject to national law and regulations.

**Social science evidence on indirect discrimination**
The prohibition of *indirect* sex discrimination is the most important innovation of British and European labour law (Redmond, 1986; Pitt, 1992; Hepple, 1996). British courts adapted slowly to dealing with discrimination cases that are not based on overt prejudice and to taking account of European law in their judgements. Perhaps most important, indirect discrimination cases necessarily involve

arguments about an employer's requirements having broadly similar or disproportionate effects on women compared to men and hence statistical evidence on the proportions meeting the requirement. Yet there are no arrangements for judges to have access to relevant social science or statistical advice. This has undoubtedly been one factor in the courts' reluctance to address statistical evidence and in judgements that appear ill-informed to the social scientist. The absence of social science expertise in the British courts, and even the ECJ, is in marked contrast to North America, where indirect discrimination cases frequently involve consideration of regression analyses of large datasets of a kind more common in social science journals than law journals (Redmond, 1986; Willborn, 1989). The gulf separating labour lawyers and labour sociologists is illustrated by a debate in the *Industrial Law Journal* on the employment rights of full-time and part-time employees under British legislation then applying: statistical comparisons of the characteristics of the full-time and part-time workforces clashed with the labour lawyer's focus on the rights of individual workers (Hakim, 1989a; Disney and Szyszczak, 1989).

Sometimes the statistical evidence is simple. A landmark decision by the House of Lords in March 1994 (*R v Secretary of State for Employment, ex parte Equal Opportunities Commission*, [1994] IRLR 176) ruled that British laws excluding part-timers working fewer than 16 hours a week from certain statutory employment rights failed the European non-discrimination principle. Indirect discrimination was easily proven in this case, as the majority of employees working over 16 hours a week are men and the great majority of those working less than 16 hours a week are women. The decision thus rested on whether there was any objective justification for the exclusion of part-timers working fewer than 16 hours, and as the government chose to rely once again on economic theory with no supporting factual evidence that the exclusion resulted in greater availability of part-time jobs, the government lost. The irony of this case is that the House of Lords decision forced the government to accept more extensive employment rights for part-time employees than had been proposed by the EC's Social Charter and Directives on atypical workers that the government had previously rejected (Hakim, 1995a: 440-1). Similarly in 1989 the ECJ ruled that the German government failed to offer objective justification for the exclusion from sick pay schemes of part-timers working less than

10 hours a week or less than 45 hours a month, the majority of whom are women (*Rinner-Kühn v. FWW Spezial-Gebaudereinigung GmbH & Co. KG*, 171/88 [1989] IRLR 493).

In other cases the statistical evidence becomes slightly more sophisticated: for example it must be shown that the proportion of women (or part-timers) fulfilling certain conditions are 'considerably smaller' than the proportion of men, or that a 'much lower' proportion of women work full-time. As yet there is no agreement on appropriate measures, for example on whether a 20 percentage point difference constitutes sufficient evidence of a differential impact or of differential eligibility. Some British courts have rejected a 8-9 percentage point difference in eligibility rates as not proving indirect discrimination, while others have accepted such evidence as adequate. In 1995, the Court of Appeal ruled that the government's decision to increase the qualifying period for unfair dismissal rights from one year to two years in 1985 was in breach of the non-discrimination principle, as the two year qualifying period excluded a third of women but only a quarter of men in employment. This means an average 9 percentage point difference between men and women was accepted as sufficient proof of indirect discrimination, overruling the Divisional Court in a judicial review proceeding (*R v Secretary of State for Employment, ex parte Seymour-Smith* [1995] IRLR 464). Table 5.4 shows an 11 percentage point difference between men and women in the proportion with less than 2 years' tenure (41% versus 30%), but it also shows roughly the same difference in the proportions with less than one year's tenure with their employer (27% versus 19%), so that raising the qualifying period from one to two years did not significantly change the situation. Most social scientists would regard a 10 percentage point difference as too small to constitute a 'considerable' difference and proof of indirect discrimination. Tests of statistical significance are of course irrelevant here as the issue is substantive significance (Hakim, 1987a: 6-7) and LFS samples are large enough to ensure statistical significance for even a 3-5 percentage point difference between working men and women. In general, the statistical evidence employed in British courts (and the ECJ) is simple and the criteria applied to prove indirect discrimination seem to be haphazard, in contrast with the hairsplitting finesse of assessments of points of law. This is in marked contrast with the contribution of complex social science evidence in comparable worth lawsuits and policies in the USA.

In a sense, comparable worth policies were introduced in the USA as a result of faulty social science evidence. Equal pay was introduced in 1963 and enforced, but women's earnings remained stubbornly at an unvarying 60% of male earnings among full-time year-round workers (Goldin, 1990: 59). In the late 1970s, the Equal Employment Opportunity Commission (EEOC) requested a study of comparable worth as an alternative route to reducing the pay gap. The report of the committee duly concluded that job segregation and the practice of paying lower wages for women's occupations were the main causes of the pay gap, so that equalising earnings on the basis of comparable worth (equal value) represented the only way of closing the pay gap (Treiman and Hartmann, 1981). The report stated, on the basis of the evidence then available, that human capital factors failed to explain the pay gap, even though one study by Corcoran (1979) showed that half the pay gap was explained by work history and job tenure variables and other studies showed vertical job segregation to explain one-third or more (Treiman and Hartmann, 1981: 22-3, 32-3, 55-6). Although comparable worth remained controversial in the USA, both politically and among economists, the report was persuasive enough for some 20 states and employers to adopt pay systems based on comparable worth principles that Congress had explicitly excluded from equal pay laws. This often entailed detailed analyses of the correlates of earnings within the organisation or across all state employees. As noted in Chapter 6 (page 186), comparable worth pay policies typically increase female earnings by only 5%-6%, far less than was suggested by Treiman and Hartmann's report, leading some to conclude that even the most carefully constructed job evaluation systems may not be entirely free from sexism, with a bias in favour of work done by men.

An alternative explanation is that Treiman and Hartmann's analysis was mistaken, failing to identify the real importance of human capital variables alongside sex discrimination as determinants of earnings. Historical analyses by Smith and Ward (1984) and Goldin show that female heterogeneity was the hidden factor that led to incorrect analyses. Female work rates rose in the post-War period because women with little work experience were pulled into the labour market. The pay gap stayed constant after equal pay was introduced because there was no change in average female work experience from the

1920s to the 1980s (Goldin, 1989, 1990: 30-42, 214). The pay gap then declined steadily throughout the 1980s due to increases in women's work experience, job tenure, qualifications and related human capital variables (O'Neil and Polachek, 1993). While Treiman and Hartmann were right to conclude that women's jobs were undervalued, they were wrong to conclude that discrimination was a more important explanatory factor than human capital variables.

Willborn (1989) compares the legal processes and outcomes of comparable worth lawsuits in the USA and equal value cases in Britain, focusing on two case studies: Helen Castrilli, the secretary who was the central plaintiff in the class action against the State of Washington in 1982, and Julie Hayward, the cook in the Cammell Laird shipyard who successfully brought the first equal value claim in Britain in 1984. He shows how the contribution of statistical evidence differs between class actions and individual claims, and how different are the outcomes of the two types of case in terms of wage adjustments and in terms of the breadth of application of the judgements.

In some cases, it is social science concepts, rather than statistics, that are used to prove indirect discrimination. The Meade-Hill case (*Meade-Hill and another v. The British Council* [1995] IRLR 478) is of interest also because it shows how women are using the law to *prevent* equal treatment with men. In 1990, Mrs Meade-Hill, a public official in London, was promoted from a clerical grade to the rank of Executive Officer (EO), the lowest managerial grade in white collar work. The contractual terms for this grade, like all managerial grades, included a mobility rule requiring people to work anywhere in Britain if so directed by the employer. Her employers did not in fact ask her to work outside London, but she sought to have the mobility rule judged unlawful anyway, just in case. Her argument, which was accepted by all parties as common ground, was that the mobility clause was acceptable to men, who are primary earners, but was a condition that women could not easily comply with as most women are secondary earners – hence was indirectly discriminatory. Secondary earners were defined very simply as women earning less than their husbands or partners. In her case, her husband was a computer engineer who earned considerably more than she did although she worked full-time.

The case is interesting because the secondary earner label was the key, indeed only argument for refusing to accept the usual terms and conditions of a management position, albeit the lowest grade of management. Executive Officers were a national career grade in government service, with a London salary scale of £13,500-£16,700, right on the average weekly earnings for full-time employees in Britain in 1994. The grade was large enough to be separately identified in the 1991 Census results, which showed 82,000 EOs, of whom 54% were men and 91% worked full-time. Thus Mrs Meade-Hill was an entirely representative full-time employee in an integrated career grade attracting national average earnings of the sort that constitute a breadwinner wage for men supporting a family. Because she earned less than her husband, an almost universal characteristic of wives, she was classified as a secondary earner who could legitimately be exempted from employment conditions routinely applied to men in the same occupational grade. The mobility rule is in fact disliked just as much by men, who can no longer assume their wives will necessarily be agreeable to moving with them. The case demonstrates that the law can be used to institutionalise the concept of secondary earner and to legitimise preferential treatment for women which is not entirely dissimilar from earlier protectionist legislation. This case stereotypes all working wives as secondary earners, disregarding female heterogeneity.

### The problem of female heterogeneity

The equal treatment principle implicitly treats working women as a homogeneous group in the same way that men are treated as a homogeneous group, insisting that the same rules, conditions and benefits should be applied to all workers, male and female (unless there is objective justification for doing otherwise). Given that the female adult population is heterogenous in its work orientations and labour market behaviour, and given increasing polarisation of the female workforce, the equal treatment principle will thus sometimes have unpredictable or surprising effects. One example has been given above, in a court ruling accepting that secondary earners should be treated differently from primary earners in order to avoid indirect discrimination. Another example is the ECJ's 1994 decision that part-timers cannot have their own separate overtime rates.

In *Stadt Lengerich v. Helmig* (15 December 1994) the ECJ ruled that there is no discrimination contrary to European law where a collective agreement provides overtime supplements will be paid only when the normal working hours for full-time workers are exceeded. This decision involved six joined cases from Germany on whether Article 119 requires employers to pay part-timers overtime supplements when they work in excess of their own contractual hours. Angelika Helmig, a married women with two young children, was employed as a tutor in the town of Lengerich's youth centre, normally working 19.5 hours a week compared to full-timers' 38.5 hours a week. Collective agreements for public service workers provided for 25% overtime supplements to hourly pay for people in her grade, which her employer argued were not required. The ECJ decided that as part-time and full-time workers were paid the same overtime rates, there was no unequal treatment and no discrimination. There was thus no need to consider whether discrimination could be justified, for example by the fact that overtime hours have a greater impact on the discretionary free time of full-timers than of part-timers.

The Advocate General's Opinion which preceded the ECJ ruling noted that full-time hours were uniform and fixed, by statute or collective agreement, whereas part-time hours can vary from 5 hours a week to 30 hours a week. Paying an overtime supplement to part-timers on an individual basis would create inequality of treatment, since one part-timer might be paid an overtime supplement for working an extra hour that was part of normal hours for another part-timer as well as for full-timers. Part-timers would thus be treated more favourably than full-timers, progressively so, the shorter their normal hours.

The ECJ has generally ruled that employers must give part-timers the same employment benefits as they offer to full-time workers, but it has also consistently refused to allow part-timers better than *pro rata* benefits or any transitional arrangements that would leave part-timers advantaged compared with full-timers. For example in the group of decisions in late 1994 on occupational pensions, the ECJ confirmed that part-timers had the right to join employers' pension schemes, with retrospective effect, but also that part-timers would have to pay in the appropriate backdated employee contributions in order to benefit retrospectively. There is extensive evidence that even when they are eligible to join employers' pension schemes, part-timers are much less likely to join: no more than half do so (Martin and Roberts, 1984: Table 5.14; Rubery et al, 1994: Table

6.7). Similarly, as noted in Chapter 2, part-time workers often limit their hours and earnings so as to ensure that there are no income tax or social security deductions from their earnings (Hakim, 1987b: 109-12, 192-6; Hakim, 1989b: 473, 493). Given the relatively small *pro rata* pensions earned by part-timers, this may be economically rational behaviour.

In sum, the non-discrimination principle applied as between men and women treats all women uniformly, ignoring the differences noted in Chapters 3 and 5 between employment-centred women who work continuously and home-centred secondary earners. Women who work part-time and intermittently are getting improved employment rights and benefits as a result of ECJ rulings, but these benefits will not put them on an equal level with people who work full-time and continuously in long-term careers. Some feminist lawyers reacted with surprise and anger at the ECJ ruling that part-time workers could not be paid overtime supplements on an individual basis. They overlook the fact that laws prohibiting sex discrimination do not alter the pre-existing diversity of the female population, the polarisation of the female workforce and their economic consequences.

### Conclusions

In sex discrimination cases, the ECJ only adjudicates on basic principles in the application of Article 119 of the Treaty of Rome and EC Directives, leaving national courts to deal with factual matters, including the crucial decisions on whether the employer's reasons for a given practice constitute objectively justified economic reasons unrelated to sex, correspond to a real need in the enterprise, are appropriate and necessary to the objective pursued. National differences in employment practices will thus remain. However there is no doubt that the rigorous application of non-discrimination principles is forcing everyone to review and rethink rules, customs and practices that may have been applied for decades but are discriminatory, such as unequal retirement ages for men and women. Within Europe, legislation is an important tool of social engineering. The process was strengthened by the controversial 1991 Francovich case (*Francovich v Italian Republic* [1992] IRLR 84) in which the ECJ ruled that a member state could be forced to pay damages for any harm or loss caused to individuals as a result of the state's failure to implement an EC Directive properly. However legislation is only one policy tool among the many available, and it has its limits, as feminist lawyers are beginning to recognise (Hepple and Szyszczak, 1992; Fredman, 1992; More, 1993; Sohrab, 1993; Fenwick and Hervey, 1995).

The law sets out the (new) rules of the game, but it is not pro-active: it only comes into play when a conflict has arisen and discussions are conducted in an adversarial context. There is a huge range of issues that cannot be addressed through legislation and require other tools of social engineering. One example is the 'freezing out' process which can eliminate people from sex-atypical occupations as noted in Chapter 6: the law can address overt acts of prejudice but not silent non-cooperation by colleagues. Another example is the social and psychological processes that inhibit women functioning effectively in senior positions and management posts, as noted in Chapter 4. Most important of all, European law only covers the labour force and even national law is restricted to public roles and activities. Neither European nor national law address the sexual division of labour in the household, which is taken to be a private matter in Western democracies, subject to private bargaining between partners. Employment law has no interest in these private arrangements and employers are not required to take account of them. It follows that labour law also has no role in sorting out any problems caused by female heterogeneity and the polarisation of women's employment. The principles of equal pay and equal treatment are powerful but limited instruments for redesigning sex roles and the opportunities open to men and women. The law can change the treatment of women in the workforce; it cannot change women themselves.

# 8
# Conclusions: female heterogeneity and workforce polarisation

What has been demonstrated by this review of the theory and empirical evidence on women's employment? First, that a great many true lies are told about women's employment in Britain and in industrial society generally. Second, that the most effective mechanism for subordinating women is neither exclusion from the workforce nor segregation within it but the ideology of the sexual division of labour in the home and the ideology of sexual differences. Prisons of the mind are always more effective than prisons of the body. Third, because women are so eager to raise their own children personally, it is women who are the main propagators and the main beneficiaries of the ideology of the sexual division of labour, both by precept and example. How many mothers tell their daughters that they should never marry, never have children, because they will live to regret it bitterly? And how many daughters, faced with a daily demonstration of what marriage and motherhood does to women, recoil in horror to say No! Never! Not I! and rush to enrol at the nearest college to enable themselves to be self-supporting? Fourth, the heterogeneity of women's preferences for homemaking or employment careers is pronounced and is unlikely to disappear. Fifth, this heterogeneity is the source of the polarisation in women's labour market behaviour. Sixth, sex differentials will ultimately disappear at the top of the occupational structure, where women conform increasingly to the male employment profile of continuous full-time employment, but there will be continuing sex differentials in attitudes and behaviour within the secondary labour market and within couples with a (modern) homemaker wife. Seventh, paradoxically, it is in the group at the top of the occupational hierarchy that the potential for sex discrimination remains the greatest, remaining hidden due to the lack of detailed information on professional and managerial women in national datasets, and due to the focus on the manufacturing sector in industrial relations research (Rubery and Fagan, 1995b). Eighth, there is evidence to support all three main theories explaining women's subordinate social and economic position, so that they must be seen as complementary rather than competing.

## True lies

A great many true lies are told about women. It is said that women's work is invisible in industrial society because women are family helpers, do home-based work, work in the informal economy, do voluntary work. All of this is true. The lie is the unstated implication that women are distinctive in engaging in these activities; that their important contribution is hidden from sight by not being recorded in national statistical surveys; that the activities are devalued by being excluded from the definition of economic activity. All of these conclusions are untrue. Men also do a great variety of informal and unrecorded work, sometimes displaying the same level and pattern of activity as women (as in voluntary work), sometimes doing more than women (in the case of home-based work), sometimes less than women (as illustrated by family helpers). Men and women are equally likely to have caring responsibilities for elderly or infirm people, although women devote more time to childcare. Domestic work is done by men as well as women, although women do more of it. However men do many more hours of market work than women, *in addition to* all their other informal work activities. The most recent time use surveys indicate that men do more work than women, using the term in its wide sense of activities producing goods and services. Employment statistics do not give the complete picture, but they do not give an entirely misleading picture of the balance of work between men and women. This may be part of the explanation for women living longer than men, despite the fact that women wear themselves out in childbirth. In practice, men still work more and longer hours and wear out faster. The most telling inequality in society today is the sex difference in average life expectancy, which is increasing over time. Life expectancy at birth has almost doubled in Britain, from 40 years for men and 42 years for women in 1838-54, to 74 years for men and 79 years for women in 1990-95. The sex difference in average life expectancy has more than doubled, from just under 2 years to 5.4 years in favour of women in Britain, with even higher sex differences in France (8 years), the USA (7 years), Germany, Sweden and Japan (6 years). The EU average is 7 years and the sex difference showed no signs of falling in the post-War decades (European Commission, 1995b: 36). The sex differential in life expectancy is almost as large as the social class differential, yet only the latter is treated as inegalitarian. Women in developing countries have heavy workloads; most women in industrial society do not. Case studies that focus on the minority of women with young children at home have given a misleading picture of the average housewife's workload. They also show that many full-time housewives make their own misery: their long hours include a substantial volume of unnecessary make-work. As an occupation, the job of housewife is hard to beat: short hours, reasonable security of tenure and average rewards in terms of status and income. It may be boring, but so are most jobs. The price is dependence on another person, but most housewives value their autonomy in comparison with the subservience of waged labour in the market economy. The choice is finely balanced.

Women do not make completely free choices, it is argued, hence are forced into low-paid part-time jobs or forced into marriage instead of the financial independence of wage labour. This is true in part. Again the implication is that men have real choices and more choices to make. This is the lie. Most men have little choice in how to spend their lives, being forced into the full-time continuous life-long employment career whether they like it or not, whether they take on the breadwinner role for a wife and children or not. Public disapproval for the househusband role is reflected in a status score so low that it scrapes the very bottom of the prestige scale, whereas the housewife's score is right in the middle of the scale. Women can choose to drop out of the labour market and become homemakers, full-time or in combination with a part-time job, and retain a social status not very different from the status of typically-female occupations in the market economy – such as secretary. No such choice is open to men. It is indicative that even career women refuse to marry and maintain househusbands: women who earn enough to be breadwinners themselves, who can afford to keep a non-earning or low-paid husband, and who constantly bemoan the fact that most men have the support services of a wife at home whereas they do not, even these women refuse to contemplate role reversal and become economic supporters rather than joint earners in a dual-career household. The closest approximation to this is the young woman who works as the main breadwinner while her husband goes through law, medical or business school. However she is investing in her husband's career with a view to being financially dependent for the rest of her life after he qualifies, so her role is the same as that of all wives contributing to two-person careers, whatever the nature of the career (Papanek, 1973; Finch, 1983). Goldberg is right to underline this *joint* refusal of men and women to contemplate complete role reversal at home as telling us something important about relations between the sexes (1993: 152, 192).

Sample selection bias provides one of the most fruitful sources of true lies. Find an unrepresentative minority group that demonstrates your point, study it in detail and broadcast the results as if they were relevant to women generally, rather than the particular minority group in question. Interestingly, economists are far more likely to be aware of, and seek to correct for sample selection bias than are sociologists.

**Sex and gender**
Some doubt that the Western distinction between sex and gender is universally meaningful, theoretically and empirically; however all human societies recognise biological differences between men and women and the differentiation of masculine and feminine social roles seems to be universal, with or without the possibility of an intermediate position, temporary or permanent (Moore, 1994). The most powerful evidence of what it means to be male and female in everyday life comes not from social science research but from real life natural experiments (Hakim, 1987a: 109-110): the accounts of people who undergo sex changes. These are not 'ordinary' people; they already believe, strongly enough to persuade doctors to help, that their true personality lies on the other side, and requires a physiological sex change to match. Yet even they are shocked when they cross over to the other side. Men who change over to being women discover they have become second-class citizens, are ignored, kept waiting, are treated dismissively and belittled in a never-ending stream of small daily humiliations; they also find themselves not protesting as they would when they were men. Women who change over to being men are amazed to discover

they go out into the world charged with aggressive energy when they start taking the testosterone tablets, wanting to fuck everyone and fight everything. People who cross over to the other side *in real life* confirm the fluidity of the boundaries between male and female, in terms of sex and gender; they also reveal how dramatic the differences are, in terms of felt experience. These real-life cases also underline the fact that sex and gender almost invariably go together in real life, even if it requires physiological change to get the match right, so that there is little point in the artful distinction, for most people most of the time. These and other natural experiments (Stoller, 1975; Imperato-McGinley et al, 1979; Goldberg, 1993: 167-8) contrast interestingly with the mind-games that Western intellectuals like to play (Moore, 1994: 135-150).

**Female heterogeneity**
Ideas generally have a material base. But once created,, ideas have a life and vigour of their own, as illustrated by feminist ideology itself.

Patriarchal ideology promoted the idea of bourgeois domestic femininity which contradicted the reality of most working class women's lives, but provided an ideal for everyone to aspire to. Patriarchal ideology also developed the idea of the sexual division of labour in the family which gave responsibility for the home to the wife and mother while the husband and father was responsible for income-earning market work. Cross-national comparisons show there is no necessary connection between these ideas. The sexual division of labour in the home seems to be a universally attractive idea, unconnected with other ideas on sex-roles, the personalities and abilities of men and women. This suggests that the idea is accepted because it is demonstrably efficient and fruitful for most couples, as Becker argues. But the exact specification of the family division of labour is changing. By the 1990s in the Western world the *complete* division of labour, which encouraged wives to refrain altogether from employment outside the home, had been replaced by what we have called the *modern* family division of labour which allows the modern housewife to engage in employment that is subordinate to her domestic responsibilities, either part-time and/or part-year work or a job that is less demanding than her husband's. Across Europe, about one-third of men and women support the modern division of labour as the ideal to aim for, with some variation between countries. In Britain, the modern sexual division of labour was accepted by at least half of all women by the 1990s. About half of women rejected the complete division of labour, but only a minority of women, about one-quarter, rejected the modern marriage career and differentiated sex roles, choosing instead to pursue male-style employment careers.

No-one doubts that the work orientations of the full-time housewife who stops work as soon as possible differ from the work orientations of the career woman who always works. It is much easier to overlook the fact that the motivations of the career woman and the secondary earner are also quite different. The career woman challenges the sexual division of labour and the sex-stereotyping of jobs that constrains her choice of occupation. In contrast, the secondary earner, even when working full-time, does not challenge the sexual division of labour and prefers to work in female-dominated occupations. Wage work is an *extension* of her homemaking role, not an *alternative* to it; she seeks additional family income whereas the career woman seeks personal development and personal fulfilment, competing on equal terms with men (Matthaei, 1982: 278-9).

The USA is distinctive in being the only Western society to exhibit a genuine long-term increase in female work rates (OECD, 1988: 129-30; Goldin, 1990: 119), so it might be expected to prove that female heterogeneity is a new phenomenon. On the contrary, Goldin's historical analysis of female employment reveals that female heterogeneity is of such long duration that it must be a permanent feature of the female population. It was the key (hidden) factor explaining the absence of any change in the pay gap for 15 years after equal pay was introduced in the USA, until the 1980s (Goldin, 1990: 28-35; see also Smith and Ward, 1984; O'Neil and Polachek, 1993). Female heterogeneity can no longer be ignored as it is the source of increasing polarisation within the female workforce, and has social and economic consequences that are not affected by sex discrimination legislation.

## Polarisation within the workforce

As a group, women are heterogeneous, diverse and divided. They have genuine choices to make between different styles of life, and the choice has widened since the contraceptive revolution made voluntary childlessness more accessible. Having made one choice early in life, some change their minds and turn off onto another road. A great many women 'hang loose' and refuse to choose fixed objectives, drifting with events and opportunities as they arise, pretending they can keep all their options open by refusing to close the door on any of them. This itself is an important choice, one men do not have, even if it is a poor one, leading to chaotically unplanned careers.

There has always been a minority of women who worked continuously throughout life: 15 per cent of women of working age in Britain in 1965 falling to less than 10 per cent by 1980. In the past, career women were usually those who never married. The modern employment career is far less socially restrictive and far more attractive. One-quarter of women working full-time are in professional and managerial jobs. Most of them will marry and many will have children, some dropping out of the workforce into full-time domesticity at this stage.

The homemaker career narrowly defined, which involves a permanent cessation of work early in adult life, on marriage or when children are born, is on the decline, replaced by the modern homemaker career, chosen by over half of women of working age in Britain. This group is the most dominant, in terms of numbers, though it is not the most vociferous. The attitudes, behaviour and interests of this group are in sharp contrast to the attitudes, behaviour and interests of the small minority of employment career women. These two contrasting groups are producing a polarisation of female employment in the 1990s and for the foreseeable future, in Britain, the rest of Europe, the USA and other industrial societies (Jenson, Hagen and Reddy, 1988; Rubery, 1988: 44, 96, 127, 145, 159, 278; Humphries and Rubery, 1992; Coleman and Pencavel, 1993).

Women in senior grades have invested in qualifications, work continuously and full-time, are as ambitious and determined as men, are concentrated in integrated or male-dominated occupations and have high earnings. Women who pursue the modern homemaker career are secondary earners, fail to utilise any qualifications they may have, choose jobs for their convenience factors and social interest rather than with a view to a long-term career, are concentrated in female occupations and have lower earnings. When the earnings dispersion increases, as it did in most countries in the 1980s, especially in Britain and the USA, the two groups polarise further. The current focus on low earnings as an indicator of discrimination has distracted attention from the fact that career women confront far more discrimination than secondary workers because they compete as equals with men but are often treated as uncommitted secondary earners.

This diversity makes women's employment patterns more interesting, but also much harder to study. Studies of male employment produced only a small labour economics literature until women were pulled into the picture (Blau and Ferber, 1992). Averages and measures of central tendency hide more than they reveal in relation to working women, often concealing divergent trends, as illustrated by trends in occupational segregation. This diversity also means that no single theory can hope to cover all aspects of women's work, paid and unpaid.

The absence of choice for men was highlighted in the 1980s by their obligation to work even when unemployment stood at over 2 million for over fifteen years in Britain, guaranteeing that there were no jobs for at least 12 per cent of men for over a decade. The pressure on men to seek and obtain employment does not diminish even in these circumstances. Women may take refuge, willingly or otherwise, in the alternative identity and social role of housewife or mother, but this is not possible for men. Research shows that men are *less* likely to share domestic work when they are unemployed than when they have a job (Pahl, 1984: 269, 273, 276, 327; Brines, 1994). Despite the fact that they have more time available, domestic work poses more of a threat to their male identity than when they have the security of the main income-earning role in the household. Unemployment creates more social and psychological stress for men than women (Hakim, 1982b: 449).


### Sex differentials

Even if sex discrimination were completely eliminated, sex differentials in employment would continue, partly due to female secondary earners but also due to the large group of drifters with no clear plans, whose labour market behaviour is closer to that of homemakers than to that of employment career women.

Occupational segregation and sex differentials in labour mobility, work experience, hours worked, earnings and many other employment characteristics will be maintained, or even increase, in the lower part of the occupational structure. In contrast, sex differentials will shrink at the top of the occupational structure, in the professional, technical and managerial grades that are already the most integrated and becoming more so. These opposite trends are concealed in studies that rely on averages to compare working women and men. This poses problems for the statistical evidence used in legal proceedings, as noted in Chapter 7.

**Explaining women's subordination**

Goldberg's theory of patriarchy and male dominance states that, by nature, men are without malice towards women. Faced with a race, men run harder than women, and win more often. Hartmann's patriarchy theory states that, in addition, there is a streak of malice in men which seeks to ensure that the male *team* wins the race, that women are kept from the prize, by fair means or foul. Becker's rational choice theory states that many women voluntarily drop out of the race to make babies and play with them, which obviously improves men's chances of winning. However even childless women working full-time accept the sexual division of labour at home as efficient and give priority to their husband's careers, so children and their care are not an essential feature of the sexual division of labour at home, with its consequences for differential attainment in the labour market. There is evidence to support all three main theories explaining why women are less likely to achieve positions offering wealth, power and status. So they have to be treated as complementary rather than competing alternatives. This review allows us to integrate the theories by identifying the missing link between them.

Theories should be able to answer the infinite regression question 'But *why*?'. Goldberg explains male behaviour as driven by psychophysiological factors within the boundaries set by socialisation processes. Becker explains the sexual division of labour in the family in terms of the mutual benefits of increased efficiency and outputs. But neither Hartmann nor Walby provide any explanation for the male malice that is implicit in the idea of patriarchy. Why should men seek to put women down? Hartmann and Walby describe mechanisms but not motives. Even Walby's (1990) most sophisticated account is essentially just description (Fine, 1992: 42). As Goldberg points out (1993: 148), patriarchy theory has so far failed to identify a cause for patriarchy, male dominance and male solidarity.

One possible answer is that Goldberg is right in saying men bear no malice towards women, that patriarchal processes are created accidentally and socially, and are thus malleable and reversible. Male solidarity rests on the natural instinct for people with similar interests, similar styles of behaviour and conversation to group together. Male managers select male applicants for jobs because they feel comfortable with them, know they can communicate effectively, will understand each other even if they disagree at times. Women are visibly different, talk differently, behave differently, so can be harder to understand or trust as colleagues. This explanation places the emphasis on social styles, communication styles and life interests providing the basis for the assumption of shared interests, and hence a distinct bias towards persons of the same sex as colleagues and friends in employment contexts as well as non-work contexts. This turns our attention to the source of such well defined differences in personal style.

Clearly, women as mothers play a large role in laying the foundations of sex role ideologies and behaviours. The separation of the workplace from the home in modern industrial society means that children do not have any immediate access to the labour market, to roles in the workplace and their father's activities. All children have access to the roles of men and women in the home, in particular the female role. Women are the first to give dolls to their daughters and guns to their sons. It is mothers who create housewives in their own image. Women treat their children as extensions of themselves, especially girl children. Whether they like them or not, men treat their children as independent social beings, who may well resist attempts to influence or persuade. Gilligan emphasises women's voice, insists it is benign rather than incapacitating, and claims it would be revolutionary to incorporate women's voice in the management of society. Another view is that it is precisely this woman's voice, so sensitive to other voices, that handicaps girls and women, allowing them to be easily swayed by others, initially their mothers, later men, in a world view in which everything is relative anyway, so why should women insist on their interests taking priority? Male solidarity wins because women dither in their judgements, because they are swayed by the dominant male voice and also because women are divided in their preferences and interests.

The key reason why male solidarity and male organisation are so effective is that women are diverse and divided. If men are the enemy, women make a hopeless adversary. Men gain a huge tactical advantage from women's diversity. The heterogeneity of female preferences - for a lifestyle with or without a clear sexual division of labour - opens up a fatal weakness in women's representation of their interests. The trouble is that there are at least two sets of interests, as reflected in the two women's movements in the USA, for example, with paler parallels in Britain. With the opposition so fundamentally divided *within itself*, men race to the winning line without much imagination, effort or talent. This bothers employment career women, who see men of average ability succeeding in places where women barely get through the door. It is entirely acceptable to women following the homemaker career, who are spending their spouse's earnings and profits. Women's failure to organise, and lack of solidarity, *vis a vis* men is due to their having two avenues of upward mobility and achievement in life, through the marriage market or through the labour market. At present, men are limited to the labour market, though that might conceivably change, if employment career women learn to value toyboys and househusbands in the same way that men value bimbo babes and housewives. Looking at it from the male perspective, the bias is in favour of women who become homemakers. Men see housewives living a life of relative comfort and low stress, winning positions of financial dependency without necessarily displaying much competence, effort or talent for the job of housewife and mother. This bothers employment career men, who see women succeeding in a role where men fail even to get through the door. Some men would make far better parents than women do, especially for adolescents, but women currently have a monopoly on the homemaker role and, to a large extent, on parenting, while the male monopoly on employment careers has been declared unlawful.

On the evidence, Goldberg's theory of male dominance and patriarchy is unassailable. But it is *sui generis*, linked to nothing else. Female heterogeneity of preferences and interests provides the missing link between the concept of patriarchy (since it is not really a theory) and Goldberg's theory of male dominance. Male patriarchal solidarity and male organisation to promote male interests are disproportionately successful because women are sharply divided in their objectives and fields of activity. Becker's rational choice theory provides an adequate account of what the homemaker half of the female population are doing; human capital theory accounts for the employment histories of the career women minority. The drifters' activities probably defy explanation.


## Looking ahead

Everything may change. Social science research results can give a misleading sense of inevitability: the current pattern of behaviour is readily interpreted as inevitable, institutionally determined and unchangeable rather than volatile, chosen and changeable. Without hard proof of causal connections, contemporary coincidences are nothing more than that. And *most* research goes no further than contemporary coincidences, especially in the case of multivariate analyses where even the direction of causality is left completely open. However large scale real life social experiments show that there are limits to what social engineering can achieve.

There is nothing 'traditional' about women's restriction to the domestic sphere – quite the contrary. In Britain, women were as likely to be in the workforce in 1871 as in 1971. The domestication of women was a social experiment that did not last even a century, three generations. The Chinese social experiment at encouraging all women into social work outside the home achieved greater success within half a century, but there are signs that even in the context of a policy of one child per couple, one-quarter to one-third of women are inclined to return to the sexual division of labour in the home and drop out of work beyond the domestic sphere. It appears that the heterogeneity of women's preferences for employment careers or for homemaking careers is a permanent feature which resists attempts to squeeze everyone into a single lifestyle. Public policy has to allow both options, even if it is impossible to design policies that are completely neutral between the two, as argued in Chapter 7. The fact that socialisation processes exist in all societies does not guarantee their success. Like men, women can always say No. Some women are prepared to swim against the current; others prefer to go with the flow. So women's preferences are malleable, to some extent. But on current evidence there is a substantial minority of women (20% in Britain) who will never want to have and raise children, and there is a substantial minority of women (probably no more than 10%) who would prefer to have four or more children and devote their life to mothering activities mainly. Perhaps public policy should encourage this more efficient division of labour and polarisation of fertility patterns.

Preferences determine choices, but they do not predict performance. Women who choose to compete with men in the public arena, not just the market economy but also politics and other public activities, will not necessarily have the ability to make it to the top, any more often than men do. *Most* men do not attain the top positions, even in the absence of discrimination. So it is not a sign of discrimination if *equally* few women are successful. Women's concentration in lower grade jobs does not differentiate them from men and cannot be discriminatory of itself. Similarly women who choose not to join the rat race may have to confront the possibility that they are no better as mothers and homemakers than they were (or would be) as workers. One of the great myths is that all women have a natural and benign talent for nurturance, that the mother's influence in never noxious. From a feminist point of view, it is arguable that mothers should not be allowed to raise either girls or boys beyond the age of about 12 years. Adolescents of both sexes need to break away from the mother to achieve autonomy and adult identities, not only boys as assumed by Chodorow (1978).

This review suggests that research should now focus on particular issues in women's employment. The invisible, and often unconscious, social processes that prevent women from obtaining and flourishing in senior grade posts merit far more attention than they have so far received. More generally, we should look more closely at the work and life histories of women committed to full-time continuous employment, including those in less prestigious occupations than the easily identified professional and managerial women, and including studies of sex differences in earnings. Research on occupational segregation must now move away from the long-standing concern with historical trends and fruitless obsession with measurement issues to address the causes and consequences of occupational segregation, its meaning for different groups of women, and whether its meaning for men is changing. Integrated or mixed occupations, employing both men and women, seem to be of particular interest both from a theoretical and a policy perspective. Lessons for the future must surely be found most often in this minority group of occupations in the workforce. Most challenging of all is the relationship between vertical job segregation, movement between segregated and integrated occupations across the lifecycle and the three employment profiles identified in Chapter 5. We need to know if the highest achievements are accessible to, even if restricted to, women following the male employment profile, or whether it takes a lot more than that to succeed in male dominated careers. There are now enough women sweeping into senior positions in the labour market, if not in the political arena, to enable us to consider general patterns rather than uniquely individual cases.

The key conclusion is that we are in the middle of significant restructuring of women's social and economic position. The report on the 1980 Women and Employment Survey concluded that despite important changes in women's attitudes to employment since Hunt's 1965 survey, work was still less central to women's lives than to men's; that most women were still primary domestic workers and secondary wage earners while husbands were primary wage earners; that a majority of women regarded a home and children as women's prime aim and main job, so that children took priority over a career; and that there was little evidence that women saw themselves becoming equal or joint wage earners on the same terms as their husbands (Martin and Roberts, 1984: 191-2). All these conclusions remain valid today in the mid-1990s, but only for one section of the female adult population. The polarisation process that started in the 1980s has produced a sharp divide between these home-centred women and the minority of career-oriented women for whom employment is just as central to their lives as it is for men; who do not regard a home and children as their primary aims in life; and who see themselves as independent wage earners whether or not they marry. This means that there will always be evidence to support *both* the gloomy view and the optimistic view of women's position in the labour market. Modern industrial society creates the conditions for women to make genuine choices between two polarised lifestyles, so their preferences have become an important new social factor, potentially over-riding the demographic, social, economic and institutional factors that have historically been so important. Difference and diversity are now the key features of the female population, with the likelihood of increasing polarisation between work-centred and home-centred women in the 21st century. And in a civilised society difference and diversity are positively valued.

# Bibliography

Allen S and Wolkowitz C (1987) *Homeworking: Myths and Realities*, London: Macmillan.

Althauser R P and Kalleberg A L (1981) 'Firms, occupations and the structure of labour markets' in *Sociological Perspectives on Labour Markets* (ed) I Berg, New York: Academic Press.

Alwin D F, Braun M and Scott J (1992) 'The separation of work and the family: attitudes towards women's labour-force participation in Germany, Great Britain and the United States', *European Sociological Review*, 8: 13-37.

Anderson M, Bechhofer F and Gershuny J (eds) (1994) *The Social and Political Economy of the Household*, Oxford: Oxford University Press.

Applebaum E (1987) 'Restructuring work: temporary, part-time and at-home work' pp 268-310 in *Computer Chips and Paper Clips* (ed) H I Hartmann, Washington DC: National Academy Press.

Arber S and Ginn J (1995) 'Gender differences in the relationship between paid employment and informal care', *Work, Employment and Society*, 9: 445-471.

Barron R D and Norris G M (1976) 'Sexual divisions and the dual labour market' pp 47-69 in *Dependence and Exploitation in Work and Marriage* (eds) D L Barker and S Allen, London: Longman.

Beatson M (1995) *Labour Market Flexibility*, Research Series No. 48, London: Employment Department.

Beatson M and Butcher S (1993) 'Union density across the employed workforce', *Employment Gazette*, 101: 673-689.

Becker G S (1985) 'Human capital, effort and the sexual division of labour', *Journal of Labor Economics*, 3: S33-S58.

Becker G S (1981, 1991) *A Treatise on the Family*, Cambridge MA: Harvard University Press.

Beechey V and Perkins T (1987) *A Matter of Hours: Women, Part-Time Work and the Labour Market*, Cambridge: Polity.

Beller A H (1982) 'Occupational segregation by sex: determinants and changes', *Journal of Human Resources*, 17: 371-92.

Beneria L (1981) 'Conceptualising the labour force: the underestimation of women's economic activities', *Journal of Development Studies*, 17: 10-28. Reprinted pp 372-391 in *On Work* (ed) R E Pahl, 1988, Oxford: Blackwell.

Beneria L and Sen G (1981) 'Accumulation, reproduction and women's role in economic development: Boserup revisited', *Signs*, 7: 279-298. Reprinted pp 355-371 in *On Work* (ed) R E Pahl, 1988, Oxford: Blackwell.

Bercusson B (1990) 'The European Community's Charter of Fundamental Social Rights of Workers', *Modern Law Review*, 53: 624-642.

Berk R (1983) 'An introduction to sample selection bias in sociological data', *American Sociological Review*, 48: 386-98.

Beutel A M and Marini M M (1995) 'Gender and values', *American Sociological Review*, 60: 436-448.

Bhavnani R (1994) *Black Women in the Labour Market: A Research Review*, Manchester: Equal Opportunities Commission.

Bielby D D and Bielby W T (1984) 'Work commitment, sex-role attitudes and women's employment', *American Sociological Review*, 49. 234-47.

Bielby D D and Bielby W T (1988) 'She works hard for the money: household responsibilities and the allocation of work effort', *American Journal of Sociology*, 93: 1031-59.

Bielby W T and Baron J N (1984) 'A woman's place is with other women: sex segregation within organisations' pp 27-55 in *Sex Segregation in the Workplace: Trends, Explanations, Remedies* (ed) B F Reskin, Washington DC: National Academy Press.

Blau F D and Ferber M A (1992) *The Economics of Women, Men and Work*, Englewood Cliffs NJ: Prentice-Hall.

Blaxall M and Reagan B (eds) (1976) *Women and the Workplace : The Implications of Occupational Segregation*, Chicago and London: University of Chicago Press. Reprint of supplement to Spring 1976 issue of *Signs*.

Blitz R C (1974) 'Women in the professions: 1870-1970', *Monthly Labor Review*, 97, may, 34-39.

Blossfeld H-P (1987) 'Labour market entry and the sexual segregation of careers in the Federal Republic of Germany', *American Journal of Sociology*, 93: 89-118.

Blossfeld H-P and Mayer K U (1988) 'Labor market segmentation in the Federal Republic of Germany: an empirical study of segmentation theories from a life course perspective', *European Sociological Review*, 4: 123-140.

Bonney N (1988) 'Dual earning couples: trends of change in Great Britain', *Work, Employment and Society*, 2: 89-102.

Bonney N and Reinach E (1993) 'Housework reconsidered: the Oakley thesis twenty years later', *Work, Employment and Society*, 7: 615-627.

Boris E and Daniels C R (eds) (1989) *Homework: Historical and Contemporary Perspectives on Paid Labor at Home*, Urbana and Chicago: University of

Illinois Press.

Bosch G, Dawkins P and Michon F (1994) *Times are Changing: Working Time in 14 Industrialised Countries*, Geneva: International Labour Office International Institute for Labor Studies.

Bose C E (1985) *Jobs and Gender: A Study of Occupational Prestige*, New York: Praeger.

Bose C E (1987) 'Devaluing women's work: the undercount of women's employment in 1900 and 1980' pp 95-115 in C Bose *et al* (eds) *The Hidden Aspects of Women's Work*, New York: Praeger.

Bose C E and Rossi P H (1983) 'Gender and jobs: prestige standings of occupations as affected by gender', *American Sociological Review*, 48: 316-330.

Boserup E (1970) *Women's Role in Economic Development*, London: Allen & Unwin.

Bradley H (1989) *Men's Work, Women's Work: A Sociological History of the Sexual Division of Labour in Employment*, Cambridge: Polity Press.

Brines J (1994) 'Economic dependency, gender and the division of labour at home', *American Journal of Sociology*, 100: 652-688.

Britton M and Edison N (1986) 'The changing balance of the sexes in England and Wales, 1851-2001', *Population Trends*, No. 46: 22-25.

Bruegel I (1979) 'Women as a reserve army of labour: a note on recent British experience', *Feminist Review*, 3: 12-23.

Buckley J E (1985) 'Wage differences among workers in the same job and establishment', *Monthly Labor Review*, 108/3: 11-16.

Burchell B and Rubery J (1994) 'Divided women: labour market segmentation and gender segregation' pp 80-120 in *Gender Segregation and Social Change* (ed) A M Scott, Oxford: Oxford University Press.

Burgess S and Rees H (1994) 'Lifetime jobs and transient jobs: job tenure in Britain 1975-1991', *mimeo*, University of Bristol, Department of Economics.

Butcher S and Hart D (1995) 'An analysis of working time 1979-1994', *Employment Gazette*, 103: 211-222.

Cain G G (1986) 'The economic analysis of labour market discrimination: a survey' pp 693-785 in *Handbook of Labor Economics* (ed) O Ashenfelter and R Layard, Amsterdam: North Holland.

Campbell B (1993) *Goliath: Britain's Dangerous Places*, London: Methuen.

Campbell E (1985) *The Childless Marriage*, London and New York: Tavistock.

Carrier S (1995) 'Family status and career situation for professional women', *Work, Employment and Society*, 9: 343-358.

Castle B (1993) *Fighting All The Way*, London: Macmillan.

Chamberlain E and Purdie E (1992) 'The Quarterly Labour Force Survey: a new dimension to labour market statistics', *Employment Gazette*, 100:

483-490.

Charles M (1992) 'Cross-national variations in occupational sex segregation', *American Sociological Review*, 57: 483-502.

Charles M and Grusky D B (1995) 'Models for describing the underlying structure of sex segregation', *American Journal of Sociology*, 100: 931-71.

Chauvin K W and Ash R A (1994) 'Gender earnings differentials in total pay, base pay and contingent pay', *Industrial and Labor Relations Review*, 47: 634-649.

Chiplin B (1976) 'Sexual discrimination: are there any lessons from criminal behaviour?', *Applied Economics*, 8: 121-133.

Chiplin B and Sloane P J (1974) 'Sexual discrimination in the labour market', *British Journal of Industrial Relations*, 12: 371-402.

Chiplin B and Sloane P J (1976) 'Male-female earnings differences: a further analysis', *British Journal of Industrial Relations*, 14: 77-81.

Chodorow N (1978) *The Reproduction of Mothering*, Berkeley: University of California Press.

Clogg C C, Eliason S R and Wahl R J (1990) 'Labour market experiences and labor-force outcomes', *American Journal of Sociology*, 95: 1536-76.

Cockburn C (1983) *Brothers: Male Dominance and Technological Change*, London: Pluto Press.

Cohn S (1985) *The Process of Occupational Sex-Typing: The Feminisation of Clerical work in Great Britain*, Philadelphia: Temple University Press.

Coleman M T and Pencavel J (1993) 'Trends in market work behaviour of women since 1940', *Industrial and Labor Relations Review*, 46: 653-677.

Connelly R (1991) 'The importance of child care costs to women's decision-making' pp 87-117 in *The Economics of Childcare* (ed) D M Blau, New York: Russell Sage Foundation.

Corcoran L (1995) 'Trade union membership and recognition: 1994 Labour Force Survey data', *Employment Gazette*, 103: 191-203.

Corcoran M E (1979) 'Work experience, labor force withdrawal and women's wages: empirical results using the 1976 Panel Study of Income Dynamics' pp 216-245 in *Women in the Labor Market* (eds) C B Lloyd, E S Andrews and C L Gilroy, New York: Columbia University Press.

Corcoran M and Duncan G J (1979) 'Work history, labor force attachment and earnings differences between the races and sexes', *Journal of Human Resources*, 14: 3-20.

Corcoran M, Duncan G J and Ponza M (1984) 'Work experience, job segregation and wages' pp 171-91 in *Sex Segregation in the Workplace: Trends, Explanations, Remedies* (ed) B F Reskin, Washington DC: National Academy Press.

Corti L and Dex S (1995) 'Informal carers and employment', *Employment Gazette*, 103: 101-107.

Cragg A and Dawson T (1981) *Qualitative Research Among Homeworkers*, Research Paper No. 21, London: Department of Employment.

Cragg A and Dawson T (1984) *Unemployed Women: A Study of Attitudes and Experiences*, Research Paper No. 47, London: Department of Employment.

Crompton R and Sanderson K (1990) *Gendered Jobs and Social Change*, London: Unwin Hyman.

Crull P (1987) 'Searching for the causes of sexual harassment: an examination of two prototypes' pp 225-244 in *Hidden Aspects of Women's Work* (eds) C Bose, R Feldberg, N Sokoloff, New York and London: Praeger.

Curtice J (1993) 'Satisfying work – if you can get it' pp 103-121 in *International Social Attitudes: the 10th BSA Report* (ed) R Jowell, Aldershot, Hants: Gower.

Daly P A (1981) 'Unpaid family workers: long-term decline continues', *Monthly Labor Review*, 105/10: 3-5.

Davidson M J and Cooper C L (eds) (1993) *European Women in Business and Management*, London: Paul Chapman.

Davies C (1980) 'Making sense of the census in Britain and the USA: the changing occupational classification and the position of nurses', *Sociological Review*, 28: 581-609.

Davies P and Freedland M (1984) *Labour Law: Text and Materials*, 2nd edition, London: Weidenfeld and Nicolson.

Davies P and Freedland M (1993) *Labour Legislation and Public Policy*, Oxford: Clarendon.

De Grazia R (1980) 'Clandestine employment: a problem of our times', *International Labour Review*, 119: 549-63.

De Grazia R (1984) *Clandestine Employment: The Situation in Industrialised Market Economy Countries*, Geneva: ILO.

de Neubourg C (1985) 'Part-time work: an international quantitative comparison', *International Labour Review*, 124: 559-76.

Desai S and Waite L J (1991) 'Women's employment during pregnancy and after the first birth: occupational characteristics and work commitment', *American Sociological Review*, 56: 551-566.

de Vaus D and McAllister I (1991) 'Gender and work orientation: values and satisfaction in Western Europe', *Work and Occupations*, 18: 72-93.

Dex S (1985) *The Sexual Division of Work*, Brighton: Harvester Press.

Dex S (1987) *Women's Occupational Mobility: A Lifetime Perspective*, London: Macmillan.

Disney R and Szyszczak E M (1989) 'Part-time work: Reply to Catherine Hakim', *Industrial Law Journal*, 18: 223-229.

Downes D and Rock P (1988) *Understanding Deviance*, Oxford: Clarendon.

Dubin R (1956) 'Industrial workers' worlds: a study of the central life interests of industrial workers', *Social Problems*, 3: 131-142.

Duncan O D and Duncan B (1955) 'A methodological analysis of segregation indices', *American Sociological Review*, 20: 200-17.

Dunnell K (1979) *Family Formation 1976*, London: HMSO.

Dupre M T, Hussmanns R and Mehran F (1987) 'The concept and boundary of economic activity for the measurement of the economically active population' pp IX-XVIII in *ILO Bulletin of Labour Statistics*, No. 1987-3, Geneva: ILO.

Edgeworth F Y (1922) 'Equal pay to men and women for equal work', *Economic Journal*, 32: 431-57.

Ehrenberg R G (1989) 'Empirical consequences of comparable worth' pp 90-116 in *Comparable Worth – Analyses and Evidence* (eds) M A Hill and M R Killingsworth, Ithaca NY: ILR Press.

Elias P (1988) 'Family formation, occupational mobility and part-time work' pp 83-104 in *Women and Paid Work* (ed) A Hunt, London: Macmillan.

Elias P and Gregory M (1994) *The Changing Structure of Occupations and Earnings in Great Britain, 1975-1990 – An analysis based on the New Earnings Survey Panel Dataset*, Research Series No. 27, London: Employment Department.

Elias P and Main B (1982) *Women's Working Lives: Evidence from the National Training Survey*, University of Warwick: Institute for Employment Research.

Elias P and White M (1991) *Recruitment in Local Labour Markets*, Research Paper No. 86, London: Employment Department.

Ellis E (1991) *European Community Sex Equality Law*, Oxford: Clarendon Press.

Ellison R (1994) 'British labour force projections: 1994 to 2006', *Employment Gazette*, 102: 111-121.

Employment Committee of the House of Commons, Session 1994-5 (1995) *Unemployment and Employment Statistics – Minutes of Evidence: Tuesday 2 May 1995*, 411-i, London: HMSO.

Employment Department (1976) 'Teachers' pay – how and why men and women's earnings differ', *Employment Gazette*, 84: 963-8.

Employment Department (1992) 'Economic activity and qualifications: results from the Labour Force Survey', *Employment Gazette*, 100: 101-133.

England P (1981) 'Assessing trends in occupational sex segregation 1900-1976' pp 273-295 in *Sociological Perspectives on Labor Markets* (ed) I Berg, New York: Academic Press.

England P (1982) 'The failure of human capital theory to explain occupational sex segregation', *Journal of Human Resources*, 17: 358-70.

England P (1984) 'Wage appreciation and depreciation: a test of neoclassical economic explanations of occupational sex segregation', *Social Forces*, 62: 726-49.

England P and McCreary L (1987) 'Integrating sociology and economics to study gender and work' pp 143-172 in *Women and Work: An Annual Review* (eds) A H Stromberg et al, Beverly Hills and London: Sage.

Erikson K and Vallas S (eds) (1990) *The Nature of Work: Sociological Perspectives*, New Haven and London: Yale University Press.

Erikson R and Goldthorpe J H (1993) *The Constant Flux: A Study of Class Mobility in Industrial Societies*, Oxford: Clarendon

European Commission (1984) *European Men and Women in 1983*, Brussels: Commission of the European Communities.

European Commission (1994) *Employment in Europe 1994*, Luxembourg: Office for Official Publications of the European Communities.

European Commission (1995a) *Employment in Europe 1995*, Luxembourg: Office for Official Publications of the European Communities.

European Commission (1995b) *The Demographic Situation in the European Union*, DG V-COM(94)595, Luxembourg: Office for Official Publications of the European Communities.

Fawcett M G (1918) 'Equal pay for equal work', *Economic Journal*, 28: 1-6.

Felstead A and Jewson N (1995) 'Working at home: estimates from the 1991 Census', *Employment Gazette*, 103: 95-99.

Fenwick and Hervey (1995) 'Sex equality in the single market: new directions for the European Court of Justice', *Common Market Law Review*, 32: 611.

Finch J (1983) *Married to the Job: Wives' Incorporation in Men's Work*, London: Allen & Unwin.

Fine B (1992) *Women's Employment and the Capitalist Family*, London and New York: Routledge.

Fiorentine R (1987) 'Men, women and the premed persistence gap: a normative alternatives approach', *American Journal of Sociology*, 92: 1118-39.

Firestone S (1974) *The Dialectic of Sex: The Case for Feminist Revolution*, New York: Morrow.

Fogarty M (1985) 'British attitudes to work' pp 173-200 in *Values and Social Change in Britain* (eds) M Abrams, D Gerard and N Timms, London: Macmillan.

Fogarty M, Allen A J, Allen I and Walters P (1971) *Women in Top Jobs*, London: Allen & Unwin for Political and Economic Planning.

Fredman S (1992) 'European Community discrimination law: a critique', *Industrial Law Journal*, 21: 119-134.

Friedan B (1963) *The Feminine Mystique*, New York: Norton.

Fuchs V R (1986) 'His and hers: gender differences in work and income, 1959-1979', *Journal of Labor Economics*, 4: S245-S277.

Furnham A (1990) *The Protestant Work Ethic: The Psychology of Work-*

*Related Beliefs and Behaviours*, London: Routledge.

Galbraith J K (1975) *Economics and the Public Purpose*, Harmondsworth: Penguin.

Gallie D and White M (1993) *Employee Commitment and the Skills Revolution*, London: Policy Studies Institute.

Gershuny J (1983a) *Social Innovation and the Division of Labour* , Oxford: Oxford University Press.

Gershuny J (1983b) 'Technical change and social limits' pp 23-44 in *Dilemmas of Liberal Democracies* (eds) A Ellis and K Kumar, London: Tavistock.

Gershuny J (1988) 'Time, technology and the informal economy' pp 579-597 in *On Work* (ed) R Pahl, Oxford: Blackwell.

Gershuny J (1992) 'Are we running out of time?', *Futures*, 3-22.

Gershuny J (1993) 'Post-industrial convergence in time allocation', *Futures*, 578-586.

Gershuny J, Godwin M and Jones S (1994) 'The domestic labour revolution: a process of lagged adaptation', pp 151-197 in *The Social and Political Economy of the Household* (eds) M Anderson, F Bechhofer and J Gershuny, Oxford: Oxford University Press.

Gilligan C (1982, 1993) *In a Different Voice: Psychological Theory and Women's Development*, Cambridge MA and London: Harvard University Press.

Glass J and Camarig V (1992) 'Gender, parenthood and job-family compatibility', *American Journal of Sociology*, 98: 131-151.

Goddard E (1994) *Voluntary Work*, London: HMSO for OPCS.

Goldberg S (1973) *The Inevitability of Patriarchy*, William Morrow.

Goldberg S (1993) *Why Men Rule: A Theory of Male Dominance*, Chicago: Open Court.

Goldin C (1987) 'The gender gap in historical perspective' pp 135-70 in *Quantity and Quiddity: Essays in Honour of Stanley Lebergott* (ed) P Kilby, Middletown, Conn.: Wesleyan University Press.

Goldin C (1989) 'Life-cycle labor force participation of married women: historical evidence and implications', *Journal of Labor Economics*, 7: 20-47.

Goldin C (1990) *Understanding the Gender Gap*, New York: Oxford University Press.

Goldin C and Polacheck S (1987) 'Residual differences by sex: perspectives on the gender gap in earnings', *American Economic Review*, 77: 143-151.

Goldschmidt-Clermont L (1982) *Unpaid Work in the Household: A Review of Economic Evaluation Methods*, Women, Work and Development Series No. 1, Geneva: ILO.

Goldschmidt-Clermont L (1987) *Economic Evaluations of Unpaid Household Work: Africa, Asia, Latin America and Oceania*, Women, Work and Development Series No. 14, Geneva: ILO.

Goldschmidt-Clermont L (1989) 'Valuing domestic activities', *ILO Bulletin of Labour Statistics*, No. 1989-4, Geneva: ILO.

Goldschmidt-Clermont L (1990) 'Economic measurement of non-market household activities', *International Labour Review*, 129: 279-99.

Goldthorpe J H (1987) 'The class mobility of women' pp 277-301 in J H Goldthorpe, *Social Mobility and Class Structure in Modern Britain*, Oxford: Clarendon Press.

Goldthorpe J H (1990) 'A response' pp 399-438 in *John H Goldthorpe: Consensus and Controversy* (eds) J Clark, C Modgil and S Modgil, London: Falmer Press.

Goldthorpe J and Hope K (1972) 'Occupational grading and occupational prestige' in K Hope (ed) *The Analysis of Social Mobility*, Oxford: Clarendon Press.

Goldthorpe J H and Hope K (1974) *The Social Grading of Occupations: A New Approach and Scale*, Oxford: Clarendon Press.

Green H (1988) *Informal Carers*, London: HMSO for OPCS.

Gregg P and Wadsworth J (1995) 'A short history of labour turnover, job tenure and job security, 1975-93', *Oxford Review of Economic Policy*, 11: 73-90.

Gregory M B and Thomson A W J (eds) (1990) *A Portrait of Pay 1970-1982: An Analysis of the New Earnings Survey*, Oxford: Clarendon Press.

Grint K (1988) 'Women and equality: the acquisition of equal pay in the Post Office 1870-1961', *Sociology*, 22: 87-108.

Gronau R (1980) 'Home production: a forgotten industry', *Review of Economics and Statistics*, 62: 408-14.

Grossman A S (1980) 'Women in domestic work: yesterday and today', *Monthly Labor Review*, 103/8: 17-21.

Gunderson V (1994) *Comparable Worth and Sex Discrimination*, Geneva: ILO.

Hakim C (1979) *Occupational Segregation: A Study of the Separation of Men and Women's Work in Britain, the United States and Other Countries*, Research Paper No. 9, London: Department of Employment.

Hakim C (1980) 'Census reports as documentary evidence: the census commentaries 1801-1951', *Sociological Review*, 28: 551-580.

Hakim C (1981) 'Job segregation: trends in the 1970s', *Employment Gazette*, 89: 521-529.

Hakim C (1982a) *Secondary Analysis*, London: Allen & Unwin.

Hakim C (1982b) 'The social consequences of high unemployment', *Journal of Social Policy*, 11: 433-467.

Hakim C (1985) *Employers' Use of Outwork: A Study using the 1980 Workplace Industrial Relations Survey and the 1981 National Survey of Homeworking*, Research Paper No. 44, London: Department of

Employment.

Hakim C (1987a) *Research Design*, London: Allen & Unwin/Routledge.

Hakim C (1987b) *Home-Based Work in Britain: A Report on the 1981 National Homeworking Survey and the DE Research Programme on Homework*, Research Paper No. 60, London: Department of Employment.

Hakim C (1987c) 'Trends in the flexible workforce', *Employment Gazette*, 95: 549-560.

Hakim C (1988a) 'Self-employment in Britain: recent trends and current issues', *Work, Employment and Society*, 2: 421-450.

Hakim C (1988b) 'Homeworking in Britain' pp 609-632 in *On Work: Historical, Comparative and Theoretical Approaches* (ed) R Pahl, Oxford: Blackwell, .

Hakim C (1989a) 'Employment rights: a comparison of part-time and full-time employees', *Industrial Law Journal*, 18: 69-83.

Hakim C (1989b) 'Workforce restructuring, social insurance coverage and the black economy', *Journal of Social Policy*, 18: 471-503.

Hakim C (1990a) 'Workforce restructuring in Europe in the 1980s', *International Journal of Comparative Labour Law and Industrial Relations*, 5/4: 167-203.

Hakim C (1990b) 'Core and periphery in employers' workforce strategies: evidence from the 1987 ELUS survey', *Work, Employment and Society*, 4: 157-188.

Hakim C (1991) 'Grateful slaves and self-made women: fact and fantasy in women's work orientations', *European Sociological Review*, 7: 101-121.

Hakim C (1992) 'Explaining trends in occupational segregation: the measurement, causes and consequences of the sexual division of labour', *European Sociological Review*, 8: 127-152

Hakim C (1993a) 'The myth of rising female employment', *Work, Employment and Society*, 7: 97-120.

Hakim C (1993b) 'Segregated and integrated occupations: a new framework for analysing social change', *European Sociological Review*, 9: 289-314.

Hakim C (1993c) 'Refocusing research on occupational segregation: reply to Watts', *European Sociological Review*, 9: 321-324.

Hakim C (1994) 'A century of change in occupational segregation 1891-1991', *Journal of Historical Sociology*, 7: 435-454.

Hakim C (1995a) 'Five feminist myths about women's employment', *British Journal of Sociology*, 46: 429-455.

Hakim C (1995b) '1991 Census SARs: opportunities and pitfalls in the labour market data', *Work, Employment and Society*, 9: 569-582.

Hakim C (1995c) 'Theoretical and measurement issues in the analysis of occupational segregation' *Beiträge zur Arbeitsmarkt- und Berufsforschung*

(Monographs on Employment Research) No. 186, Nürnberg: Federal Employment Services (IAB).

Hakim C (1996) 'Labour mobility and employment stability: rhetoric and reality on the sex differential in labour market behaviour', *European Sociological Review*, 12: 45-69.

Hakim C and Dennis R (1982) *Homeworking in Wages Council Industries: A Study of Pay and Earnings based on Wages Inspectorate Records*, Research Paper No. 37, London: Department of Employment.

Haller M and Hoellinger F (1994) 'Female employment and the change of gender roles: the conflictual relationship between participation and attitudes in international comparison', *International Sociology*, 9: 87-112.

Haller M and Rosenmayr L (1971) 'The pluridimensionality of work commitment', *Human Relations*, 24: 501-518.

Hansard Society (1990) *Women at the Top*, London: Hansard Society.

Harding P and Jenkins R (1989) *The Myth of the Hidden Economy*, Milton Keynes: Open University Press.

Harding S, Phillips D and Fogarty M (1986) *Contrasting Values in Western Europe: Unity, Diversity and Change*, London: Macmillan.

Hartmann H (1976) 'Capitalism, patriarchy and job segregation by sex' pp 137-179 in *Women and the Workplace: The Implications of Occupational Segregation* (eds) M Blaxall and B Reagan, Chicago: University of Chicago Press. Reprinted 1976, *Signs*, 1: 137-69. Reprinted in *Capitalist Patriarchy and the Case for Socialist Feminism* (ed) Z R Eisenstein, 1979, New York and London: Monthly Review Press.

Hartmann H (1979) 'The unhappy marriage of Marxism and feminism: towards a more progressive union', *Capital and Class*, 8: 1-33. Reprinted in *Women and Revolution* (ed) L Sargent, 1981, London: Pluto Press.

Hartmann H (1981) 'The family as the locus of gender, class and political struggle: the example of housework', *Signs*, 16: 366-94.

Hawrylyshyn O (1977) 'Towards a definition of non-market activities', *Review of Income and Wealth*, 23: 78-96.

Hennig M and Jardim A (1978) *The Managerial Woman*, London: Marion Boyars.

Hepple B A (1990) 'The implementation of the Community Charter of Fundamental Social Rights', *Modern Law Review*, 53: 643-654.

Hepple B A (1996) 'Equality and discrimination' in *Comparative Principles and Perspectives of European Community Labour Law* (ed) P Davies, S Schiarra and S S Simitis, Oxford: Oxford University Press.

Hepple B A and Hakim C (1996) 'Working time in the United Kingdom', in R Blanpain, J Rojot and E Kohler (eds) *Legal and Contractual Limitations on Working Time*, Antwerp: Kluwer.

Hepple B A and Szyszczak E (eds) (1992) *Discrimination: The Limits of the Law*, London: Mansell.

Hochschild A (1990) *The Second Shift: Working Parents and the Revolution at Home*, London: Piatkus.

Hofstede G (1980, 1994) *Culture's Consequences: International Differences in Work-Related Values*, Beverly Hills and New York: Sage.

Hofstede G (1991) *Cultures and Organisations*, London: HarperCollins.

Holcombe L (1973) *Victorian Ladies at Work: Middle Class Working Women in England and Wales 1850-1914*, Hamden, Connecticut: Archon Books.

Horrell S (1994) 'Household time allocation and women's labour force participation' pp 198-224 in Anderson M, Bechhofer F and Gershuny J (eds) (1994) *The Social and Political Economy of the Household*, Oxford: Oxford University Press.

Humphries J (1981) 'Protective legislation, the capitalist state and working-class men: the case of the 1842 Mines Regulation Act', *Feminist Review*, 7: 1-35. Reprinted pp 95-124 in *On Work* (ed) R E Pahl, 1988, Oxford: Basil Blackwell.

Humphries J (1987) 'The most free from objection . . . the sexual division of labour and women's work in nineteenth-century England', *Journal of Economic History*, 47: 929-949.

Humphries J and Rubery J (1992) 'The legacy for women's employment: integration, differentiation and polarisation' pp 236-255 in *The Economic Legacy of Thatcherism* (ed) J Michie, London: Academic Press.

Hunt A (1968a,b) *A Survey of Women's Employment: Report and Tables*, 2 vols, London: HMSO.

Hunt A (1975) *Management Attitudes and Practices towards Women at Work*, London: HMSO.

Husbands R (1992) 'Sexual harassment law in employment: an international perspective', *International Labour Review*, 131: 535-559.

Hussmanns R (1989) 'International standards on the measurement of economic activity, employment, unemployment and underemployment', *ILO Bulletin of Labour Statistics*, No. 1989-1: IX-XX.

Hutson S and Cheung W (1991) 'Saturday jobs: sixth-formers in the labour market and in the family' in *Household and Family: Divisions and Change* (eds) S Arber and C Marsh, London: Macmillan.

Huws U (1984) 'New technology homeworkers', *Employment Gazette*, 92: 13-17.

IER (1995) *Review of the Economy and Employment: Occupational Assessment*, Coventry: University of Warwick Institute for Employment Research.

ILO (1962) 'Discrimination in employment or occupations on the basis of marital status', *International Labour Review*, 85: 368-89.

ILO (1990a) *Statistical Sources and Methods: Economically Active Population, Employment and Hours of Work*, Geneva: ILO.

ILO (1990b) 'Methodology of labour force surveys in 70 countries', *ILO Bulletin of Labour Statistics*, No. 1990-2: XVIII-XXIV.

Imperato-McGinley J et al (1979) 'Androgens and the evolution of male-gender identity among male pseudohermaphrodites with 5a reductase deficiency', *New England Journal of Medicine*, 300/22: 1233-37.

IRRR (1991) 'Long-term earnings trends 1971-91', *Industrial Relations Review and Report*, No. 500: 2-8.

Irvine J, Miles I and Evans J (eds) (1979) *Demystifying Social Statistics*, London: Pluto Press.

Jacobs J A (1989a) 'Long-term trends in occupational segregation by sex', *American Journal of Sociology*, 95: 160-173.

Jacobs J A (1989b) *Revolving Doors: Sex Segregation and Women's Careers*, Stanford: Stanford University Press.

Jacobs J A and Lim S T (1992) 'Trends in occupational and industrial sex segregation in 56 countries, 1960-1980', *Work and Occupations*, 19: 450-86. Reprinted pp 259-293 in *Gender Inequality at Work* (ed) J Jacobs, Thousand Oaks: Sage.

Jacobs S (1995) 'Changing patterns of sex segregated occupations throughout the life-course', *European Sociological Review*, 11: 157-171.

James D R, Taeuber K E. (1985) 'Measures of segregation' pp 1-31 in *Sociological Methodology* (ed) N B Tuma, San Francisco: Josey Bass.

Jenson J, Hagen E and Reddy C (eds) (1988) *Feminization of the Labour Force: Paradoxes and Promises*, New York: Oxford University Press.

Jones R M (1971) *Absenteeism*, Manpower Paper No. 4, London: HMSO.

Jonung C and Persson I (1993) 'Women and market work: the misleading tale of participation rates in international comparisons', *Work, Employment and Society*, 7: 259-274.

Joseph G (1983) *Women at Work*, Oxford: Philip Allen.

Joshi H E (1981) 'Secondary workers in the employment cycle: Great Britain, 1961-1974', *Economica*, No. 189, 48: 29-44.

Joshi H E, Layard R and Owen S J (1985) 'Why are more women working in Britain? ', *Journal of Labor Economics*, special issue on *Trends in Women's Work, Education and Family Building* (eds) R Layard and J Mincer, 3: S147-S176.

Joshi H E and Owen S (1987) 'How long is a piece of elastic? The measurement of female activity rates in British censuses, 1951-1981', *Cambridge Journal of Economics*, 11: 55-74.

Kahn P and Meehan E (eds) (1992) *Equal Value/Comparable Worth in the UK and the USA*, London: Macmillan.

Kalleberg A L (1977) 'Work values and job rewards: a theory of job satisfaction', *American Sociological Review*, 42: 124-143.

Kanter R M (1977) *Men and Women of the Corporation*, New York: Basic Books.

Kay H (1984) 'Is childminding real work?', *Employment Gazette*, 92: 483-6.
Kay J A and King M A (1978) *The British Tax System*, Oxford: Oxford University Press.
Kiernan K (1992) 'Men and women at work and at home' pp 89-112 in *British Social Attitudes: the 9th Report* (eds) R Jowell et al, Aldershot, Hants: Dartmouth.
Kilbourne B S, England P, Farkas G, Beron K and Weir D (1994) 'Returns to skill, compensating differentials and gender bias: effects of occupational characteristics on the wages of white women and men', *American Journal of Sociology*, 100: 689-719.
Killingsworth M R (1990) *The Economics of Comparable Worth*, Kalamazoo MA: W E Upjohn Institute.
King M C (1992) 'Occupational segregation by race and sex, 1940-88', *Monthly Labor Review*, 115/4: 30-37.

Lane C (1983) 'Women in socialist society with special reference to the German Democratic Republic', *Sociology*, 17: 489-505.
Laufer J (1993) 'Women in business and management – France' pp 107-32 in *European Women in Business and Management* (eds) M J Davidson and C L Cooper, London: Paul Chapman.
Leete L and Schor J B (1994) 'Assessing the time-squeeze hypothesis: hours worked in the United States, 1969-89', *Industrial Relations*, 33: 25-43.
Leighton P (1983) *Contractual Arrangements in Selected Industries: A study of employment relationships in industries with outwork*, Research Paper No. 39, London: Department of Employment.
Lewin-Epstein N and Semyonov M (1992) 'Modernization and subordination: Arab women in the Israeli labour-force', *European Sociological Review*, 8: 39-51.
Lewis J (1984) *Women in England 1870-1950: Sexual Divisions and Social Change*, Brighton: Wheatsheaf and Bloomington: Indiana University Press.
Lewis J (1992) *Women in Britain Since 1945 – Women, Family, Work and the State*, Oxford: Blackwell.
Lewis R (1986) *Labour Law in Britain*, Oxford: Blackwells.
Lipset S M, Trow M A and Coleman J S (1956) *Union Democracy: The Internal Politics of the International Typographical Union*, Garden City NY: Anchor Books.
Loveridge R (1983) 'Labour market segmentation and the firm' pp 155-175 in *Manpower Planning: Strategy and Techniques in an Organisational Context*, Chichester: John Wiley & Sons.
Loveridge R (1987) 'Stigma – the manufacture of disadvantage' and 'Social accommodation and technological transformations – the case of gender' pp 2-17 and 176-197 in *The Manufacture of Disadvantage: Stigma and*

*Social Closure* (eds) G Lee and R Loveridge. Milton Keynes: Open University Press.

Ma Youcai, Wang Zhenyu, Sheng Xuewen and Shinozaki Masami (1994) *A Study of Life and Consciousness of the Contemporary Urban Family in China: A Study in Beijing with Comparisons with Bangkok, Seoul and Fukuoka*, Beijing: Chinese Academy of Social Sciences with Kitakyushu Forum on Asian Women.

Macarov D (1982a) 'The work personality: a neglected element in research', *International Journal of Manpower*, 3(4): 2-8.

Macarov D (1982b) *Worker Productivity: Myths and Reality*, Beverly Hills: Sage.

Madden J F (1981) 'Why women work closer to home', *Urban Studies*, 18: 181-194.

Main B (1988a) 'The lifetime attachment of women to the labour market' pp 23-51 in *Women and Paid Work* (ed) A Hunt, London: Macmillan.

Main B (1988b) 'Women's hourly earnings: the influence of work histories on rates of pay', pp 105-122 in *Women and Paid Work* (ed) A Hunt, London: Macmillan.

Maret E (1983) *Women's Career Patterns*, Lanham MD: University Press of America.

Marshall H (1993) *Not Having Children*, Melbourne: Oxford University Press Australia.

Martin J and Roberts C (1984) *Women and Employment: A Lifetime Perspective*, London: HMSO.

Martin J K and Hanson S L (1985) 'Sex, family wage-earning status and satisfaction with work', *Work and Occupations*, 12: 91-109.

Matheson J (1990) *Voluntary Work*, GHS-17/A, London HMSO for OPCS.

Matthaei J A (1982) *An Economic History of Women in America: Women's work, the sexual division of labour and the development of capitalism*, New York: Schocken/Brighton: Harvester.

Mayhew K and Rosewell B (1978) 'Immigrants and occupational crowding in Great Britain', *Oxford Bulletin of Economics and Statistics*, 40: 223-48.

McCrudden C (ed) (1987) *Women, Employment and European Equality Law*, London: Eclipse.

McCrudden C, Smith D J and Brown C (1991) *Racial Justice at Work: The Enforcement of the Race Relations Act 1976 in Employment*, London: Policy Studies Institute.

McRae S (1991) *Maternity Rights in Britain*, London: Policy Studies Institute.

Mellor E F and Parks W (1988) 'A year's work: labor force activity from a different perspective', *Monthly Labor Review*, 111/9: 13-18.

Meulders D, Plasman R and Vander Stricht V (1993) *The Position of Women on the Labour Market in the European Community*, Aldershot: Dartmouth Publishing.

Meulders D, Plasman O and Plasman R (1994) *Atypical Employment in the EC*, Aldershot: Dartmouth Publishing.

Middleton C (1988) 'The familiar fate of the *Famulae*: Gender divisions in the history of wage labour' pp 21-47 in *On Work* (ed) R Pahl, Oxford: Blackwell.

Mikes G (1966) *How to be an Alien: A Handbook for Beginners and Advanced Pupils*, Harmondsworth: Penguin.

Milkman R (1987) *Gender at Work: The Dynamics of Job Segregation by Sex During World War II*, Urbana and Chicago: University of Illinois Press.

Miller J B (1976) *Toward a New Psychology of Women*, Boston: Beacon.

Millward N, Stevens M, Smart D and Hawes W R (1992) *Workplace Industrial Relations in Transition: The ED/ESRC/PSI/ACAS Surveys*, Aldershot: Dartmouth.

Mincer J (1962) 'Labor force participation of married women: a study of labor supply' pp 63-73 in *Aspects of Labor Economics*, Princeton: Princeton University Press, reprinted pp 41-51 in *The Economics of Women and Work* (ed) A H Amsden, 1980, Harmondsworth: Penguin.

Mincer J (1985) 'Intercountry comparisons of labor force trends and of related developments: an overview', *Journal of Labor Economics*, special issue on *Trends in Women's Work, Education and Family Building*, S1-S32.

Mincer J and Ofek H (1982) 'Interrupted work careers: depreciation and restoration of human capital', *Journal of Human Resources*, 17: 3-24.

Mincer J and Polachek S (1974) 'Family investments in human capital: earnings of women', *Journal of Political Economy*, 82: S76-S110

Mogensen G V (ed) (1990) *Time and Consumption*, Copenhagen: Danmarks Statistik.

Molm I D (1986) 'Gender, power and legitimation: a test of three theories', *American Journal of Sociology*, 91: 1356-86.

Moore H L (1994) *A Passion for Difference: Essays in Anthropology and Gender*, Cambridge: Polity Press.

More G C (1993) 'Equal treatment of the sexes in European Community law: what does 'equal' mean?', *Feminist Legal Studies*, 1: 45-74.

Morell C M (1994) *Unwomanly Conduct: The Challenges of Intentional Childlessness*, New York and London: Routledge.

Morgan S P and Waite L J (1987) 'Parenthood and the attitudes of young adults', *American Sociological Review*, 52: 541-547.

Morse N C and Weiss R S (1955) 'The function and meaning of work and the job', *American Sociological Review*, 20: 191-198.

Mott F L (ed) (1978) *Women, Work and Family*, Lexington, MA: D C Heath.

Mott F L (ed) (1982) *The Employment Revolution: Young American Women of the 1970s*, Cambridge, MA: MIT Press.

MOW (Meaning of Work) International Research Team (1987) *The Meaning of Working*, London: Academic Press.

Mueller C W, Wallace J E and Price J L (1992) 'Employee commitment: resolving some issues', *Work and Occupations*, 19: 211-36.

Myrdal A and Klein V (1956, 1968) *Women's Two Roles: Home and Work*, London: Routledge.

Naylor K (1994) 'Part-time working in Great Britain – an historical analysis', *Employment Gazette*, 102: 473-484.

Naylor M and Purdie E (1992) 'Results of the 1991 Labour Force Survey', *Employment Gazette*, 100: 153-172.

Nielsen R and Szyszczak E (1991) *The Social Dimension of the European Community*, Copenhagen: Handelshojskolens Forlag.

Nuss S and Majka L (1983) 'The economic integration of women: a cross-national investigation', *Work and Occupations*, 10: 29-48.

Nyberg A (1994) 'The social construction of married women's labour-force participation: the case of Sweden in the twentieth century', *Continuity and Change*, 9: 145-156.

Oakley A (1974, 1985) *The Sociology of Housework*, Oxford: Blackwell.

Oakley A (1976) *Housewife*, Harmondsworth: Penguin.

OECD (1984) 'Employment turnover and job tenure', *Employment Outlook*, Paris: OECD.

OECD (1985) *The Integration of Women into the Economy*, Paris: OECD.

OECD (1987) 'Occupational differentials in earnings and labour demand', *Employment Outlook*, Paris: OECD.

OECD (1988) 'Women's activity, employment and earnings: A review of recent developments', *Employment Outlook*, Paris: OECD.

OECD (1989) 'Job tenure by industry', *Employment Outlook*, Paris: OECD.

OECD (1990) 'Maternity and parental leave', *Employment Outlook*. Paris: OECD.

OECD (1991) 'Absence from work reported in labour force surveys', *Employment Outlook*, Paris: OECD.

OECD (1993) 'Enterprise tenure, labour turnover and skill training' and 'Earnings inequality: changes in the 1980s', *Employment Outlook*, Paris: OECD.

OECD (1994) *Women and Structural Change: New Perspectives*, Paris: OECD.

O'Leary B and McGarry J (1993) *The Politics of Antagonism: Understanding Northern Ireland*, London: Athlone.

O'Neill J (1985) 'The trend in the male-female wage gap in the United States', *Journal of Labor Economics*, 3: S91-S116.

O'Neill J and Polachek S (1993) 'Why the gender gap in wages narrowed in the 1980s', *Journal of Labor Economics*, 11: 205-28.

OPCS (1983) *General Household Survey 1981*, London: HMSO for OPCS.

OPCS (1988) *Census 1971-1981: The Longitudinal Study – England and Wales*, CEN81LS, London: HMSO for OPCS.

OPCS (1991) *Standard Occupational Classification, Vol 3: Social Classifications and Coding Methodology*, London: HMSO for OPCS.

OPCS (1992) *GHS: Carers in 1990*, OPCS Monitor SS92/2, London: OPCS.

OPCS (1994) *1991 Census – Economic Activity Great Britain*, London: HMSO.

OPCS (1995) *General Household Survey 1993*, London: HMSO.

Oppenheimer V K (1970) *The Female Labor Force in the United States*, Westport, Conn.: Greenwood Press.

Osmond M W and Martin P Y (1975) 'Sex and sexism: a comparison of male and female sex-role attitudes', *Journal of Marriage and the Family*, 37: 744-58.

Owen D (1994) *Ethnic Minority Women and the Labour Market: Analysis of the 1991 Census*, Manchester: Equal Opportunities Commission.

Owen S J and Joshi H (1987) 'Does elastic retract: the effect of recession on women's labour force participation', *British Journal of Industrial Relations*, 25: 125-143.

Pahl J M and Pahl R E (1971) *Managers and their Wives*, Harmondsworth: Penguin.

Pahl R E (1984) *Divisions of Labour*, Oxford: Blackwell.

Pahl R E (ed) (1988) *On Work: Historical, Comparative and Theoretical Approaches*, Oxford: Basil Blackwell.

Papanek H (1973) 'Men, women and work: reflections on the two-person career', pp 90-110 in *Changing Women in a Changing Society* (ed) J Huber, Chicago and London: University of Chicago Press.

Payne M (1995) 'Patterns of pay: results of the 1995 New Earnings Survey', *Labour Market Trends*, 103: 405-412.

Pfau-Effinger B (1993) 'Modernisation, culture and part-time employment: the example of Finland and West Germany', *Work, Employment and Society*, 7: 383-410.

Phelps E S (1972) 'The statistical theory of racism and sexism', *American Economic Review*, 62: 659-661

Phillips A and Taylor B (1980) 'Sex and skill: notes towards a feminist economics', *Feminist Review*, 6: 79-88.

Pitt G (1992) *Employment Law*, London: Sweet and Maxwell.

Polachek S W (1979) 'Occupational segregation among women: theory, evidence and a prognosis' pp 137-70 in *Women in the Labor Market* (ed) C B Lloyd, E S Andrews and C L Gilroy, New York: Columbia University Press.

Pollert A (1981) *Girls, Wives, Factory Lives*, London: Macmillan.

Pott-Buter H A (1993) *Facts and Fairy Tales about Female Labor, Family and Fertility: A Seven-Country Comparison, 1850-1990*, Amsterdam: Amsterdam University Press.

Power M (1988) 'Women, the state and the family in the US: Reaganomics and the experience of women', pp 140-162 in J Rubery (ed.) *Women and Recession*, London: Routledge & Kegan Paul.

Prechal S and Burrows N (1990) *Gender Discrimination Law of the European Community*, Aldershot, Hants: Gower.

Pringle R (1988, 1989) *Secretaries Talk: Sexuality, Power and Work*, London & New York: Verso.

Purcell J (1993) 'The end of institutional industrial relations', *Political Quarterly*, 64: 6-23.

Redclift N (1985) 'Gender, accumulation and the labour process' in *Beyond Employment* (eds) E Mingione and N Redclift, Oxford: Blackwell, reprinted 1988 in *On Work* (ed) Pahl R E, Oxford: Blackwell, pp 428-448.

Redmond M (1986) 'Women and minorities' pp 472-502 in *Labour Law in Britain* (ed) R Lewis, Oxford: Blackwells.

Reskin B (ed) (1984) *Sex Segregation in the Workplace: Trends, Explanations, Remedies*, Washington DC: National Academy Press.

Reskin B F and Hartmann H I (eds) (1986) *Women's Work, Men's Work: Sex Segregation on the Job*, Washington DC: National Academy Press.

Reskin B and Padavic I (1994) *Women and Men at Work*, Thousand Oaks, CA: Pine Forge.

Reskin B F and Roos P A (1990) *Job Queues, Gender Queues: Explaining Women's Inroads into Male Occupations*, Philadelphia: Temple University Press.

Rexroat C (1992) 'Changes in the employment continuity of succeeding cohorts of young women', *Work and Occupations*, 19: 18-34.

Rexroat C and Shehan C (1984) 'Expected versus actual work roles of women', *American Sociological Review*, 49: 349-358.

Riboud M (1985) 'An analysis of women's labour force participation in France: cross-section estimates and time series evidence', *Journal of Labor Economics*, special issue on *Trends in Women's Work, Education and Family Building*, 3: S177-S200.

Roberts E (1984) *A Woman's Place: An Oral History of Working Class Women 1890-1940*, Oxford: Blackwell.

Robinson J P and Gershuny J (1994) 'Measuring hours of paid work: time-diary vs. estimate questions' pp xi-xvii in *Bulletin of Labour Statistics*, 1994-1, Geneva: ILO.

Rodgers G and Rodgers J (eds) (1989) *Precarious Jobs in Labour Market Regulation*, International Institute for Labour Studies, Geneva: International Labour Office.

Rogers B (1981) *The Domestication of Women: Discrimination in Developing*

*Societies*, London: Tavistock.

Roos P A (1983) 'Marriage and women's occupational attainment in cross-cultural perspective', *American Sociological Review*, 48: 852-64.

Rose M (1994) 'Skill and Samuel Smiles: changing the British work ethic', pp 281-335 in *Skill and Occupational Change* (eds) R Penn, M Rose and J Rubery, Oxford: Oxford University Press.

Rosenfeld R (1983) 'Sex segregation and sectors', *American Sociological Review*, 48: 637-56.

Rosenfeld R A and Kalleberg A L (1990) 'A cross-national comparison of the gender gap in income', *American Journal of Sociology*, 96: 69-106.

Rosenfeld R A, Spenner K I (1992) 'Occupational segregation and women's early career job shifts', *Work and Occupations*, 19: 424-49, reprinted pp 231-258 in *Gender Inequality at Work* (ed) J A Jacobs, 1995, London: Sage: 231-258.

Rossi A (1977) 'A biosocial perspective on parenting', *Daedalus*, 106: 1-31.

Routh G (1965, 1980) *Occupation and Pay in Great Britain 1906-79*, London: Macmillan.

Routh G (1987) *Occupations of the People of Great Britain, 1801-1981*, London: Macmillan.

Rubery J (ed) (1988) *Women and Recession*, London: Routledge & Kegan Paul.

Rubery J and Fagan C (1993) *Occupational Segregation of Women and Men in the European Community*, *Social Europe*, Supplement 3/93, Luxembourg: Office for Official Publications of the European Communities.

Rubery J and Fagan C (1994) *Wage Determination and Sex Segregation in Employment in the European Community*, *Social Europe*, Supplement 4/94, Luxembourg: Office for Official Publications of the European Communities.

Rubery J and Fagan C (1995a) 'Gender segregation in societal context', *Work, Employment and Society*, 9: 213-240.

Rubery and Fagan C (1995b) 'Comparative industrial relations research: towards reversing the gender bias', *British Journal of Industrial Relations*, 33: 209-236.

Rubery J, Horrell S and Burchell B (1994) 'Part-time work and gender inequality in the labour market' pp 205-234 in *Gender Segregation and Social Change* (ed) A M Scott, Oxford: Oxford University Press.

Rytina N F. (1981) 'Occupational segregation and earnings differences by sex', *Monthly Labor Review*, 104/1: 49-53.

Sandell S and Shapiro D (1980) 'Work expectations, human capital accumulation and the wages of young women', *Journal of Human Resources*, 15: 335-53.

Saunders C and Marsden D (1981) *Pay Inequalities in the European Communities*, London: Butterworths.

Sayer A (1984) *Method in Social Science: A Realist Approach*, London: Routledge.

Scott A M (ed) (1994) *Gender Segregation and Social Change*, Oxford: Oxford University Press.

Scott A M and Burchell B (1994) 'And never the twain shall meet? - Gender segregation and work histories' pp 121-156 in *Gender Segregation and Social Change* (ed) A M Scott, Oxford: Oxford University Press.

Scott J (1990) 'Women and the family' pp 51-76 in *British Social Attitudes: the 7th Report* (eds) R Jowell et al, Aldershot, Hants: Gower.

Scott J, Braun M and Alwin D (1993) 'The family way' pp 23-47' in *International Social Attitudes: The 10th BSA Report* (eds) R Jowell et al, Aldershot, Hants: Dartmouth.

Shaw L B (ed) (1983) *Unplanned Careers*, Lexington MA: D C Heath.

Shaw L B and Shapiro D (1987) 'Women's work plans: contrasting expectations and actual work experience', *Monthly Labor Review*, 110/11: 7-13.

Sieling M S (1984) 'Staffing patterns prominent in female-male earnings gap', *Monthly Labor Review*, 107/6: 29-33.

Siltanen J (1994) *Locating Gender: Occupational Segregation, Wages and Domestic Responsibilities*, London: UCL.

Sloane P J (1990) 'Sex differentials: structure, stability and change', pp 125-171 in *A Portrait of Pay, 1970-1982: An Analysis of the New Earnings Survey* (eds.) M B Gregory and A W J Thomson, Oxford: Clarendon Press.

Sly F (1993) 'Women in the labour market', *Employment Gazette*, 101: 483-502.

Sly F (1994) 'Mothers in the labour market', *Employment Gazette*, 102: 403-413.

Smart C (1976) *Women, Crime and Criminology: A Feminist Critique*, London: Routledge.

Smart C and Smart B (eds) (1978) *Women, Sexuality and Social Control*, London: Routledge.

Smith J P and Ward M P (1984) *Women's Wages and Work in the Twentieth Century*, Santa Monica, CA: Rand Corporation.

Smith S J (1982) 'New worklife estimates reflect changing profile of labor force', *Monthly Labor Review*, 105/3: 15-20.

Smith S J (1983) 'Estimating annual hours of labor force activity', *Monthly Labor Review*, 106/2: 13-22.

Sohrab J A (1993) 'Avoiding the exquisite trap: a critical look at the equal treatment/special treatment debate in law', *Feminist Legal Studies*, 1: 141-162

Sorensen A and McLanahan S (1987) 'Married women's economic dependency, 1940-1980', *American Journal of Sociology*, 93: 659-87.

Sorensen A and Trappe H (1995) 'The persistence of gender inequality in earnings in the German Democratic Republic', *American Sociological Review*, 60: 398-406.

Sorensen E (1989) 'The wage effects of occupational sex composition: a review and new findings', pp 57-89 in *Comparable Worth: Analyses and Evidence* (eds) M A Hill and M R Killingsworth, Ithaca NY: ILR Press.

Sorensen J B (1990) 'Perceptions of women's opportunity in five industrialised nations', *European Sociological Review*, 6: 151-164.

Spence A (1992) 'Patterns of pay: results of the 1992 New Earnings Survey', *Employment Gazette*, 100: 579-591.

Spitze G D and Waite L J (1980) 'Labor force and work attitudes', *Work and Occupations*, 7: 3-32.

Stafford F P (1980) 'Women's use of time converging with men's', *Monthly Labor Review*, 103(12): 57-9.

Statistics Sweden (1995) *Women and Men in Sweden*, Orebro: Statistics Sweden Publication Services.

Steinberg R (1988) 'The unsubtle revolution: women, the state and equal employment' pp 189-213 in *Feminisation of the Labour Force: Paradoxes and Promises* (eds) J Jenson, E Hagen and C Reddy, New York: Oxford University Press.

Stephan P E and Schroeder L D (1979) 'Career decisions and labour force participation of married women' pp 119-135 in *Women in the Labor Market* (eds) C B Lloyd *et al*, New York: Columbia University Press.

Stewart M B and Greenhalgh C A (1984) 'Work history patterns and the occupational attainment of women', *Economic Journal*, 94: 493-519.

Stinson J F (1990) 'Multiple jobholding up sharply in the 1980s', *Monthly Labor Review*, 113/7: 3-10.

Stockman N, Bonney N and Sheng Xuewen (1995) *Women's Work in East and West: The Dual Burden of Employment and Family Life*, London: UCL.

Stoller R J (1975) *The Transexual Experiment*, London: Hogarth Press.

Stolzenberg R M and Waite L J (1977) 'Age, fertility expectations and plans for employment', *American Sociological Review*, 42: 769-783.

Strom S H (1989) 'Light manufacturing: the feminisation of American office work, 1900-1930', *Industrial Labor Relations Review*, 43: 53-71.

Summerfield P (1984) *Women Workers in the Second World War*, London: Croom Helm.

Sutherland S (1978) 'The unambitious female: women's low professional aspirations', *Signs*, 3: 774-94.

Thomas J J (1992) *Informal Economic Activity*, LSE Handbooks in Economics, Herts: Harvester Wheatsheaf.

Tijdens K (1993) 'Women in business and management – the Netherlands' pp 79-92 in *European Women in Business and Management* (eds) M J Davidson and C L Cooper, London: Paul Chapman.

Tilly L A and Scott J W (1990) *Women, Work and Family*, London:

Routledge.

Tokyo Metropolitan Government (1994) *International Comparative Survey of Issues Confronting Women*, Tokyo: Tokyo Metropolitan Government.

Tomaskovic-Devey D (1993) *Gender & Racial Inequality at Work: The Sources and Consequences of Job Segregation*, Ithaca: ILR Press.

Treadwell P (1987) 'Biologic influences on masculinity' pp 259-285 in *The Making of Masculinities* (ed) H Brod, Boston and London: Allen & Unwin.

Treiman D J and Hartmann H I (eds) (1981) *Women, Work and Wages: Equal Pay for Jobs of Equal Value*, Washington DC: National Academy Press.

Tsoukalis L (1993) *The New European Economy: The Politics and Economics of Integration*, Oxford: Oxford University Press.

Tzannatos Z and Zabalza A (1984) 'The anatomy of the rise of British female relative wages in the 1970s: evidence from the New Earnings Survey', *British Journal of Industrial Relations*, 22: 177-94.

United Nations (1995) *Human Development Report 1995*, Oxford: Oxford University Press.

Vaessen M (1984) *Childlessness and Infecundity*, World Fertility Survey Comparative Studies No. 31, Voorburg: International Statistical Institute.

Vanek J (1974) 'Time spent in housework', *Scientific American*, 231: 116-120, reprinted pp 82-90 in *The Economics of Women and Work* (ed) A H Amsden, Harmondsworth: Penguin.

Veevers J E (1973) 'Voluntarily childless wives: an exploratory study', *Sociology and Social Research*, 57: 356-66.

Vogler C (1994a) 'Segregation, sexism and labour supply', pp 39-79 in *Gender Segregation and Social Change* (ed) A M Scott, Oxford: Oxford University Press.

Vogler C (1994b) 'Money in the household', pp 225-66 in *The Social and Political Economy of the Household* (eds) M Anderson, F Bechhofer and J Gershuny, Oxford: Oxford University Press.

Waite L J and Berryman S E (1986) 'Job stability among young women: a comparison of traditional and non-traditional occupations', *American Journal of Sociology*, 92: 568-595.

Waite L J and Stolzenberg R M (1976) 'Intended childbearing and labor force participation of young women: insights from nonrecursive models', *American Sociological Review*, 41: 235-252.

Waite L J, Haggstrom G W and Kanouse D (1986) 'The consequences of parenthood for the marital stability of young adults', *American Sociological Review*, 50: 850-857.

Walby S (1986) *Patriarchy at Work: Patriarchal and Capitalist Relations in Employment*, Cambridge: Polity Press.

Walby S (1990) *Theorising Patriarchy*, Oxford: Blackwell.

Waring M (1988) *Counting for Nothing: What Men Value and What Women are Worth*, Wellington: Allen & Unwin/Port Nicholson.

Warr P (1982) 'A national study of non-financial employment commitment', *Journal of Occupational Psychology*, 55: 297-312.

Watson G (1992) 'Hours of work in Great Britain and Europe: Evidence from the UK and European Labour Force Surveys', *Employment Gazette*, 100: 539-57.

Watson G (1994) 'The flexible workforce and patterns of working hours in the UK', *Employment Gazette*, 102: 239-247.

Watson G and Fothergill B (1993) 'Part-time employment and attitudes to part-time work', *Employment Gazette*, 101: 213-220.

Wellington A J (1994) 'Accounting for the male/female wage gap among whites: 1976 and 1985', *American Sociological Review*, 59: 839-848.

Werner B (1986) 'Family building intentions of different generations of women: results from the General Household Survey', *Population Trends*, 44: 17-23.

Werner B and Chalk S (1986) 'Projections of first, second, third and later births', *Population Trends*, 46: 26-34.

Wicker A (1969) 'Attitudes versus actions: the relationship of verbal and overt behavioral responses to attitude objects', *Journal of Social Issues*, 25: 41-78.

Willborn S L (1989) *A Secretary and a Cook: Challenging Women's Wages in the Courts of the United States and Great Britain*, Ithaca, NY: ILR Press.

Williams C L (1989) *Gender Differences at Work: Women and Men in Nontraditional Occupations*, Berkeley and London: University of California Press.

Williams G (1976) 'Trends in occupational differentiation by sex', *Sociology of Work and Occupations*, 3: 38-62.

Willis P (1977) *Learning to Labour: How Working Class Kids Get Working Class Jobs*, Farnborough, Hants: Saxon House.

Witherspoon S (1988) 'Interim report: a woman's work', pp 175-200 in *British Social Attitudes: the 5th Report*, (eds) Jowell R et al, Aldershot, Hants: Gower.

Witherspoon S and Prior S (1991) 'Working mothers: free to choose?' pp 131-154 in *British Social Attitudes: the 8th Report* (eds) R Jowell et al, Aldershot, Hants: Gower.

Wood R G, Corcoran M E, Courant P N. (1993) 'Pay differences among the highly paid: the male-female earnings gap in lawyers' salaries', *Journal of Labor Economics*, 11: 417-41.

Wright E O, Baxter J and Birkelund G E (1995) 'The gender gap in workplace authority: a cross-national study', *American Sociological Review*, 60: 407-435.

Yankelovich D (1985) *The World at Work*, New York: Octagon Books.

Young M and Willmott P (1973) *The Symmetrical Family*, London: Routledge, reprinted 1975, Penguin.

Zabalza A and Arrufat J (1985) 'The extent of sex discrimination in Great Britain' pp 70-96, 120-137 in *Women and Equal Pay: The Effects of Legislation on Female Employment and Wages in Britain*, A Zabalza and Z Tzannatos, Cambridge: Cambridge University Press.

Zabalza A and Tzannatos Z (1985a) 'The effect of Britain's anti-discriminatory legislation on relative pay and employment', *Economic Journal*, 95: 679-99.

Zabalza A and Tzannatos Z (1985b) *Women and Equal Pay: The Effects of Legislation on Female Employment and Wages*, Cambridge: Cambridge University Press.

Zabalza A and Tzannatos Z (1988) 'Reply to comments on the effects of Britain's anti-discrimination legislation on relative pay and employment', *Economic Journal*, 98: 839-843.

Zelizer V A (1989) 'The social meaning of money: special monies', *American Journal of Sociology*, 95: 342-37.

# Subject Index

# Author Index

# THE MAGIC OF
# PALM READING

SWEETWATER
PRESS

*The Magic of Palm Reading*

Copyright © 2007 Cliff Road Books, Inc.
Produced by arrangement with Sweetwater Press

Design by Miles G. Parsons

Printed in The United States of America

ISBN-13: 978-1-58173-539-0
ISBN-10: 1-58173-539-1

# THE MAGIC OF
# PALM READING

**Ian Alan**

SWEETWATER
PRESS

# TABLE OF CONTENTS

# THE UNKNOWN REVEALED

Let me ask you a few questions.

Does the unknown attract and fascinate you? Do you feel the lure of hidden things? Have you always felt that you have an exceptional human gift of some kind, like ESP or clairvoyance? Would you like to uncover the deepest secrets of your own mind's twilight world or—more importantly—divine the secrets of another's mind?

During the sweep of centuries mankind has developed the skills necessary to insure survival. The ability to predict the weather and the seasons put him in touch with those latent sensitivities that told him when to plant, when to harvest, and when to seek shelter. His dealings with others led him to develop a sixth sense that told him when to trust, when to fear, when to flee, and when to fight. As primitive man's innate sensitivities developed further, he created various systems of divination to help him refine his abilities. Perhaps the oldest system of divination known to early man is the subject of this book: Palmistry.

If you answered "Yes" to any of the questions above, then this is the book for you. Who among us wouldn't like to know what life has in store for us, what forces are at work beneath the surface of our own personalities, and what untapped abilities we have? Better yet, I am certain that you would like to possess the ability to uncover the most intimate secrets of others.

If you had the ability to uncover the deepest secrets of mind and personality, where might it lead you? Would you like to access the complete record of the past and be able to predict the future? With skill at Palm Reading, also known as Chiromancy, you can accomplish all these things and so much more.

The hand, as you are about to learn, is a transcendental clock that determines the time of life and the forces that shape that life. Within the clockwork mechanism of lines, mounds, and swirls, your fortune and fate are clearly presented.

Your palm also reveals when events are likely to occur in your life. That is, if you know what to look for. It is a fascinating study and one upon which you are about to embark.

Welcome to the world of Palm Reading!

# How to Give a Palm Reading

The language of Palmistry is intuitive. Therefore, you must learn to not only speak the language of intuition but also learn to listen intuitively to the subject's body language and subtle physical clues as you read a palm.

The reading that follows is my variation on a presentation that has been used by professional magicians and palm readers for almost sixty years. It is a script that will serve as the foundation and starting point for all of your explorations in palmistry. Memorize it "as is" or rewrite it to fit your personality. Every successful palm reader has his or her own manner of speaking and the script should reflect who you are.

Take your time with this. Start by memorizing one or two statements at a time. In short order you'll have all of them under your belt. Through this reading, you will accomplish three things:

1) Learn to speak like a palm reader;

2) Build skill at intuitively reading your subject;

3) Convince your subject that you can see his or her most hidden attributes.

Each section contains a statement that is designed to get a reaction out of your subject. Specifically, they will agree or disagree with the statements you make. This will lead you to specific responses. If you deliver the statements and responses with confidence, your subject will be convinced that you can see things about them that others cannot see. This will build a bond between you and your subject that will make it easier to actually interpret the lines and formations in their palm. In point of fact, it will supercharge your palm reading!

This skill, called cold reading, is a fundamental ability that every great palm reader possesses. After you learn it you will be able to easily apply actual palm reading knowledge along the way. Armed with cold reading ability and a detailed knowledge of the landscape of the hand that follows, you will become a member of the ancient fraternity of palm readers.

*"The study of the human hand is worth the while of an elevating and enquiring mind."*

*Alexander the Great*

# THE BASIC PALM READING

Here is a suggested script for a basic cold reading.

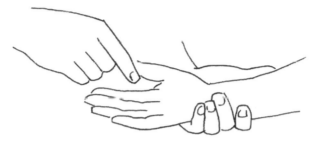

"Hello.

"Let's see what secrets your palm reveals.

"Please give me the hand that you use to explore the world in which you live.

"If you are right-handed your left hand is your Inner Hand. It reveals your natural talents and inclinations. Your Inner Hand contains a record of your power and your potential. Your right hand is your Outer Hand. It shows us where your natural inclinations, power, and talents are destined to take you.

"With left-handed people the right hand is the Inner Hand and the left is the Outer.

"Keep your hand open and relaxed so that I can interpret it properly.

"Hmm...This is very interesting. I see conflicting indicators, which by itself isn't unusual. But these particular groupings are intriguing."

## First Statement

"Your palm seems to indicate that sometimes you are outgoing and social, yet at other times not so much."

*If your subject's body language or facial expression says "yes" then you reply:*

"These lines tell me that you are sensitive and aware in social situations and tend to go with the flow of what's happening around you."

*If your subject's body language or facial expression says "no" then you reply:*

"You are pretty steady inside aren't you? However, your palm reveals that you are also a bit of a chameleon, as well. I see changing lines in your palm that mean you can change—or at least appear to—with the situation."

## Second Statement

"What's the best thing to do, right now?" (Pause and stare intently at the subject's hand.) "You ask yourself that question as well, don't you? Frequently, you have reservations."

*If your subject's body language or facial expression says "yes" then you reply:*

"People trust you much more than you know. They see your talents and strengths. They also see your weaknesses, but they don't worry about them. Your palm shows trust."

*If your subject's body language or facial expression says "no" then you reply:*

"You project a bit too much and you second-guess yourself, but you are very focused. If you set your mind to a task, then you get it done. Your palm shows great determination."

## Third Statement

"The crosses in your palm show that you've learned the dangers of letting your guard down and being too honest with people."

*If your subject's body language or facial expression*
*says "yes" then you reply:*

"You've been hurt in the past. Secrets were betrayed. According to the crossed lines in your palm it appears that you got too close to an untrustworthy person and got hurt badly. It taught you to be cautious. I see caution and circumspection in the lines and swirls of your palm."

*If your subject's body language or facial expression*
*says "no" then you reply:*

"Having said that, the number of crosses in your palm tells me that you can keep confidences. Your palm shows that you'd make a great spy! Yes, you can keep a secret when you have to."

## Fourth Statement

"The combination of lines and whorls in your palm tell me that you like the flux and flow of life's changes."

*If your subject's body language or facial expression says "yes" then you reply:*

"However, you don't like to be inhibited or confined. I can see that you do not like complications and red tape."

*If your subject's body language or facial expression says "no" then you reply:*

"Yet, you like things to be orderly and organized. I also see from your palm that you don't appreciate the craziness of change just for the sake of change."

## Fifth Statement

"The shape and proportion of your palm and hand tell me that at heart you are a clear-thinking and free individual. Your hand also tells me that you don't blindly accept what other people tell you."

*If your subject's body language or facial expression*
*says "yes" then you reply:*

"There is an intuitive configuration in the structure of your palm. It is a hand that reflects the heart and soul. It shows someone who doesn't like pushy and ego-driven people."

*If your subject's body language or facial expression*
*says "no" then you reply:*

"But, your palm also reveals that you are a good listener. You have the ability to connect deeply with others. You will take stock of their wisdom, advice, and counsel."

## Sixth Statement

"I see by your palm and the shape of your fingers that you have many untapped talents and latent, or hidden, skills."

*If your subject's body language or facial expression says "yes" then you reply:*

"You tend to put things off a little, but the lines in your palm don't indicate that this is necessarily bad. In fact, it's OK. It allows you to think things through so you can make the best possible decision for yourself."

*If your subject's body language or facial expression says "no" then you reply:*

"Sometimes you feel like you have pushed yourself to the brink, the end of your rope. Remember, though, if you can break out of your own prison then you can truly be yourself. There is great power in being yourself. Your palm shows me the truth of it."

## Seventh Statement

"The mounts of your palm indicate that you are cool, calm, and collected on the outside, but nervous and tense on the inside. Perhaps, you're a little self-conscious?"

*If your subject's body language or facial expression says "yes" then you reply:*

"Your palm shows a history of sleepless nights and nervous habits. It also indicates an overly busy mind. It is time to relax a bit more and enjoy your life."

*If your subject's body language or facial expression says "no" then you reply:*

"Over the years, however, your outward behavior in dealing with life has shaped your personality for the better. I can see it in your palm. Be careful, though. You wouldn't want to become too detached and collected."

## Eighth Statement

"It seems from studying the details of your palm that you really want people to like you. Is that true?"

*If your subject's body language or facial expression says "yes" then you reply:*

"It appears that you want everything to go smoothly. Your hand's overall structure reveals that, in a difficult situation, you will compromise first. In difficult situations you will apologize first as well, even if you were not the one at fault."

*If your subject's body language or facial expression says "no" then you reply:*

"Don't get upset if people misread you. Your palm tells me that you have great depth, a depth that most people will never see. They would be lucky for the opportunity to get to know you."

## Ninth Statement

"The length of your fingers and the texture of your palm tell me that some of your closely held goals, wishes, and dreams are inclined to be a bit impractical."

*If your subject's body language or facial expression says "yes" then you reply:*

"But, that's fine. Your palm reveals a marvelously developed sense of mental resourcefulness and ingenuity. You can accomplish wonders, so dare to dream. Try to see things as they are; that will be of great help to you in the future."

*If your subject's body language or facial expression says "no" then you reply:*

"But, that's fine. Your palm indicates a mature individual who is aware of your gifts as well as your deficits. You plan ahead even more than you know."

## Tenth Statement

"Like each of us, the lines and swirls of your palm reveal shortcomings in your character. But it also shows that you know how to deal with them."

*If your subject's body language or facial expression says "yes" then you reply:*

"I'm not quite sure what it is, but I see clues in your palm that point to a secret weapon that helps you come out of any situation smelling like a rose. Things have worked out for you in the past because of it, and it will work for you in the future."

*If your subject's body language or facial expression says "no" then you reply:*

"Deep inside you have the strength to push through your weaknesses. I see it clearly in the lines of your palm. You possess great inner strength and fortitude, much more than you are aware of. You only have to release it."

## Eleventh Statement

"I see from the unique contours of your hand that you are liable to be a bit hard on yourself. Is that true?"

*If your subject's body language or facial expression says "yes" then you reply:*

"I know that you look for flaws in yourself but I have to say that I really don't see that many in your palm. Just remember that when you are overly critical of yourself, you end up being overly critical of others."

*If your subject's body language or facial expression says "no" then you reply:*

"But instead of being a bad thing, it has actually helped you to overcome great obstacles in your life. Your palm shows that you have stepped over quite a few pitfalls without ever knowing that you were in danger. Good work!"

## Closing

"All of this and so much more is revealed by the landscape of these hands; these hands that you have used to explore your world and navigate your life. Truly, you do—indeed—hold the world in the palm of your hand.

Thanks so much for the opportunity to read your palm."

That's all there is to it! Take your time when delivering this basic reading. It will put your subject at ease and give you time to analyze the lines, mounts, stars, and crosses in their palm. Soon you will begin to get intuitive flashes about the subject that you can include in the reading.

Now that you can give a reading based on your subject's subconscious reactions, it's time to delve into the venerable science of interpreting the structure, shape, and markings of the hand.

# READING THE SIZE AND SHAPE OF THE HANDS AND FINGERS

A professional palm reading begins with an examination of the overall shape and proportion of the subject's hands and fingers. Once you have the basic palm reading memorized well enough to present it, then you can inject an interpretation of the hands and fingers at any time during the reading.

Certainly you can base an entire reading on the interpretations that follow and dispense with the cold reading altogether. But they work best when they are combined. Presented in this way, the actual knowledge that you have regarding the size and shape of the hands and fingers will appear even more miraculous than it already is.

Take your time learning this information. Read and re-read it until it starts to sink in. Make a daily hobby out of looking at the size and shape of people's hands. Compare them to your own. Study every nuance of hand movement they make as well as their overall structure. Study the face, body, and mannerisms of each hand's owner. This is an important part of your education as a palm reader.

If you relax while delivering the basic palm reading then the information regarding the hands and fingers contained in this chapter will bubble to the surface. Eventually you will be able to access all of this ancient wisdom.

# TYPES OF HANDS

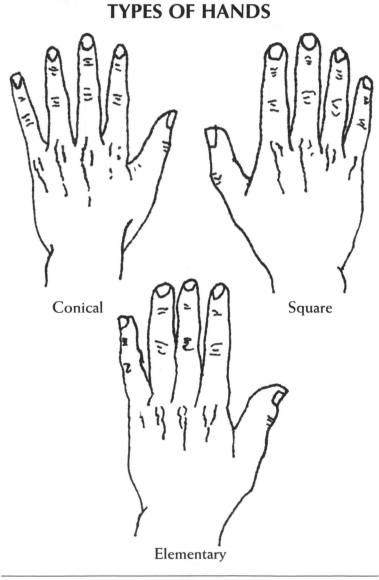

Conical

Square

Elementary

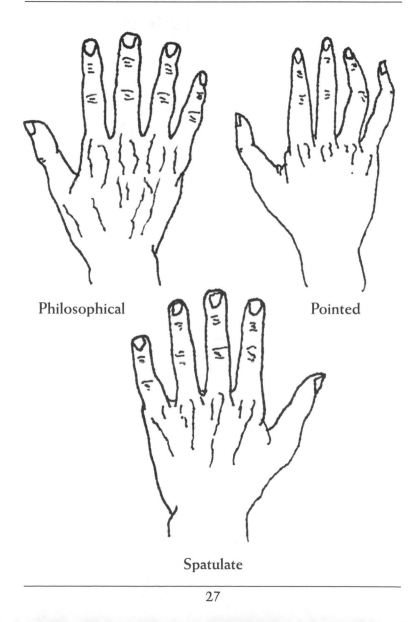

Philosophical

Pointed

Spatulate

# TYPES OF FINGER JOINTS

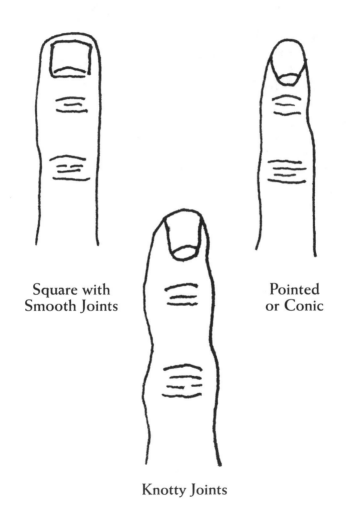

Square with
Smooth Joints

Pointed
or Conic

Knotty Joints

# TYPES OF THUMBS

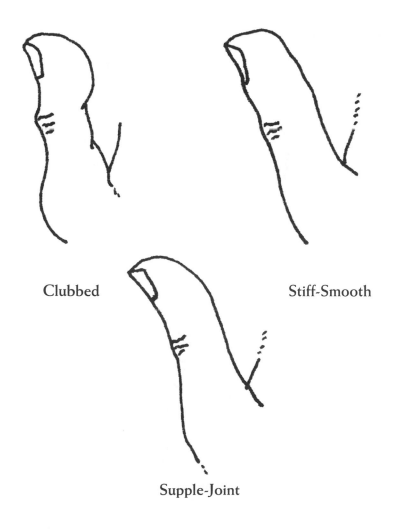

Clubbed

Stiff-Smooth

Supple-Joint

# TYPES OF THUMBS

Knotty-Jointed

Thick

Waisted

# TYPES OF NAILS

Very Broad-
Meddlesome

Short-Critical

Very Short-
Irritable

Long-
Artistic, Idealistic

Wedge-
Very Sensitive

Fluted-
Over-Exertion

# HAND INDICATORS

- **Well-proportioned** – healthy personality, poised, clear, and direct

- **Too long** – troublesome, interfering, meddling, tends towards maniacal behavior

- **Too short** – hot tempered, untrustworthy, many character flaws

- **Narrow (woman's hand)** – uncomfortable in intimate relationships, dislikes confining places and situations

- **Large for the body** – cleverness, cunning, devious, crafty

- **Short with fat fingers** – lazy, neglectful, prone to dizziness, sleepy personality

- **Fleshy and well-defined** – indicates a long and productive life

- **Hollow and undefined** – indicates a short and unproductive life

- **Long, narrow, and thin** – egotistical, pushy, likes to be in charge, unfriendly, inaccessible

- **Short and thin** – greedy, frugal, given to rumor and idle chatter

- **Fat and well-proportioned** – superior personality, unusual and valuable talents

- **Twisted and badly shaped** – strange personality, outlandish behavior, wild

- **Bulging** – very lucky, good with money, life is easy

- **Swarthy and soft** – unfaithful, double-dealing

- **Smooth and cold** – egotistical, insensitive, brash, unthinking

- **White and pale (even in motion)** – constant, unfaltering, determined

- **Pliant, supple, and slightly wrinkled** – kind, warmhearted, charitable, a good person

- **Inflexible, hard, and very wrinkled** – belligerent character, pugnacious, bellicose

# FIRST FINGER INDICATORS

- **Long** – authoritarian personality, pushy, a slave driver, a tyrant

- **Short** – tendency to give up, cut and run, a quitter, likes to play hooky

- **Average size** – very industrious, alert, enterprising with a keen disposition

- **Set low** – socially awkward, tends towards inappropriate behavior

- **Angles toward the thumb** – craving for more independence and personal freedom

- **Angles toward the second finger** – great self-esteem, self-gratifying, tends toward egotism

- **Longer than second finger** – overbearing, likes to be in control, power hungry

- **Shorter than second finger** – quiet disposition, secretive, hesitant, bashful

- **Equal in length with second finger** – obsessed with power and authority

- **Longer than third finger** – overly aggressive, excessive enthusiasm, given to unbridled excitement, unhealthy desire for success

- **Shorter than third finger** – a boring and unexciting life

- **Equal in length with third finger** – obsessed with popularity, money, and notoriety

# SECOND FINGER INDICATORS

- **Long** – dark, depressive disposition, gloomy, tends to brood

- **Short** – compliant, lenient, tends towards hedonism

- **Average size** – wise, sensible, a cautious personality

- **Crooked** – cold, distant, very calculating, brutal, a difficult personality

- **Angled toward first finger** – capricious, unpredictable, forceful with a hint of resignation and depression

- **Angled toward third finger** – macabre, unhealthy preoccupation with death and dying, focuses on the frightening and the dreadful

- **Longer than first finger** – sadness, silliness, moody disposition

- **Shorter than first finger** – desire for great success in life, very earnest

- **Equal in length with first finger** – passionate, takes the initiative, driven, and determined.

- **Longer than third finger** – fixated on being popular, boastful, a braggart, self-aggrandizing

- **Shorter than third finger** – impetuous, rash behavior, imprudent, headstrong

- **Equal in length with third finger** – takes chances, risk taking, speculation, a natural gambler

# THIRD FINGER INDICATORS

- **Long** – possesses the gambling instinct, tends to theorize, given to conspiracy theories and wild conjecture

- **Short** – love of money, obsessed with riches and fame

- **Average size** – wise, discreet, far-sighted, very shrewd negotiator

- **Crooked** – false sense of self, feigns accomplishment to impress others, given to phony creativity

- **Angled toward second finger** – vain, egotistical, morbidly conceited, condescending

- **Angled toward fourth finger** – possesses a solid artistic sense, skilled in business matters, able to identify with the common man

- **Longer than first finger** – love of creativity, passionately artistic, should own artwork

- **Shorter than first finger** – unguided passion, given to blind enthusiasm

- **Equal in length to first finger** – thirsts for popularity and acceptance, desires great fame and notoriety

- **Equal in length to fourth finger** – indicates a profound inner struggle, moral conflicts

- **Much shorter than fourth finger** – very artistic, creative, the promise of success as an artist

- **Longer than second finger** – rash, incautious, engages in dangerous behavior, insecure, touchy

- **Much shorter than second finger** – lack of motivation to succeed, frustration, feelings of inadequacy

- **Equal in length with second finger** – possesses a penchant for gambling

# FOURTH FINGER INDICATORS

- **Long** – cleverness, very sly, a penchant for deceitfulness, tricky, practical joker

- **Short** – apathetic, insensitive, reckless, tends toward egocentric behavior

- **Average size** – possessing a flexible nature and adaptable personality, resilient, a peace-maker and bridge builder

- **Crooked** – untruthful, cunning, deceitful, dishonest, a very tricky person, a schemer

- **Angled toward third finger** – prone to a life of business and commerce, creative with business, artistic

- **Equal in length with first finger** – tactful, calculating, very cunning, polite, clever

- **Equal in length with second finger** – very methodical, objective, possessing an experimental nature, scholarly

- **Equal in length with third finger** – cautious with an ability to see the big picture, public speaker, tends toward public service, a politician

# THUMB INDICATORS

- **Large thumb** – indicates a realistic life, pragmatic, useful, sensible, a solid existence

- **Small thumb** – emotional, romantic, given to affectionate displays, very passionate

- **Long** – caring, mindful, contemplative, tendency to be introspective

- **Short** – mental failings and impairment, vulnerable, defenseless, given to feeble reasoning and moral relativism

- **Very long** – stubborn, contradictory, inflexible, very opinionated

- **Very short** – faithless, flighty, inconstant, capricious, and changeable

- **Curves high** – indicates a stiff personality, unable to roll with the punches

- **Curves very high** – foolhardy, insane, half-witted

- **Thumb close to fingers** – given to avarice, tends toward excessiveness, ravenous, selfish

- **Thumb away from fingers** – very indulgent, wasteful, lavish, given to absurdity, tends to overdo

- **Flexible thumb** – given to uncommon behavior, unique, a non-conformist, unorthodox, individualistic

- **Stiff thumb** – obstinate behavior, headstrong, unyielding, inflexible personality, self-willed, tenacious

- **Slender thumb** – cultured, gracious, suave, elegant, civilized behavior

- **Thick thumb** – given to rude behavior, boisterous, impolite, wildness

- **Thumb bends back easily** – generous nature, charitable, honest, kind, tolerant, and magnanimous

- **Broad thumb** – given to destructive behavior, belligerent, brutal, roughness indicator

- **Flat thumb** – anxious, angry outbursts, moodiness, a penchant to worry, uneasiness

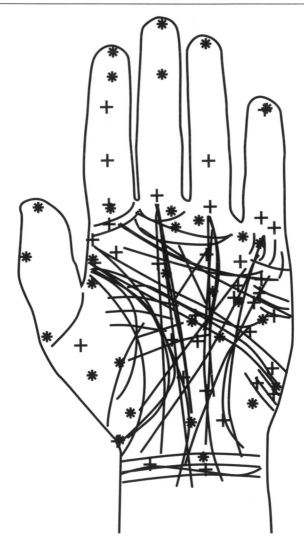

**The Celestial Dragon Palm**

# THE ART OF CHINESE PALM READING

Chinese Palm Reading is closely linked to the arts of Feng Shui and Chinese astrology. The life force of the subject is revealed in the palm, knuckles, and joints of the hand. The color and placement of the lines of the palm reveal the details of the subject's personality, as well as the overall direction of his or her life. The left hand reveals fundamental personality traits and inherited characteristics. The right hand shows mannerisms and habits that have been developed during the course of the subject's life.

It is important to note that these indicators are reversed if the subject is left-handed. However, many people will have a dominant hand that is the opposite of the hand that they normally use for writing. Over time, you will be able to discern which hand is dominant and therefore reveals fundamental personality traits.

Deep red lines show bountiful and powerful life force energy while shallow and pale lines indicate a propensity to lose or waste life energy. If there are numerous crosses, stars, branches, or breaks in a line, then the life force energy is leaking out of the subject and must be corrected if they are to live a long and healthy life. Interpreting all of these marks and formations is referred to as Taming the Celestial Dragon.

I chose Chinese Palm Reading for this chapter because it is a secret craft and is therefore relatively unknown among palm readers. It also lends an exotic flavor to any palm reading session. Remember, dispense this knowledge within the flow of the basic reading and your subject will credit you with great insight. In truth, knowledge of Chinese Palm Reading will indeed grant you access to the personality and inner life of the subject.

*Thus, he that Nature rightly understands,*
*May from each line imprinted in his hands,*
*His future Fate and Fortune come to know,*
*And what Path it is his Feet shall go.*
*His secret Inclination he may see,*
*And to what Vice he shall addicted be.*
*To th' End that when he looks into his Hand,*
*He may upon his Guard the better stand;*
*And turn his wandering steps another way;*
*Whene'er he finds he does from Virtue stray.*

*From "Aristotle's Masterpiece"*

# CHINESE PALMISTRY FORMATIONS

## Metal/Gold Star Band

If this band is well-developed and pronounced, it indicates vivid and often lucid dreams. This band also indicates an elaborate and vivid imagination, especially regarding romantic and sensual encounters. The presence of a pronounced Metal Band also reveals moodiness and melancholy.

## Water Star Line

If the Water Star Line is deep and well formed, it indicates
vitality for life and elevated levels of energy and passion.
However, if it is shallow and not well defined, it predicts a
lack of drive and motivation.

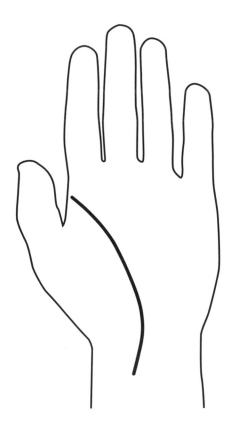

## Wood Star Loop

If a well-developed or pronounced Wood Star Loop is present, it indicates a lonely life. It predicts periods of solitude, isolation, and separation from family and society.

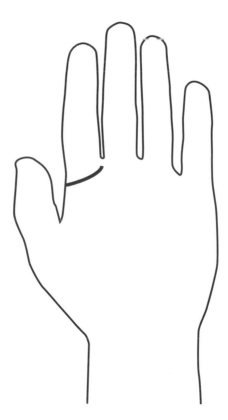

## Fire Star Line

If this line is present it shows personal drive,
determination, and aggressiveness. This line supports both
the Water Star Line and the Life Line. It shows a deep
vitality that struggles to rise to the surface.

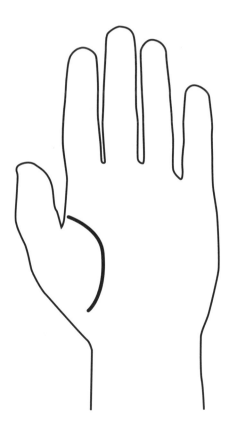

## Earth Star Loop

The Earth Star Loop indicates a troubled life filled with difficulties and hardships. This is the loop of tribulation.

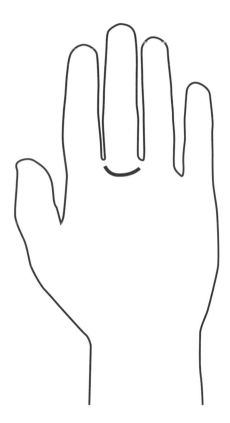

## Force Line

If the Force Line is strong, it indicates a need to have power and control over others. If, on the other hand, it is weak or non-existent it indicates a "live and let live" personality and the desire to let other people be who they are.

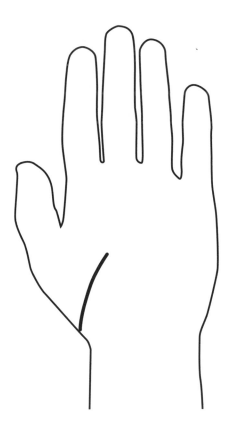

## Life Line

In Chinese Palm Reading the length of this line does not point to the length of the subject's life; rather, it is an indicator of the strength of one's life. If it is strong, straight, and deep it reveals great life force. If it shallow or broken it predicts variance and confusion in the life energy of the subject.

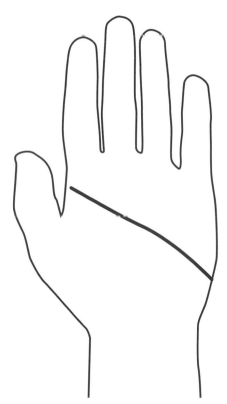

## Head Line

The Head Line relates to mental prowess and the ability to understand the complex. A deep line indicates great focus and the ability to concentrate. A straight line reveals a very good student, and if it slopes downward, it indicates a communicative, expressive, and sensual personality.

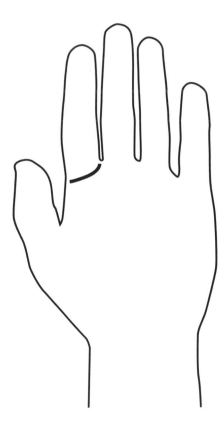

## Fortune Line

A well-defined Fortune Line indicates inner peace and great harmony in the subject's life. This line is an indicator of happiness and contentment. Branching lines are very auspicious. They predict a very happy destiny filled with interest and variety.

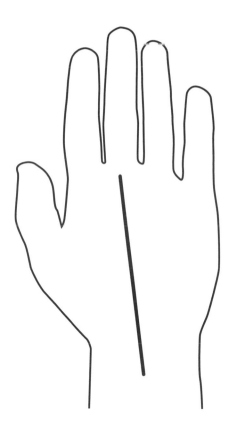

## Children Lines

This formation reveals the number and gender of your children. If the lines are deep, broad, and well-defined they foretell the arrival of sons. However, if the lines are narrow and fine then daughters are destined. The number of lines in this formation indicates the number of children the subject is destined to have.

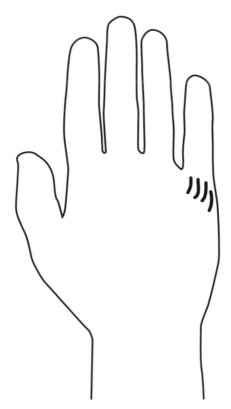

## Worry Lines

If one or more of these lines are present, it indicates elevated levels of worry, fear, and insecurity. If, however, none are present, it indicates a confident personality. Deep worry lines show how deep the insecurities and worries have penetrated the subject's personality.

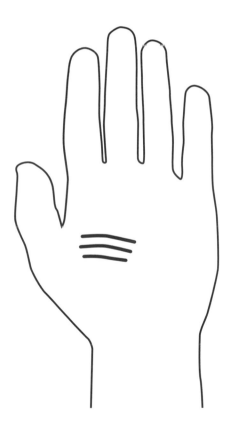

## Ill Health Lines

This is one line that you don't want on your palm. Its absence is an indicator of good health. However, its presence points to a weak constitution and the need to actively protect one's health.

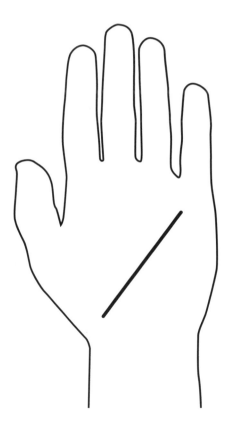

## Line of Sensuality

This line is sometimes called the Passion Line. It indicates great fire and passion if it is pronounced. If it is very pronounced it points to an over indulgent personality given to outbursts, emotional gushing, and excess.

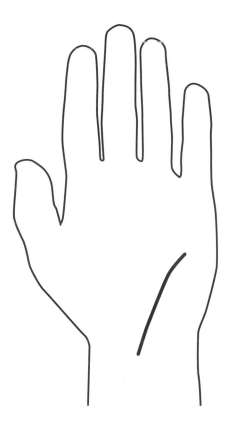

## Lines of Opposition

These lines, if present, indicate a life that is filled with contradiction and complexity. But conflict isn't universally undesirable. This can point to a varied and adventuresome life if the conflicts encountered are met head-on and not avoided.

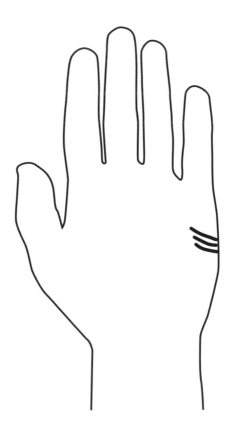

## Success Line

If this line is strong and deep, it indicates a strong personality with great influence over people. A single line means consistent success, while a broken line or multiple lines points to a turbulent and checkered career.

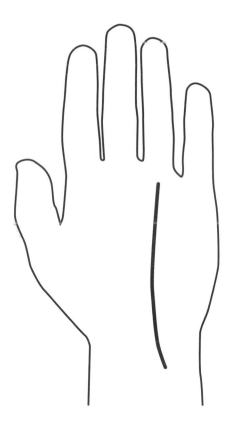

## Intuition Line

If this line is deep and pronounced it indicates an elevated intuitive sense and the ability to see the hidden side of life. If very pronounced, it indicates that the subject has the gift of prophecy.

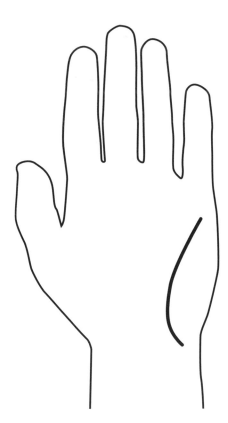

## Marriage Line

If this line is pronounced, straight, and clear, it indicates a very happy married life. However, if the line is crooked or broken, then extra measures must be taken to avert difficulties and assure a tranquil domestic life.

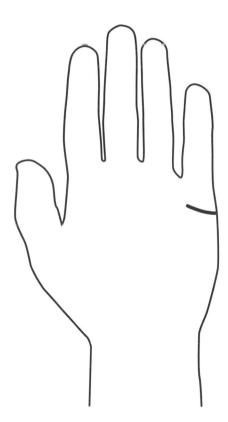

## Journey Lines

These lines predict travel and adventure. Journey Lines, as well as lines branching off the Life Line, indicate great change and predict an interesting and varied life.

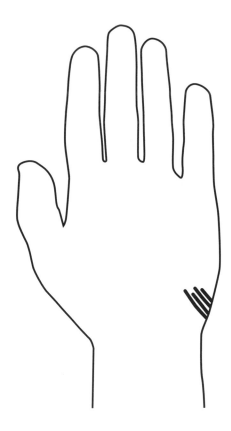

## Ten Character Crossed Lines

When this formation presents itself on a palm, it indicates mystical talent and the gift of profound intuition. It is a powerful symbol of a deeply gifted individual with great sensitivity and magical talent.

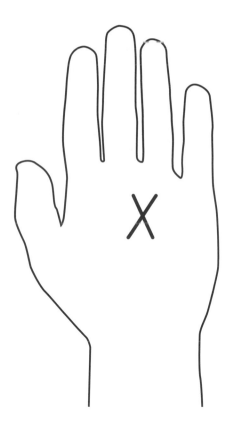

## Red Heart Line

Sometimes called the Emotion Line, the Red Heart Line
can indicate many things. If it is short it indicates an aloof
and reserved personality. A long line reveals emotional
intensity and volatility. One line indicates one great love in
your life, while broken and interwoven lines point to
romantic variety.

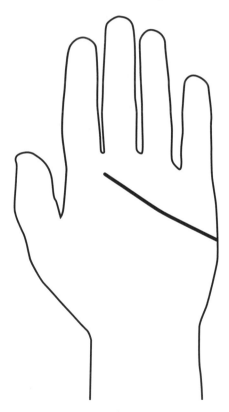

## Wrist Lines

Wrist Lines are indicators of overall physical and mental health. If the first line down from the base of the palm goes all the way around the wrist, it is an indication of robust health. If not, then steps need to be taken to insure health and prevent illness.

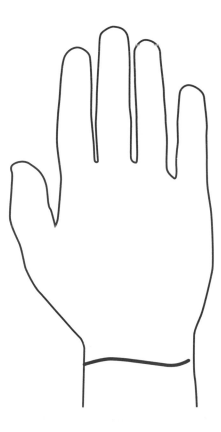

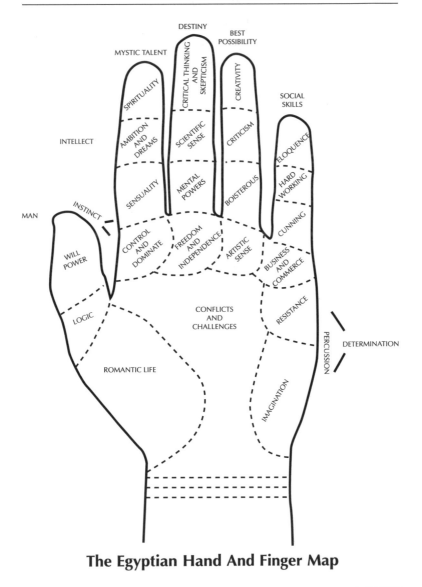

**The Egyptian Hand And Finger Map**

# Egyptian Palm Reading

Finger and hand mapping has its roots in ancient Egyptian palmistry. Simply put, it involves looking for the number and size of stars and crosses in different areas of the palm as well as lines that connect one area of the palm to another.

Generally speaking, crosses indicate conflicts in an area and stars indicate an amplification of the basic energies that the palm area represents. For example, a cross in the area that governs romantic life indicates contentious romantic relationships, while the presence of stars predicts an active and enjoyable love life. If the area of the thumb contains a cross, it indicates a lack of will power. However, stars in the same area reveal a formidable will.

Large crosses indicate great conflict while smaller ones point to internal conflicts. By the same token, a large star is more positive than a smaller one.

An abundance of either stars or crosses indicates that the energies are turning into their opposites. A single cross, for example, is considered negative and inauspicious, while an abundance of crosses in a given area is considered to be very positive.

Lines that connect areas of the palm can reveal interesting character traits. For example, a line that connects the areas of "artistic sense" with "business and commerce" might reveal a talent for managing art galleries. If a line runs from the center of the palm to the base of the second finger, it reveals an individual that is fighting to assert his or her independence and personal freedom.

Once you memorize the sites on the hand and finger map you will be able to easily interpret the inner workings of the subject's personality.

## Other Marks on the Egyptian Hand and Finger Map

- Bars and dots – obstacles, walls, and roadblocks

- Circles – obstruct the energy of the site

- Small lines – amplify the qualities of the site

- Squares – indicate the energy of the site is reserved or protected

- Islands – a symbol of weakness

- Horizontal lines – weaken the energy of the site

- Triangles – strengthen the energy of the site

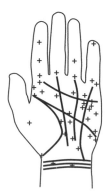 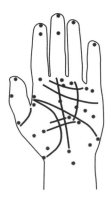

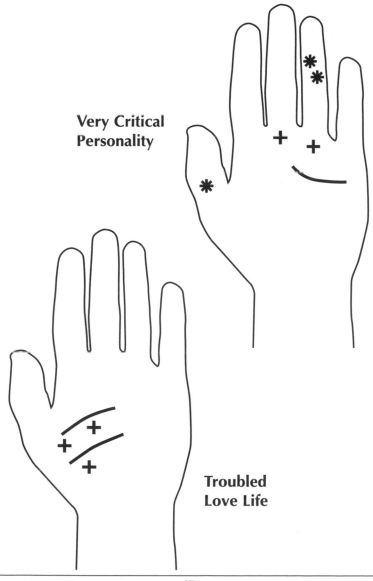

**Very Critical Personality**

**Troubled Love Life**

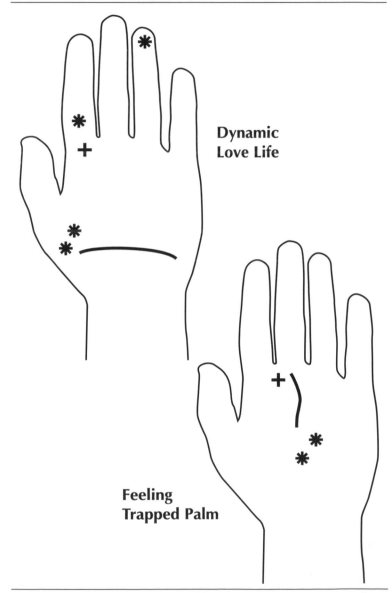

**Dynamic
Love Life**

**Feeling
Trapped Palm**

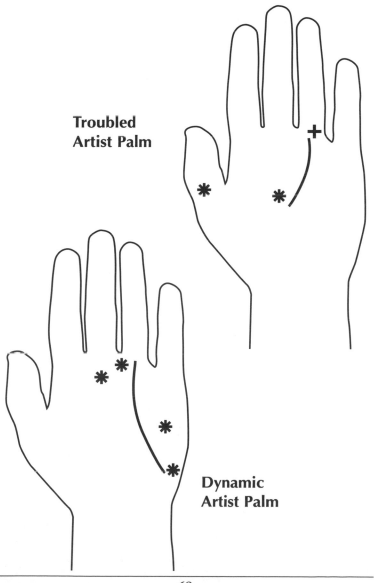

**Troubled
Artist Palm**

**Dynamic
Artist Palm**

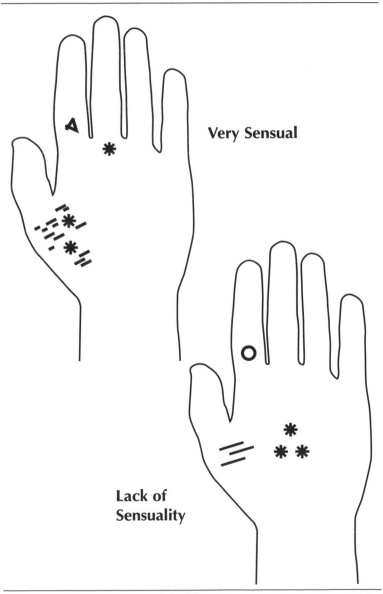

**Very Sensual**

**Lack of
Sensuality**

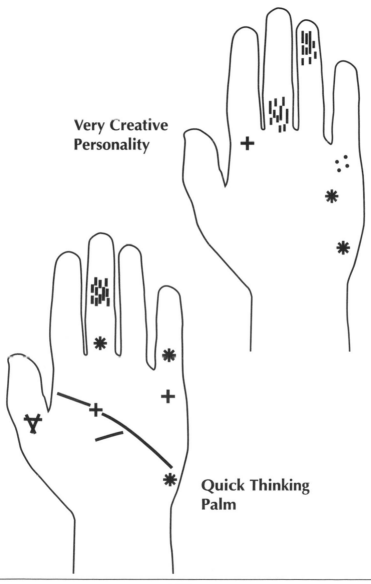

Very Creative
Personality

Quick Thinking
Palm

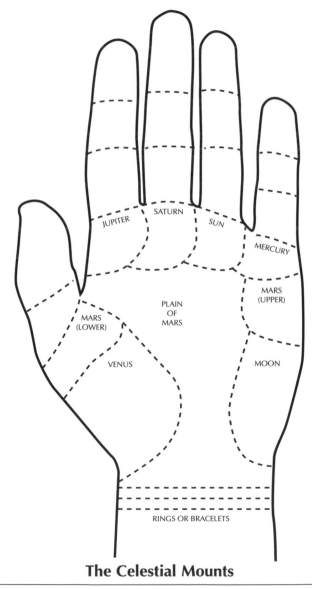

# The Celestial Mounts

# THE CELESTIAL MOUNTS

The science of palmistry divides the palm into nine specific areas and associates each with a different heavenly body. The Celestial Mounts, as they are called, are the master keys that unlock the secrets of our natural talents and abilities. The mounts also reveal the details of our emotional life.

Each of the nine mounts is an area of energetic convergence that corresponds to the inner workings of the entire body and mind. These areas form reservoirs of magnetic force reflective of the force of your personality, lifestyle, dreams, and aspirations. They also contain a subtle record of your life experience.

The nine mounts and their locations are:

- Mount of Jupiter – located at the base of the first finger

- Mount of Saturn – located at the base of the middle finger

- The Solar Mount – located at the base of the ring finger

- Mount of Mercury – located at the base of the little finger

- Upper Mount of Mars – located below the mount of Mercury

- Lower Mount of Mars – located at the base of the thumb

- The Plain of Mars – located in the remainder of the palm

- The Lunar Mount – located below the upper mount of Mars

- Mount of Venus – located below the lower mount of Mars

Generally, mounts that are raised or preeminent indicate an abundance of life energy. If mounts are flat or slightly sunken they are indications of a deficiency of life energy. If they are very sunken they represent the opposite of the qualities each one represents.

One mount that is larger than the others is an indication of the represented quality exerting a dominant influence. If, however, a mount is significantly larger than the others it denotes an excessive condition that damages the body, mind, and spirit.

The random appearance of dots, crosses, stars, lines, and other markings on these nine areas are indications that the intuition is trying to speak regarding a specific situation. These markings signal the rise of unconscious insight and wisdom into the field of the conscious mind.

# THE MOUNT OF JUPITER

This mount represents ambition, social prestige, honors, and awards. If it is well-proportioned it indicates verve and a joy for life. This well-formed area also indicates happy marriages and relationships with great emotional and physical rewards.

- Excessively raised – superstitious, pride in oneself, desire to be in charge, boisterous

- Excessively depressed – loss of self-respect and dignity

- Leans toward Saturn – spiritual aspirations, mystical leanings, religious

- Absorbs Mount of Saturn – desires to be a winner no matter the cost

## Marks on Jupiter

- Dots – ambition leading to disaster, indicates a loss of position

- Cross – indicates impending happiness and love

- Stars – indicates impending pleasure and satisfaction

- Triangle – indicates impending need to be a peacemaker

- Bar – thwarted plans and opportunities

- Crossed lines – upcoming unhappiness on the home front

- Straight upward lines – impending great success

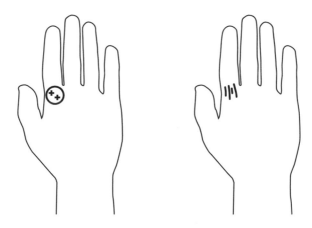

*Julius Caesar reportedly used palmistry as a means for evaluating his men.*

# THE MOUNT OF SATURN

This mount is the symbol of decorum, good manners, and modesty. Caution, reserve, and love of a solitary lifestyle are reflected in a well-proportioned Mount of Saturn. This area is the symbol of individual human destiny.

- Excessively raised (very rare) – resentful, embittered

- Smooth, naturally full and plain emblematic of a peaceful and quiet lifestyle

- Leans toward Jupiter – possesses a bad reputation, forceful determination

- Leans toward the sun – creative and artistic, will choose form over function, tends toward depression

## Marks on Saturn

- Dots – indicate approaching unhappiness or even death

- Cross – indicates the approach of fatalistic thinking

- Stars – indicate the threat of impending sickness, pain, and discomfort

- Triangle – the symbol of an approaching mystical event, skill at mysticism

- Straight upward lines – an unusual event, indicates a deeply philosophical mind

- Crossed lines – indicate too much outside interference

- Square – approaching danger from fire

- Grille-shaped lines – approaching problems with authority

*"Thus, in arming yourself with this science, you arm yourself with a great power, and you will have a thread that will guide you into the labyrinth of the most impenetrable hearts."*

*Balzac*

# THE SOLAR MOUNT

The Solar Mount, sometimes called the Mound of Apollo, represents artistic talent and a full appreciation for all the arts. A well-developed mount suggests great achievement in any chosen field of endeavor. Glory and the wealth that come with it are also indicated.

- Excessively raised – no artistic success, destined to be destitute, infamy

- Sunken – conflicts abound, the energy of obscurity, great achievement will not be easy, disdain for art and the artistic temperament

- Plain and slightly developed – indicates a peaceful and solitary life, lack of excitement or notoriety

## Marks on the Solar Mount

- Dots / Holes – back pain, disorders of the kidneys and bladder

- Stars – impending danger, triumph at great cost

- Triangle – great talent for art

- Bar – egotism, vanity, impotence, troublesome events that interfere

- Upward lines – a good omen of things to come, success, and achievement

- Irregular lines – filled with energy, filled with boldness, lighthearted, carefree

- Small mount on the bottom – triumph, wealth, riches, adultery

*Palmistry is an ancient practice dating back thousands of years. Evidence of the practice of palmistry has been found even in prehistoric caves, where large quantities of hands have been found painted on cave walls. Archaeological finds from ancient civilizations include hands made of stone, wood, and ivory.*

# THE MOUNT OF MERCURY

The Mount of Mercury represents the healing arts. Doctors, nurses, and caregivers of all kinds have a well-developed mount. It also signals great intelligence and personal magnetism, as well as a very successful career in medicine.

- Excessively raised – arrogant, pretentious personality, given to stealing and deception, impending financial ruin, deviousness, calculating

- Sunken or missing – indicates none of the abilities reflected in a well-formed mount

- Bulging and leaning toward edge of hand – indicates a beneficial confluence of innate skill, clear thinking, artistic talent, and persuasiveness

## Marks on Mercury

- Cross – given to thievery, taking credit for the work of another

- Bar – involved in embezzlement as a perpetrator or a victim

# THE UPPER MARTIAN MOUNT

Located between the Lunar Mount and the Mount of Mercury is the Upper Martian Mount. This portion of your hand embodies bravery and endurance. It also typifies the qualities of restraint and firm resolution. The energy of the Upper Martian Mount is the passive and feminine side of those energies that swirl and collect on the Lower Martian Mount.

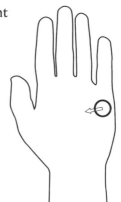

Its energies center around the aggressive and masculine. The Plain of Mars keeps the energy of these two opposing indicators separate and balanced.

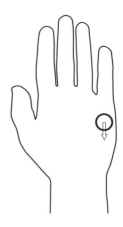

- Excessively raised – possesses a penchant for callousness and cruelty, an inordinate propensity for physical aggressiveness

- Sunken or missing – macabre personality, depressive, unhealthy habits, overly sensitive, easily offended, a paranoid personality

- Higher and more pronounced than Mercury – indicates a person who will not be defeated, typifies persistence

- Leans toward center – indicates over aggressiveness and a tendency toward violent outbursts

- Leans toward lunar – public speaker, very persuasive, eloquent, and very clever with words; employs inspirational rhetoric and demonstrates formidable legal skill

- Leans toward percussion – the ability to adapt, always on the ready, able to tap into great physical and emotional reserves

## Marks on Upper Martian

- Single vertical line – valor, fearlessness in the face of danger

- Parallel lines – savagery, cold-blooded, sadistic

- Short horizontal lines – indicates having made many enemies, blocked by barriers, obstacles and many difficulties

- Long horizontal lines – indicates an impending confrontation

- Cross – argumentative and quarrelsome

- Triangle – indicates an honorable warrior

- Circle – carries many physical or emotional scars

*"The hand is the servant of the brain. By continual use, the nerves from the brain to the hand become highly developed. Our hands are the photographic plates upon which our brain writes our impulses, whether good or bad."*

*Frances Kienzle*

# THE LOWER MARTIAN MOUNT

The Lower Martian Mount represents will power. Specifically, it is an indication of whether one has the strength of character to fight valiantly for God, country, and family. This is the seat of will power in all physical, intellectual, and emotional struggles.

- Well-developed in a man's hand – courageous, forthright, and true

- Well-developed in a woman's hand – aggressive, protector of family

- Bulging and over-developed – rude, offensive, insulting, pushy, and egotistical

- Flat or depressed – apprehensive, nervous, timid personality, jittery

## Marks on Lower Martian Mount

- Dots – fearful, introverted, and reserved

- Stars – impending death of a close friend

- Square – clever, quick-witted

- Grille-shaped lines – awkward, easily offended

- Many stars – signals an accident in the mountains

*"The brain which admittedly houses the mind, is intimately related with the hand—its most constant servant—that from this point alone, it may be realized that the hand outwardly reflects the personality more revealingly than any other part of the anatomy."*

*Rita Van Alen*

# THE MARTIAN PLAIN

The center of the palm is known as the Martian Plain. It is seen as a field of energy balancing the energy of the Upper and Lower Martian mounts. Great forces gather on the Martian Plain that affect the reading of the entire palm.

- High and distinct – signals great self-control with a gift for maintaining a balance of strength, imagination, and emotion. Great military generals usually have a distinct and high Martian Plain.

- Depressed or hollow palm – reveals a reticent and fearful personality who needs the input of others to make even the simplest of decisions.

- Flat and indistinct – reveals a pessimist who regards most everyone and everything with quiet disdain.

## Marks on the Martian Plain

- Dots – obstacles, impediments to Martian energy

- Squares – symbols of protection and inner strength

- Stars – amplifies positive qualities and blunts negative ones

- Circles – blocked life energy
- Small horizontal lines – emotional, physical, or psychic imbalance

*"The line where flesh ends and nail begins, contains the inexplicable mystery of the constant transformation of fluids into horn, showing that nothing is impossible to the wonderful modifications of the human substance."*

*Balzac*

# THE LUNAR MOUNT

This mount represents creative ability, imagination, and intuitive sense. This mount requires careful examination. The number of stars, crosses, and lines that connect it to other parts of the hand are all important indicators. If this area is filled with blood, it indicates robust characteristics. If, on the other hand, it is pale, then a deficiency of the indicated characteristics is indicated. If it is bluish in color, it indicates a gloomy personality given to melancholy.

- Bulging percussion – indicates a pressing need for creative physical activity

- Full, developed leaning toward Upper Mars – a dreamer, imaginative; indicates a need to creatively apply oneself, apply imagination to common activities

- Flat and undeveloped – indicates complacency, satisfaction with life, and an unwillingness to excel

- Leans toward Venus – tender, loving, feeling, passionate, and emotional

- Developed and near the wrist – given to romantic fantasy

- Leans toward Martian Plain – determined, aggressive, boisterous, willing to do anything to succeed

## Marks on the Lunar Mount

- Fine lines – prone to nervousness and tension

- Lines running obliquely – dreams of travel and far-away places

- Small crosses – indicates poetical skill, dramatic, given to fantasy, superstitious, given to neurosis and worry

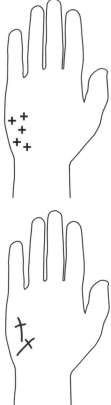

- Large crosses – imaginative, flamboyant, often given to spontaneous and often reckless behavior

- Stars – abundant conflicts between the lunar indicators

- Triangles – unusual skills, latent talents that will change everything, determination and success

- Grille-shaped lines – capricious, changeable, inconsistent

- Squares – should avoid traveling by boat or plane, indicates fear of water

*Studies of the hand often reveal more than personality traits or the future. Medical researchers studying skin patterns have noted a relation between genetic abnormalities and unusual markings of the hand. Research has confirmed a link between certain fingerprint patterns and heart disease. The palm has often been viewed as an instrument of healing because it provides a link between God and man.*

# THE MOUNT OF VENUS

The Mount of Venus reveals the intimate characteristics of the romantic life. This area of the palm, which is surrounded by the Line of Life, is the largest mount on the hand. It is the seat of human vitality and essence that attracts us to lovers and pleasures of the senses. This mount represents sensual love, leaving the fancies of sentimental love to be inscribed on the line of the heart.

- Evenly developed and well-centered – the best configuration, signals abundant vitality and success in all phases of sensual life

- Leaning toward or connected to Lower Martian Mount – great capacity for sympathy, sensual love, and passion

- Flat or depressed – dispassionate, cold, aloof, and unable to commit to a relationship

- Leaning toward Lunar Mount – hedonistic, indulgent, and pleasure-seeking

- Puffy and cushioned – makes a great companion and considerate lover

- Flat, muscular, and inflexible – easily irritated, disgruntled, intolerant of the opinions and ideas of others

## Marks on the Venusian Mount

- Dots – signal impending accidents and mishaps

- Bar – indecent, lewd, very lustful, perverse

- Triangle – cold and calculating, manipulative, shallow

- Small cross – great unhappiness in love

- Large cross – indicates a very happy married life abounding with love

- Curved lines running parallel with Life Line – indicates that friends and relatives will figure prominently in your overall happiness

- Grille-shaped lines – very passionate

- Small lines on the grille – worrisome

- Small lines on the mount – indicates numerous short-term affairs

- Lines from thumb base to Life Line – indicates multiple lovers

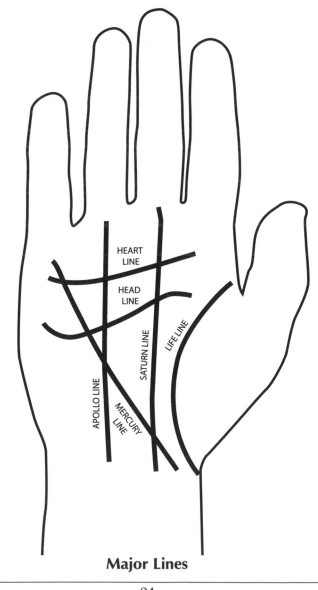

HEART
LINE

HEAD
LINE

SATURN LINE

LIFE LINE

APOLLO LINE

MERCURY
LINE

## Major Lines

# READING THE LINES OF FATE

Reading the major lines on the palm of the hand is called Reading the Lines of Fate.

There are six lines that make up the fate lines:

1) The Line of Life

2) The Line of The Head

3) The Line of The Heart

4) The Line of Saturn

5) The Line of Apollo

6) The Line of Mercury

A line should be clear and easy to see. It should be evenly colored, not too deep, and not too wide. Any number of marks can appear on the Lines of Fate. The same rules that apply to Egyptian Palmistry regarding stars and crosses apply here as well.

Palm readers call these lines, formed in the maternal womb and placed by the universe on each of our hands, "The Great Revealers." And each hand is different. It takes a lifetime of study to decipher the code of events that are revealed in our palms. The following examples are the most noticeable.

Accompanying each illustration is a short description of what each line means. I've also included important key words and phrases that will help you to better understand the implication of the lines and what personality traits are reflected in them.

*The recognition that each hand is unique has had practical applications as well as spiritual ones. As early as 1823, the University of Breslau's Professor Jan Evangelista Purkyne published a thesis acknowledging nine distinct fingerprint patterns. In 1892, Sir Francis Galton advocated use of this information in forensic science. That same year, the first fingerprint identification in a criminal case was made. By 1901, the famous Scotland Yard had established its own Fingerprint Bureau, followed by use of the procedure in the United States the next year.*

# THE LINE OF LIFE

## Deep and Thick

A deep and thick life line indicates a strong, healthy, and vigorous person. It also predicts victory in overcoming hardships and obstacles. If the line is red it means that the subject has unused strength and will power.

Key words: solid, durable, hard working, resilient, productive, determined, strong

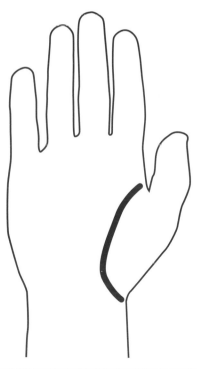

## Shallow and Thin

Life lines that are shallow and thin are indications of deep-seated fear and insecurity. They also reflect the subject's shallow grasp of the fullness of life and all it has to offer.

**Key words:** reclusive, solitary, guarded, self-protective, hidden, avoidance

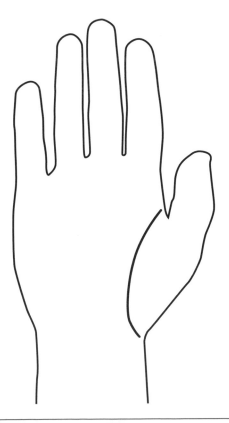

## Sweeping Out

A life line that curves deeply into the palm is called a sweeping out line. It indicates an eagerness for living life to the fullest. Compassion and helpfulness describe the subject with a sweeping out life line.

**Key words:** mentor, teacher, passion, a can-do attitude, eager, a little reckless

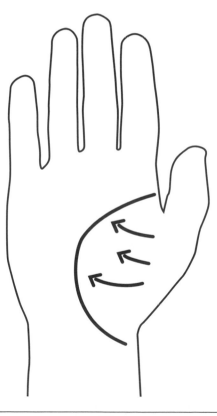

## Sweeping In

A life line that hugs the thumb is called a sweeping in line. It indicates an emotionally closed and overly conservative approach to life. The subject with this kind of life line avoids personal contact with others and often rejects them for no good reason.

**Key words:** unaware, dismissive, self-centered, stubborn, penchant for self-destruction

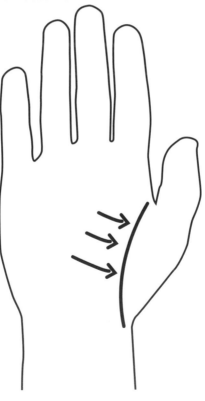

## Long Life Line

A long life line predicts a long and healthy life. It indicates a productive personality, great creative skill, and a desire to work very hard.

**Key word:** stimulation, firm, strength, nurture, nourishment, talent, skill, opportunity

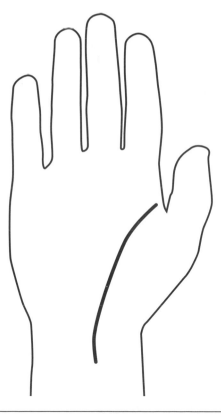

# THE LINE OF THE HEAD

## Long Head Line

A long head line indicates a reasoned and thoughtful personality. It also represents a keen intellect and the innate ability to solve complex problems quickly and easily.

**Key words:** keen, quick-witted, insightful, mentally sharp, able to understand the "big picture"

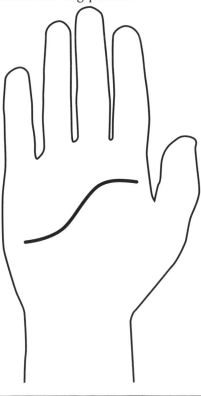

## Short Head Line

A short head line indicates a concise and focused thinker who is not given to flights of fancy. An affinity for the predictable and the known is also represented by this configuration and is sometimes called a "habit line."

**Key words:** measured, steady, rational, objective, down to earth, likes routine tasks

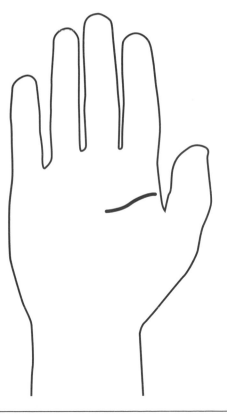

## Thick and Straight

Time to mentally get to work! This line indicates a person who is squandering his or her God-given talents. It also appears on the palm of explorers, woodsmen, and adventurers.

**Key words:** reckless, wasteful, relaxed, informal, live for today, wander

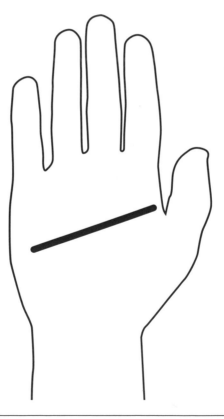

## Faint and Thin

A faint and thin head line is indicative of someone who lacks determination and the desire to get the job done. This line also reveals a tendency towards muddled thinking.

**Key words:** lackluster, unmotivated, unable to finish things, disappointed, a victim

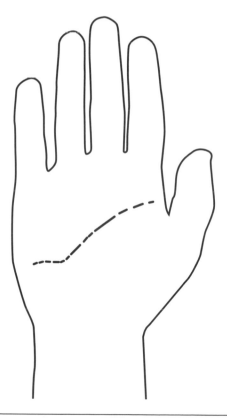

## Broken

Broken head lines reveal a series of heartbreaking incidents.
If the lines are well-defined it also indicates that the bearer
is his or her own worst enemy. It's time to enjoy the
company of friends and family.

**Key words:** foolish, a spendthrift, easily cheated,
misfortune in the future, family conflicts, divorce

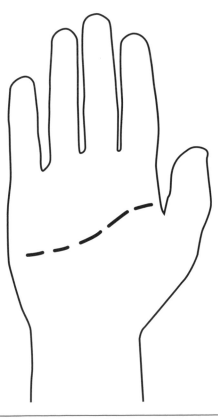

# THE LINE OF THE HEART

## Deep and Long Heart Line

A deep and long heart line indicates great passion and a zest for living. A subject with this line is compassionate and caring. It also predicts a great opportunity to correct an injustice.

Key words: tender, caring, controlled, helpful, self-sacrificing, empathetic

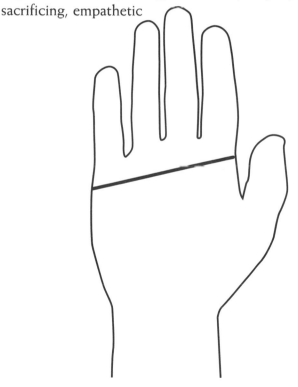

## Sweeping Low

A heart line that runs lower than usual in the palm is said to be low sweeping. This kind of heart line indicates a propensity to be a victim. It predicts the impending arrival of charlatans, confidence men, and other insecure people into the subject's life.

**Key words:** beware, think before you act, stay alert, prudence

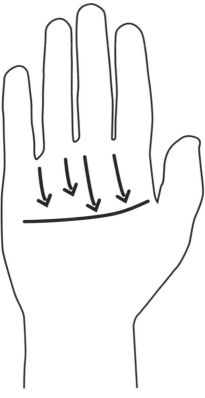

## Sweeping High

A heart line that rides high on the palm is said to be high sweeping. This line indicates a subject that is careful and attentive regarding love and the emotions of others.

**Key words:** prudent, calculating, wise of heart, cautious, safe, realistic in love

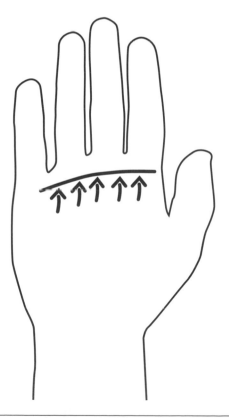

## Rising

A heart line that extends into the base of the first finger is called a rising heart line. This line reveals the subject's propensity to love but not love well. It indicates a sincere and idealistic personality that often is blind to the bad intentions of others.

**Key words:** pure, innocent, lofty, decent, caring, righteousness, fairness

## Pointed

A heart line that extends into the base of the second finger is called a pointed heart line. This line reveals the subject's propensity to be over-protective and a little bit selfish. This is particularly true regarding family and close friends.

**Key words:** controlling, jealous, unwilling to share, clinging, resentful, chip on the shoulder

# THE LINE OF SATURN

## Straight

A straight Saturn line is indicative of a team player that can easily step back and see the big picture. This line reveals a personality that likes things to be organized, neat, and tidy. For maximum comfort, the subject with this configuration needs everything to be in its place.

**Key words:** contentment, controlled, designer, overview thinking, architect, engineer

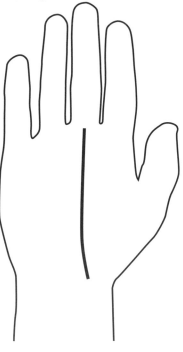

## Crooked or Wavy

The line of Saturn determines your fate. A crooked or wavy Saturn line is indicative of a confused person that is buffeted about by the winds of change and the forceful will of others. If you have this line in your palm, endeavor to stay calm and focused if you want to counter its characteristics.

Key words: uncertain, capricious, flighty, over-worked, meek, pulled apart, puts out fires

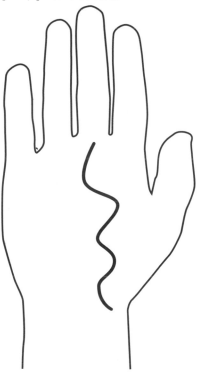

## Long and Pointed

A Saturn line that rises from the wrist and moves well into the second finger is said to be long and pointed. This kind of line reveals a great reservoir of talent and skill in a variety of airs. These talents reveal themselves at the peak of hard work and focused determination.

**Key words:** follow your bliss, ignore detractors, seize the day, good fortune

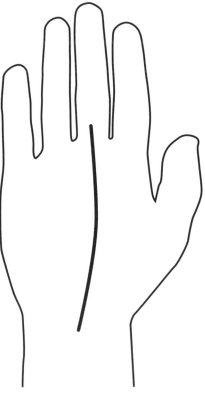

## Short Saturn Line

A short Saturn line that doesn't extend into the lower palm indicates a life filled with conflict and intense struggle. Great care should be taken to avoid pessimism and depression.

**Key words:** warlike, disagreeable, antagonistic, contentious, pushes and tries too hard

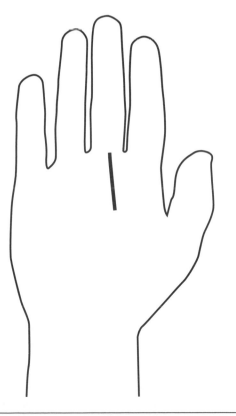

## Points to Ring Finger

This Saturn line, which is usually shorter than normal, indicates trauma or hardship in early life. Indicative of a nervous or wary individual, this line calls for a happy home life to balance out past problems.

**Key words:** introspective, cautious, brooding, unfulfilled

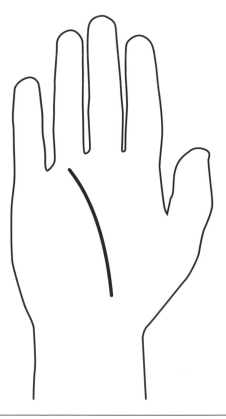

# THE LINE OF APOLLO

## Irregular Apollo Line

The irregular Apollo line reveals the existence of hidden skills that lie just beneath the surface. It signals a great capacity for spontaneity and creativity if the subject's inner reserves are tapped. The person whose palm has this configuration has a gift for wasting time.

**Key words:** procrastinate, outcast, uneven personality, bound in self-doubt

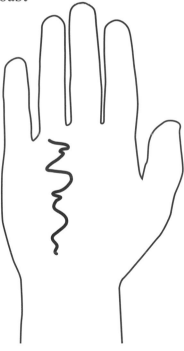

## Short and Low

An Apollo line that is short and runs low on the palm indicates a person that has inborn gifts and natural talent. It also represents immense flexibility that is revealed in difficult situations.

**Key words:** talented, gifted, sell yourself short, needs confidence, inner struggle

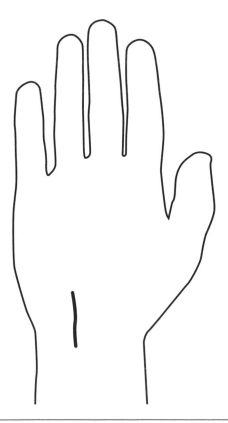

## Full Moon Line

The full moon line is an Apollo line that arcs from the Lunar Mount and points toward the ring finger. It signifies an extremely charismatic person.

**Key words:** charming, charisma, persuasive, inspiring, loyal, popular

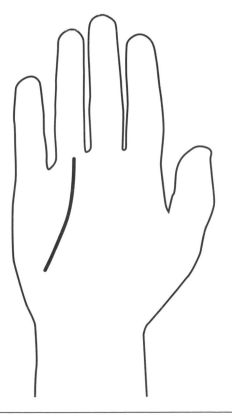

## Conflict Lines

The presence of two Apollo lines converging toward the base of the ring finger signals a life of conflict and indecision. Its appearance can also represent an upcoming opportunity to reap big rewards from a difficult situation.

**Key words:** easily swayed, confused, uncertainty, signals the presence of too many options

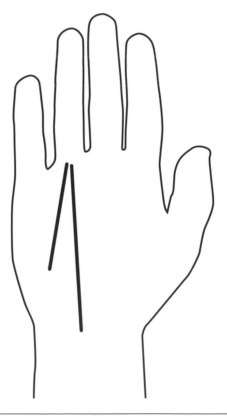

## Inner Life Lines

An Apollo line that becomes broken and divided near the base of the ring finger indicates a person with a rich inner life filled with imaginative wanderings. This configuration of lines also represents a person who is at home anywhere they go.

**Key words:** eclectic, adventuresome, keen senses, capricious, emotionally flexible

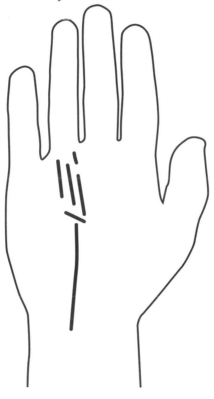

# THE LINE OF MERCURY

## Indecision Line

This formation on the line of Mercury signals conflict between your inner and outer worlds. This conflict is easily overcome by focusing on the needs of others. Doctors and nurses frequently display this formation in their palms.

**Key words:** compassionate, helping, a caretaker, driven, tunnel vision

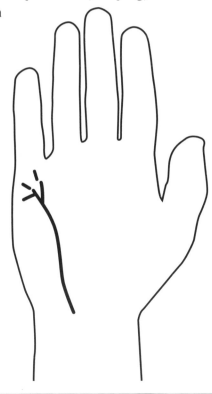

## Sweeps Out

When a Mercury line sweeps toward the percussion, it
indicates a tendency to put your trust in nefarious
characters. This formation comes with a warning: Protect
yourself.

**Key words:** confrontation, puts on airs, haughty, refuses to
confront a problem, succumbs to the will of others

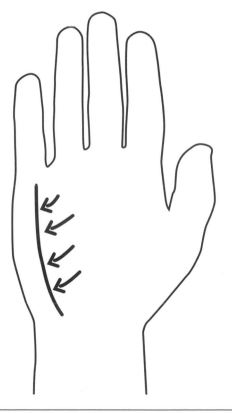

## Fallen Line

A fallen Mercury line lies low in the palm. This reveals a person who values rest and repose—perhaps too much. This formation presents itself in a person who comes alive when everyone else has turned in for the night.

**Key words:** unfocused, carefree, sedate, quiet, introspective, a night owl

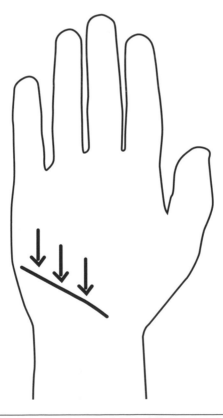

## Danger Line

When the Mercury line sends branches in the directions indicated by the illustration it warns of becoming obsessive compulsive. It also predicts the arrival of dark times and emotional strife.

**Key words**: beware, let it go, relax, shuts out friends, behavior characterized by over focus

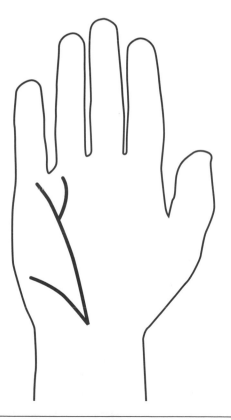

## Sensitivity Line

A Mercury line that begins close to the wrist line and projects to the base of the little finger near the edge of the palm indicates great sensitivity and awareness. This heightened awareness grants the bearer deep insight into the physical, emotional, and mental workings of others.

**Key words:** empathy, thoughtfulness, diplomatic, a good listener

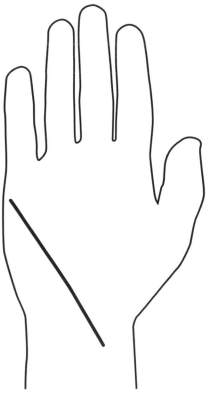

# Advanced Palmistry

Whether you like it or not, your hands, palms, and fingers are infallible indicators of your true personality. The full panorama of precisely who you are and how you live your life is faithfully indexed in whorls, ridges, lines, and flesh. Shakespeare was talking about the hands when he said, "There's a divinity that shapes our ends, rough-hew them how we will." He meant that it is very difficult to reshape the contours and characteristics of the hands. It is true that a person may undergo a shift in temperament and lifestyle, but even then the changes in his hands will only be slight. It takes a dramatic change in character—so radical as to be called a rebirth—before the lines and marks of the hand will permanently change.

Highly skilled Chiromancers are able to read special groups of formations that are made up of the various lines, marks, and mounts of each hand. In fact, the materials we've covered so far make up the building blocks of these special formations. How those building blocks combine lay bare the innermost thoughts and desires. The quietest thought or the most violent mental disruption can be seen in the palm if you know what to look for. These composite formations are called Personality Portraits. They form twin maps of destiny that we carry with us throughout our lives.

If you are able to successfully interpret these portraits, you will be able to see the virtue and vices of literally anyone you meet. Indeed, you will be able to fully glimpse their inner being and pierce the veil that hides future events from them. The following portraits will set you on the path.

# PERSONALITY PORTRAITS

Here are some common personality types and the hand characteristics you'll likely notice with each.

## Architect's Personality
- The second finger is long.
- The third finger is long and straight with a spatulate tip.
- The nails are long and square.
- A strong Venusian Mount is visible.
- There is a strong Solar Mount.
- The Head Line is straight.
- The hand is spatula shaped.
- The fingertips are square and well-defined.

## Artist's Personality (Successful)
- The first finger is pointed.
- The third finger is long and straight.
- The hands are average in size and conical shaped.
- The palms taper slightly.
- The first phalanx of the third finger is especially long.
- There is a strong Lunar Mount.
- All of the fingers have a strong and firm base.

## Artist's Personality (Unsuccessful)
- The hands are thick and soft.
- The fingers are short and conical.
- The first phalanx of the thumb is unusually short and small.
- The palms are frequently larger than the fingers.
- The Head Line droops downward.
- The Head Line is weak or broken.
- The Mount of Venus is small
- The Solar Mount is under-developed .
- The Mount of Jupiter is over-developed.

## Star Gazer's Personality
- The fingers are large and knotted.
- The palms are hollow or hard.
- There is a philosophical shape to the hands.
- The fingertips are square.
- The thumbs are large and strong.
- There are very pronounced mounts of Saturn and Mercury.
- A prominent Head Line is visible.

## Benevolent Personality
- The nails are long and well-defined.
- The hands are soft.
- The Heart Line is well-defined.
- The Heart Line is forked.
- The Heart Line begins on the Mount of Jupiter.
- The Jupiter Mount is strong and well-developed.

- The Venusian mount is prominent.
- The Saturn Line begins within the Mount of Venus.

## Teacher's Personality
- The thumbs are long and well-shaped.
- The fingers are knotty.
- The fingertips are square.
- The Head Line and Heart Line are thin and faint.
- The Head Line and Life Line do not touch near the thumb.
- The Solar Mount appears faint but well-developed.
- The Mount of Mars is very developed.
- The Mount of Mercury feels firm.
- Jupiter and Venus Mounts contain many fine markings.

## Greedy Personality
- The hands are thin and hard.
- The fingertips are square.
- Fingers are knotted and boney.
- All mounts are deficient.
- The Heart line is either broken or absent.
- If present, the Heart Line stops on the Mount of Mercury.
- A thick and prominent Head Line is present.

## Coercive Personality
- The hands are long and thin.
- The fingers are pointed.
- The fingernails are broad.

- The fingers are crooked and have knotty joints.
- There is excessive flesh on the Jupiter and Solar Mounts.
- Crosses appear on a strong Mount of Mercury.

## Chaste Personality
- The hands are smooth and thin.
- The first finger is pointed and well-defined.
- The fingernails are either long or wedge-shaped.
- All of the Mounts seem small and under developed.
- Crosses are visible on the third finger.

## Avant-Garde Personality
- The palms are soft and supple.
- The hands are small.
- The first finger is short and blunt.
- The Lunar Mount is overly developed.
- The Mount of Venus is strong or bulging.
- The thumbs are flexible and curve backward.

## Business Personality
- The hand shape is elementary.
- The fingers are frequently longer than the palm.
- The fourth finger is very long.
- The fingertips are square.
- The Head Line is strong and deep.
- The Mount of Mercury on both hands is very prominent.
- The Solar Mount is well-developed.
- The thumb's first phalanx is very strong.

- The Fate Line branches with one branch reaching for the Mount of Mercury.
- A forked Head Line moves towards the Mount of Mercury.

## Psychic Personality
- The hands are soft and almond shaped.
- The fingers are smooth and short.
- The thumbs are small.
- An abundance of small crosses throughout the palms can be seen.
- The Lunar Mount is very prominent.
- The Heart Line is weak.
- The Head Line curves slightly downward.
- A whorl can be seen under the first finger.
- Strong and deep lines are present within the Lunar Mount.

## Intuitive Personality
- Hands that are thin and soft.
- Conical-shaped fingers are short and smooth.
- The fingernails range from short to very short.
- The thumbs are strong and conical.
- The first phalanx of each finger is long.
- The Lunar Mount is strong.
- The Mount of Mercury is strong.
- The Lunar Mount displays triangular marks.
- Prominent marks can be seen on the Mount of Saturn.
- The Head Line curves slightly downward.

## Belligerent Personality
- The palms are square.
- The fingers are short and smooth.
- Fingernails are broad and short.
- The fingertips are spatulate.
- Large crosses are visible on the palm.
- The Upper Martian Mount is overly developed.
- The Saturn Lines are deep and red.

## Legal Personality
- The palm is flat and smooth.
- The fingernails are short.
- The fingers are long and close together.
- The fourth finger is more prominent than the others.
- The thumb is long and straight.
- The Mounts of Mercury and Mars are large.
- The Head Line is straight and forks at the end.
- The Head Line and Life Line do not touch near the thumb.

## Gambler's Personality (Compulsive)
- The hands are soft.
- The fingers are short and smooth.
- The third and second fingers are of equal length.
- The Lunar Mount is well-developed.
- A Head Line curves dramatically downward.

# OTHER INDICATORS

Here are some other items you'll want to take note of during your readings, plus what each means.

## Hair
- Hairy woman's hands indicate a cruel disposition.
- Hairy hands on a man indicate a violent temper.
- Hair appearing on all of the fingers indicates a passionate or zealous nature.
- Hair on the thumbs indicates latent genius.
- Hair on the lower phalanges indicates a pretentious personality.
- Dark hair indicates vital energy.
- Light hair indicates inherent weakness.

## Nails
- Breaking nails indicate weak or failing health.
- Naturally colored nails indicate faithfulness and dependability.
- Oddly shaped and twisted nails indicate a materialistic personality.
- Long and dark nails indicate a treacherous person.
- Short, pointed nails on thin fingers indicate weak lungs.
- Short nails reveal an argumentative personality.
- Short and hard nails reveal a bad temper.
- Soft nails indicate an absence of willpower.
- A little fingernail that is weaker than the others indicates weak digestion.

- Nails that are pale and round indicate a very dangerous personality.
- Broad and flat nails that are slightly curved at the ends reveal deviousness.

## Skin Color

- Pink skin in which the veins can be seen points to a caring person.
- White skin that is slightly transparent indicates indifference.
- Red skin indicates optimism and confidence.
- Dark red or purple skin reveals ill health and indolence.
- Dark color with shades of green or yellow indicates a foul temper.
- Swarthy color with pink and red tints indicates robust health and moral strength.

# VIRTUES AND VICES UNREALIZED

Some palm readers rely on the fourth or little finger to reveal the innermost talents or shortcomings that lie hidden at the center of each of us. These virtues and vices are usually buried deep within and have not yet been realized by the subject. If a reading points to a virtuous talent, then the subject can take steps to bring it forward in their lives. However, if the hidden tendency is a negative one, the subject can work to keep it from ever manifesting in their lives.

* Excessively long fourth fingers indicate a latent penchant for cleverness and intrigue.

* Excessively short fourth fingers are an indication of inconsiderate and foolish behavior at work below conscious awareness.

* Fourth fingers that are the same length as the first finger shows a latent talent for diplomacy and consensus building.

* Fourth fingers that are the same length as the second finger point to hidden scientific and mathematical talents.

* Fourth fingers that are the same length as the third finger show an unrealized talent for the world of politics.

* A bent or crooked fourth finger is an indication of latent dishonesty and duplicitous behavior.

* A strong fourth finger that is slightly larger than normal points to an adaptable and flexible nature, the benefits of which have yet to be realized.

## Planetary Unions

When the hand of a subject shows two mounts that are equally developed more than the others, it is called a Mount Combination or Planetary Union. Interpreting these formations requires a keen eye and sensitive touch. These combinations reveal, among other things, our dreams and ambitions.

Jupiter united with Saturn reveals academic ambitions.

Jupiter united with Mercury reveals utilitarian ambitions.

Jupiter united with the Lunar Mount reveals artistic and creative ambitions.

Jupiter united with Venus reveals dreams of great accomplishments.

Jupiter united with Upper Mars reveals courageous ambition and dreams of valor.

Saturn united with the Solar Mount reveals a dream to be wise.

Saturn united with Mercury reveals dreams for great knowledge.

Saturn united with the Lunar Mount reveals dreams of mystic encounters.

Saturn united with Venus reveals dreams of practical knowledge.

Saturn united with Upper Mars reveals an ambition to engender trust.

Sun united with Mercury reveals business ambitions.

Sun united with the Lunar Mount reveals creative ambitions.

Sun united with Venus reveals artistic ambitions.

Sun united with Lower Mars reveals self-development ambitions.

Sun united with Upper Mars reveals dreams of courage and bravery.

Mercury united with the Moon reveals ambitions to be an inventor.

Mercury united with Venus reveals dreams of intimacy and companionship.

Mercury united with Lower Mars reveals business ambitions.

Mercury united with Upper Mars reveals dreams of great personal achievement.

Moon united with Venus reveals social ambitions.

Moon united with Lower Mars reveals repressed ambitions.

Venus united with Lower Mars reveals patriotic ambitions.

Venus united with Upper Mars reveals dreams of strength, insight, and confidence.

# Putting It All Together

OK; so now you can read palms. Now what?

To be a true palm reader you must be confident of your ability. You must sincerely believe in your mind that you can, indeed, divine someone's deepest secrets merely by looking at their palms, hands, and fingers. This confidence is very important and you must exude it.

Please remember that as a Chiromancer you are the master of the situation. Take your time when reading a palm. Never become flustered. Be respectful of your subject. Remember, they have put their lives and imagination under your direct control. You have special knowledge and skill, so act that way. If they lose confidence in you, your intuition will dry up and you won't be able to read them successfully.

When you first begin to read palms, it'll be easier to read strangers than friends. This is because your friends already know you and, most importantly, you know them. Consequently, there isn't much mystery. Strangers, however, don't know how long you have been reading palms or how much skill you actually have. If you are calm and confident, you will automatically project great expertise.

I believe that, ultimately, you must really like people in order to be a good palm reader. Having the ability to speak in front of an audience is also helpful. Your own hands should be clean and well-maintained. After all, you will be making physical contact with your subjects. Speak to them politely and give them your fullest attention. Always assure your subjects that you have no wish to embarrass them in any way. Be mature and professional. Whether you know it or not, people will expect this of you.

Palm reading is an art, and you should treat it like one. Don't try to reveal too much in one reading. Tell your subject four or five things at most and then, as if it is getting difficult to read the signs, end the reading on a positive note. Said another way, it's far better to stop short than to fill the glass to the brim. Handled in this way, their short palm reading session with you will be a fun and enjoyable experience that they will never forget.

Now go out and join hands with the world. All of its secrets are waiting.

# ABOUT THE AUTHOR

Ian Alan is a psychic investigator and gifted clairvoyant who has spent a lifetime researching the mysterious side of existence and uncovering its deepest secrets. When not delving into the world's great enigmas, he teaches ancient art and philosophy. A prolific freelance writer and magician, he is also the author of a series of books on regional ghost stories. Ian Alan lives and writes in Birmingham, Alabama.